The Complete Book of Canoeing

D1220986

"This is a great book on canoeing, even for people who actually want to do it. The inverted-canoe-as-dining-room-table tip alone is worth the book's price."

—*Daily TRAVEL News*

"Provides an abundance of helpful tips for beginners, making good use of illustrations . . . clear graphic explanations help clear up the mysteries of form . . . simple illustrations also cleanly show how different strokes control a canoe's direction . . . there is an excellent chapter on paddling with kids. . ."

—*The Grand Rapids Press*

"This fully illustrated guidebook offers lucid advice on trip planning, paddling techniques, "reading the water," portaging, and much more."

— *Sierra* magazine *(San Francisco, CA)*

"Grab this book, sit down by the fire, and let a wilderness canoe guide share a life-time of paddling experience. Whether it's draws and sweeps, portages and paddles, camp cooking or Kevlar, Herb's knowledgeable tips explain it all with color and style."

—Kevin McCarthy,
national trip leader for the Sierra club

Help Us Keep This Guide Up to Date

Every effort has been made by the author and editors to make this guide as accurate and useful as possible. However, many things can change after a guide is published—establishments close, phone numbers change, hiking trails are rerouted, facilities come under new management, etc.

We would love to hear from you concerning your experiences with this guide and how you feel it could be made better and be kept up to date. While we may not be able to respond to all comments and suggestions, we'll take them to heart, and we'll also make certain to share them with the author. Please send your comments and suggestions to the following address:

The Globe Pequot Press
Reader Response/Editorial Department
P.O. Box 833
Old Saybrook, CT 06475

Or you may e-mail us at:

editorial@globe-pequot.com

Thanks for your input, and happy travels!

THE COMPLETE BOOK OF CANOEING

The Only Canoeing Book You'll Ever Need

Second Edition

by

I. Herbert Gordon

The Globe Pequot Press

Old Saybrook, Connecticut

Library of Congress Cataloging-in-Publication Data

Gordon, I. Herbert.
    The complete book of canoeing / by I. Herbert Gordon.—2nd ed.
        p.   cm.
    "An East Woods book."
    Includes index.
    ISBN 0-7627-0052-1
    1. Canoes and canoeing.   I. Title.   II. Series.
    GV783.G68   1997   96-31520
    797.1'22—dc20   CIP

Manufactured in the United States of America
Second Edition/First Printing

To the memory of Frank Jones,
whose passionate belief that livery canoeing
should be a safe as well as rewarding activity
helped set national standards that have made that belief a reality;
and to Scott, Hilary, and Rebecca.

Contents

Foreword

CANOEING MADE EASY should have the following warning on the cover: "Caution—the contents of this book may change your life and fill your leisure time with excitement, joy, and adventure."

Maybe it was because I know Herb as a friend and colleague and enjoy his tales of wilderness adventure; maybe it was because he wrote about my favorite subject; or maybe it was the mood created by the crackling fire, freshly fallen snow, and nothing else to do but enjoy a good read. Whatever the reason, I was captured by *Canoeing Made Easy* and read it from beginning to end in one sitting.

I was told this book was designed to entice would-be paddlers into their first canoe. Even professional guides with millions of paddling strokes behind them on streams, rivers, lakes, and salt water, however, will find this book offers a most enjoyable opportunity for reverie and learning to do old things in new and better ways. I kept finding myself saying things like: "I remember when that happened to me," and "Ah-ha, that's the way it is done," or "I'll have to try that next time I go canoeing."

I have never taken a canoe trip without something memorable happening. Whether it was the eagle standing guard over his catch of the day, a beaver slapping his tale to warn others of his kind of our presence, an otter rolling over on his back and waving as we floated by, or a gaggle of geese loudly chiding us for intruding on their private beach party, something unique has happened every time I have paddled.

A wise university professor once challenged me when I complained that I had to stay home and work in my yard instead of going with him on a canoe trip. "Twenty years from now, what are you going to remember? Cutting grass or floating the Red?" I will never forget that canoe trip!

Canoe travels are the stuff from which lifetime memories are made. The great psychologist Maslow would have called them rare peak experiences. In this book Herb Gordon shares many of his memorable experiences and teaches us, often in a humorous way, how to avoid the common mistakes beginners make. Each chapter insures that all our future "sea stories" will be joyous ones.

Reading this book will not be a vicarious paddling experience. The closet adventurer is invited to step out into the wonderful world of wilderness travel. The timid soul who has always wanted to paddle his or her own canoe will find in these pages the knowledge to take that first step, and the advanced paddler will find a potpourri of suggestions for making the next journey even more enjoyable.

So, go ahead. Read it today. You will find yourself paddling tomorrow. That's a promise.

Jim Thaxton
Executive Director, Professional Paddlesports Association
Board member, American Recreation Coalition in Washington.

Preface

The May breeze swept through the open windows of our well-used blue passenger van bouncing north on NY97, a curving highway that parallels the beautiful Delaware River where it bonds New York and Pennsylvania. The thick forests on the low mountains that flank the Delaware Valley were bursting with the fresh green of late spring.

It was a magical day to begin a weekend canoe trip. There were ten of us in the van on a Sierra Club outing. We would spend two days canoeing the sparkling river and one night camping under the trees on the riverbank. Listening to the chatter of the group, I recalled what naturalist George W. Sears, writing under the Indian name Nessmuk, said in his outdoor classic, *Woodcraft,* more than a century ago: "We do not go to the green woods and crystal waters to rough it, we go to smooth it. We get it rough enough at home."

The tension of city life slipped away during the morning drive like a river mist vanishing in the early sun. A few hours earlier we had been strangers, driving separately to our common meeting place at a canoe livery in the village of Barryville.

We left our cars and camping equipment at the Wild & Scenic Canoe livery parking lot under a row of spreading elm trees and climbed into the livery van for the drive upriver about 12 miles. Our put-in was at a shaded beach section of the Delaware known as Ten Mile River. On the ride we were becoming friends, united by a wonderful activity new to most of the group—a canoe weekend.

In a special trailer behind the van were five sleek, modern 16½-foot-long ABS canoes, direct descendants of the birchbark canoes the Lenape Indians once paddled along this same waterway.

First occupied by white settlers in the late seventeenth century, the upper reaches of the Delaware are still a sparsely settled land of a few small farms and tiny villages.

In the 1980s this scenic river valley was given permanent protection from further development when some 75 miles of the river was added to the nation's Wild and Scenic Rivers system.

The van topped a long rise and the beautiful valley opened up for a view of miles of wooded slopes bisected by the clear water. As we drove down the highway, the van reached a dirt side road. The driver swung onto the road toward a popular canoe-launching site. We rounded a bend to see a couple of large vans parked beside the river, each with a canoe trailer attached. The area was alive with people, carrying canoes to the river's edge, loading personal gear into the craft, sorting paddles, creating an air of warmth and excitement as they moved about, talking and trying on life jackets.

Our driver stopped. We climbed out and helped carry our canoes to the muddy bank, selected paddles, fastened our life jackets to make certain they fit properly, and placed our personal belongings beside the canoes. Then it was time for some discussion of paddling techniques, since our group was basically a cluster of novices. They included the following:

Abe and Nancy, in their forties, were off for a weekend without the kids. Canoeing experience: Nancy had canoed once in summer camp. Abe had never touched a canoe.

Marge, a striking woman in her late thirties, was an assistant buyer at a major department store and had rafted once on Idaho's Salmon River. As for canoes? "Well, our raft carried eight people and a guide. But these canoes look awfully small."

Beside her stood Charles, a silver-haired lawyer in his early fifties. Divorced a year before, he had recently taken up skiing, backpacking, and now canoeing.

Two happy, if somewhat nervous, young women in their twenties, totally innocent of the ways of paddle or canoe, were part of the group. They worked together in an accountant's office.

Beside them stood a broad-shouldered man in his late forties. He was powerfully built and said he needed to keep his arms in shape, so he wanted to try canoeing. There was some jesting about hoping he wouldn't get mad at a canoe or he'd crush it. Next to him was his son. Dad was "Big Mike," a long-distance truck driver, and his son was "Little Mike," a twenty-year-old student studying engineering. "Little Mike," it turned out, was an experienced canoeist and kayaker and had talked his dad into this trip.

Then there was Stan, a skilled canoeist and my good friend and co-leader. Wearing a full beard, dressed in ragged shorts and torn shirt, he looked more the bedraggled river rat than a successful printing-firm executive in his 9:00 A.M. to 5:00 P.M., Monday-through-Friday life.

So that was our group. Young. Mature. Inexperienced. Skilled. An average canoe group for a great weekend.

For the next half hour we talked about how to handle a paddle to make a canoe go where you want it to go when you want it to go there and how to stop when you want to stop without ramming head-on into a rock or the bank.

Questions?

"Yeah," said one of the young women, Lisa. "Is it dangerous? It doesn't look dangerous. I mean, it looks so flat and smooth and easy."

"You can have problems." I held up my life jacket. "That's why we wear our life jackets. At all times."

A group of perhaps a dozen canoes was pushing out into the

river. Paddlers climbing in. Paddles flashing. Talk and laughter filling the air.

"Watch," I said, pointing to them. "They're all novices."

"How can you tell? By the way they're paddling?"

"Nope. They're mostly sitting on their life jackets. If they were veterans, they'd have life jackets on before putting in."

Now it was time to pair off and stow our gear on the canoes, carefully tying the plastic bags with our extra clothing to the thwarts.

The sun was warm as we slid our canoes into the briskly moving water. It was an ideal day for the start of a trip.

We rounded a bend. I waved for the canoes to make their way over to me. We practiced basic strokes for the bow and stern. Slowly but steadily, as we began moving again downstream, these inexperienced strangers to canoeing acquired better and better control over their crafts, proving once again my permanent prophecy: Anyone can learn to canoe. I had seen it happen before, many times—seniors getting into a canoe for the first time and learning, in a day or two, to be very good, controlled paddlers; excited teenagers picking up skills so quickly it made me jealous; families learning together the first time Mom and Dad get into a canoe.

And so our tiny flotilla continued downriver, past the heavily wooded shores. At midday we found a private sanctuary, a 50-foot stretch of beach between two house-sized boulders. We beached our canoes and scrambled ashore.

Two paddlers had been assigned as cooks for the day. They spread out a poncho and took the lunch out of a pack protected from splashing water by an inner plastic bag. You will enjoy every trip you make by canoe if you eat well. And so we did: a creamy Brie cut into wedges and served up on English water crackers, sliced salami with a spicy mustard, juicy purple plums, powdered lemonade mixed with the spring water we had brought in a plastic jug, and miniature candy bars, plus a crisp and refreshing Fetzer Chardonnay, cooled in the river's currents.

Nearby, a small stream flowed into the river. I gathered our half-novice group alongside its waters for a lesson in how to canoe light rapids—light, but not necessarily gentle rapids. Not if you go belly-up in them. I pointed out the wave patterns on the stream and explained what lay ahead. "Always aim for the Vs to go through safely," I finished.

By midafternoon we were paddling up to the shore where we would make camp for the night, near where we had left our cars at the livery parking lot. Drivers hiked up to bring the cars down a dusty road through a stretch of woods to the river's edge. Tents were quickly put up, equipment stored, and a fire started. A fine meal, befitting fine canoeists, was served up by the two designated cooks.

Night settled gently over the valley. We sat around a small glowing campfire long after dark, recalling the day, telling stories, sharing dreams. I heard Nancy tell her husband: "We've got to take the kids canoeing." And handsome George was smiling at Marge, who was quite attentive to his charms, while "Little Mike" ignored everyone but the two young women.

The fire burned down. By ones and twos everyone drifted off to their tents. Stan and I shared a last sip of cognac, then walked down to where the canoes had been pulled ashore and flipped over, flashing our lights on them. "Everything look secure?"

"Looks fine to me. Well, good night, Stan."

"Good night, Herb."

I crawled into my tent, slipped off my clothes, and climbed into my sleeping bag. Through the insect netting of the tent's door filtered a soft glow from a wondrously bright moon. I listened to the sound of tiny waves lapping at the shore. That was the last I remembered until the dawn.

About this Book

Canoeing is for everyone. It's for kids in summer camp and for a family that wants to paddle the wilderness. It's as easy for Grandma to learn as it is for a sturdy truckdriver. It's a sport whose enthusiasts set their own level of adventure. Extreme canoeists maneuver their modern version of a native American craft through roaring waters that no sober, intelligent paddler would touch with anything but a camera with a 300mm lens. And it is a skill that weekenders enjoy on quiet rivers.

No one else but you paddles your canoe, if it's a solo craft, or you and your partner when enjoying the fun of tandem canoeing. Whatever level you choose, wherever you paddle, it's your own ability and effort that makes canoeing an enriching experience.

It's the one outdoor activity in which only a small number pay out the bucks to own their own equipment. Canoes, paddles, and life jackets usually are rented for a few hours, days, or weeks from more than 2,000 liveries in the United States and Canada.

The growing lure of the paddle is national. Throughout the United States and Canada, there are great rivers and remote wilderness regions that attract participants who enjoy the freedom of the waters.

Two weeks. 150 miles. Ah, the sad joy when a glorious Sierra Club wilderness adventure on Canada's Megiscane River came to an end.

In the first study of its kind, the National Survey on Recreation and the Environment (NSRE) reported in 1996 that approximately 24.2 million Americans relish outdoor pleasure in canoes, kayaks, or rafts. Of this astounding total, 13.2 million are canoeists (approximately the same number of Americans who are Alpine skiers), 1.4 million paddle kayaks, whereas another 15.2 million favor rafting.

Breaking down self-propelled water sports by regions, the NSRE study found that 13.7 percent of paddlers are in the Midwest, 12.1 percent are in the Northeast, another 11.9 percent are in the South, and, finally, the West attracts 10.7 percent of the enthusiasts.

Once you discover the glorious pleasure of canoeing, the sport will become a part of your life. The objective of this book is to heighten your interest in this increasingly popular sport, to teach you some basic techniques of paddling, and to give you an insight into the many ways you can enjoy canoeing. If your goal is to enjoy the pleasure of casual canoeing, you are in excellent company. According to Tom Foster, the 1990 chairman of the National Instruction Committee of the highly respected American Canoe Association, 70 percent of canoe enthusiasts prefer a gentle-water touring experience. The other 30 percent may go on to more challenging adventures on whitewater. This book has been designed to offer valuable information to both groups.

Basic Equipment

In the first chapter you will learn about the basic equipment of canoeing. Information on the parts of the canoe, shapes and types of canoe, and canoe materials will acquaint you with any craft you might use as you enjoy the sport. The section on paddles will teach you the parts of the paddle and will help you select the right shape of paddle for the kind of canoeing you are doing. You will learn about paddle materials and how to choose the proper paddle length. Tips on the care and purchase of paddles are also included.

The first chapter also contains a section on the canoeist's best friend—the PFD, or personal flotation device. Commonly known as a life preserver or life jacket, it is essential to canoeing safety. You will learn the various types of PFDs available and which of those are best suited to canoeists. Tips on size and comfort will help you purchase your own life vest or select a properly fitted one from the stock at the livery. Lastly, some words of advice are included to encourage you to wear a PFD while canoeing.

Information on accessories rounds out the chapter. You will find out which items are indispensable and which are simply nice to have along. You'll discover that much of the gear of canoeing is small, lightweight, inexpensive, and useful for other outdoor activ-

ities. You may already have a good waterproof pack from backpacking or camping experiences, for instance. A sponge, a water
jug, a sturdy rope, and a cut-off plastic bottle for use as a bailer are
all the gear you'd need to add for a day on the river.

Paddling

The second chapter gives basic instruction on different types of
paddling—bow and stern, tandem and solo. Details on getting in
and out of the craft and sitting, kneeling, standing, and changing
seats in a canoe provide a basis for safe handling skills.
Instruction on how to hold your paddle precedes individual
descriptions of canoeing strokes, and some advice on practicing the
strokes follows.

Getting Underway

Chapter 3 provides basic instruction for handling a canoe and
sound advice on basic paddling skills you should have before you
go out on the water. You will learn about the International Rating
System's classification of rapids, water level and flow, and
canoeists' skill. It will help you assess your own capabilities and
educate you as to the level of difficulty you might encounter on a
particular route. You will also learn how to load and balance your
craft and how to put in, ferry, and take out in quiet water and swift
currents. You'll learn how to adjust your course and read water formations. What's a V, anyway? You'll learn.

A section on coping with wind is important for all paddlers,
whether on open water or on sheltered rivers or streams. The section includes fun ideas for using the wind (create a canoe catama-
ran or rig a makeshift sail); it also describes the dangers of beam
seas, crosswinds, head winds, and tail winds and provides paddling instruction for dealing with each type.

Chapter 3 also provides information for advanced paddlers; it
discusses eddy turns, backpaddling, and other difficult maneuvers
in whitewater. The chapter also reviews some typical canoeing
hazards and their solutions and offers information on emergency
procedures for capsizing or person-to-person rescue. And you'll be
reassured to find out about the National Canoe Safety Patrol.

Liveries and Outfitters

Chapter 4 tells you everything you need to know about liveries
and outfitters. You'll learn how to find them and how to recognize
a good one from a bad one. You'll learn about the services they offer
and the equipment they provide; sections on costs, rain checks,

refunds, insurance, and references will help you compare various operations and select a reputable outfit to make your trips successful and safe. An extensive list of state agencies that can supply you with canoeing information and the names of liveries and outfitters is provided for your convenience.

Short Trips

If you need advice on planning your first short canoe trip—a day or a long weekend, for instance—check out Chapter 5. It gives details of what to wear and what to bring along in the way of food, first aid, and other personal gear for a day trip. It goes on to describe options like livery-arranged overnight trips or do-it-yourself overnights.

Canoeing with Kids

Sure you can take the kids along! With the help of Chapter 6, you'll discover that kids and canoeing mix well together. Advice on clothing, sleeping bags and other camp gear, food, and the kids' medicine chest is designed to make family trips easy. The chapter also includes water safety tips, PFD information, and suggestions on swimming and paddling. Sections on enjoying the outdoors and using the outdoor classroom on in-camp days as well as en route ensure that your family canoe trips will be fun.

Wilderness Travel

Many canoeists eventually travel to remote areas for a look at the beauty of the wilderness from their canoes. Chapter 7 provides a wealth of information on the wilderness experience, from planning the route to putting out the campfire. You'll learn how to prepare your maps, how to divide camp chores, how to choose a campsite and set up camp, how to portage, how to orient yourself if you lose your way, and how to pack your gear. Information on sleeping bags, camp stoves, clothing, tents, packs, and dozens of small necessities will help you equip yourself properly. Advice on protecting your food supplies, disposing of garbage, and cleaning your campsite are just a few of the issues addressed in the section called Making Camp.

Outdoor Cuisine

From freeze-dried lunches to three-course dinners alfresco, Chapter 8 describes camp and canoe food extraordinaire. You'll learn how to plan for short or long trips, how to plan nutritious menus, how to figure out quantities for large and small groups, and how to shop for and pack your selections.

Field Medicine

Whether you have a medical emergency or nasty sunburn, this chapter will come in handy on any wilderness or weekend trip. It includes suggested first-aid texts, items for a first-aid kit, a discussion of drowning and hypothermia, and advice on wild animals, bugs, bees, and poison plants.

Protecting Our Rivers

Chances are if you are a canoeist, you're also an environmentalist in spirit or in practice. Chapter 10 discusses the need for all outdoor enthusiasts to take an interest in the protection of U.S. waterways for the use and enjoyment of all generations. It includes a list of organizations to contact for further information.

Et Cetera

The appendixes of this book are intended to help you obtain any other canoeing information you may need. Clothing and equipment outlets, canoe and paddle manufacturers, books, videocassettes, maps, Wild and Scenic River agencies, conservation organizations, canoe and kayak schools, clubs, and shows are listed among them. Addresses, telephone numbers, prices, and other details are included for your convenience.

So, you want to get away from the scars and tensions of the daily bread-and-butter struggle, away from traffic, away from the frustrations of city life? Let the canoe become your magic carpet into the freedom of the outdoors. Go alone or with a friend, or invite a few friends or your family. Go ahead. Grab a paddle.

CHAPTER ONE

BASIC EQUIPMENT

CANOES, PADDLES, LIFE VESTS, AND OTHER NECESSITIES

Some half a million people paddle the nation's waterways every week during the summer, most of them using equipment rented from the two-thousand or so liveries scattered throughout the country. The basics are few: canoe, paddles, life vests, sponge, painter (rope to tie onto the canoe), plastic bags for personal items, and whatever else the individual wants to bring along, from lunch to extra dry clothes. That's about it for the one-day pleasure cruise. Camping gear rounds out the list for overnight trips.

This chapter includes basic information that will acquaint novices with basic terminology and specific variations on the equipment theme. Many canoeists rent their canoes, paddles, and life vests from responsible liveries and outfitters, but the chapter will educate you about what to expect when you arrive at the livery. You will learn about the parts and various types of canoes and paddles, life vest options, and other necessities for short and long trips. A section on accessories provides some ideas for extras that will make each trip easy and pleasurable.

If you are a beginner or novice, at least skim the chapter briefly so that you're familiar with the terms and can make a good decision when you are offered rental options. As you become more experienced, or if you are already familiar with the basics, read the chapter more thoroughly so that you feel comfortable requesting a specific variety when you rent for different kinds of trips. Eventually you may want to purchase your own equipment; at that point, review the chapter carefully to make sure you buy the right equipment for your favorite kind of canoeing.

Canoes

Whether you're a beginner about to try a day on a popular river with a group of friends, or a veteran paddler beginning to think about buying a sleek, sturdy canoe of your own, you should know something about canoes themselves.

The Parts of a Canoe

Figure 1 gives the correct names for the parts of a typical aluminum canoe. These are the same basic parts found on all canoes, no matter what they are made of.

In the old days of wood-and-canvas canoes, the bang plate on the better craft was a band of brass that protected the delicate and intricate front of the bow and, often, the stern. It is common today to see plastic canoes fitted with bang plates made of Kevlar, a material that looks much like fiberglass. A strip of Kevlar covers the bow and stern and extends a foot or two under the bottom of the craft. This reinforcement, popular on rental canoes, protects the bow against rocks and other objects that crop up to harass inexperienced paddlers. It also offers some protection to the forward bottom of the canoe, which inevitably gets scraped when being paddled onto the shore.

Note part 5, the gunwale (pronounced "gunnel"). The part of the gunwale that faces the inside of the canoe is known as the inwale; the part facing the outside, the outwale. Also note the extended keel, a feature found mainly on aluminum and wood-canvas canoes.

The Shapes of Canoes

On the canoe shown in figures 2 and 3, notice that the sides slope inward toward the gunwale. This kind of slope, called a

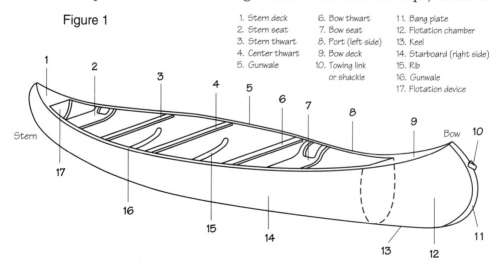

Figure 1

1. Stern deck
2. Stern seat
3. Stern thwart
4. Center thwart
5. Gunwale
6. Bow thwart
7. Bow seat
8. Port (left side)
9. Bow deck
10. Towing link or shackle
11. Bang plate
12. Flotation chamber
13. Keel
14. Starboard (right side)
15. Rib
16. Gunwale
17. Flotation device

tumble-home, was developed long ago by Indians building birchbark canoes. It helps keep water from splashing into the craft.

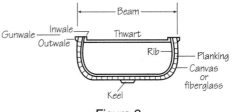

Figure 2

The part of the outwale that extends out from the canoe also helps keep water from splashing up and into the canoe. Some designs will use a slight outward flare, instead of a tumblehome, to keep water out of the craft.

If there is a general, although not always reliable, rule about the sides flaring, forming a tumblehome, or going almost straight up from bilge to gunwale, it is this: The straight side is basically for touring; the other shapes give more protection on rougher river waters.

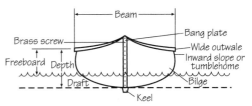

Figure 3

Like the sides of the craft, the bottoms vary in shape, as shown with some exaggeration in figure 4.

A flat bottom is a delight to the novice. It gives a canoe a feeling of stability. A flat-bottomed boat is also easier to maneuver in whitewater. When a flat-bottomed canoe tilts sharply to one side, however, it is much more apt to flip over than a round-bottomed canoe. Therefore, though the round bottoms do not have the initial feeling of stability, they are more forgiving when tipped, thus providing more total stability.

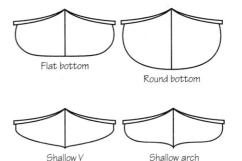

Figure 4

There also are subtle differences in hull shapes involving what are described by their designers as a shallow V and a shallow arch. The V-configuration canoes generally track (travel in a straight line) better, whereas the flatter and rounded bottoms maneuver better.

The "rocker" is the longitudinal curve of the canoe as illustrated in figure 5. The straighter the hull, the better it holds a straight course. The upswept ends are designed for greater maneuverability. Extreme curves are the choice of whitewater paddlers where swift maneuverability is required. Most canoes rented by liveries tend to have flat bottoms and a modest rocker or none at all.

Canoes differ in such areas as the depth measured from the gunwale to the bottom; the length measured from tip to tip, as well as

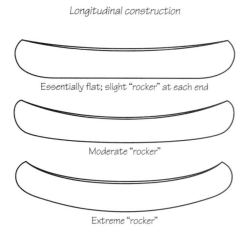

Longitudinal construction

Essentially flat; slight "rocker" at each end

Moderate "rocker"

Extreme "rocker"

Figure 5

The slight V hull marks this as a touring canoe, especially suited for long travel on flat water. The V hull is slightly more difficult to maneuver than the flat hull.

along the waterline; and the beam, the width from gunwale to gunwale in the middle of the canoe.

The great variety of shapes have more meaning to the person planning to buy a canoe than to one renting a canoe. If you have a choice, though, choose a rental canoe that meets your specific needs, whether it is a solo canoe for whitewater work or a canoe that will paddle easily day after day on a wilderness trip that does not involve whitewater.

Types of Canoes

Canoe and Kayak magazine classifies canoes into several types:

• The *casual recreation* canoe is best described as a canoe that "feels safe." It is 16 to 17 feet long, with a flat bottom and a slight rocker, is easy to maintain and store, and performs moderately well on short cruising trips and in modest currents.

• A *touring* canoe is usually somewhat longer (from 16½ to 18 feet) and has a wider beam for higher volume, to hold camping equipment. With its somewhat rounded bottom, the touring canoe is good for flat-water work and maneuvers well in light rapids.

• The *weekender* is a medium-volume canoe, about 16 to 17½ feet long, that will easily handle a total load of around 600 to 700 pounds; it tends to be a bit quicker on the water than the touring canoe. It is fairly easy to maneuver in Class II rapids.

• *Cruising* canoes are faster than touring models; they are designed for experienced canoeists who want maximum flat-water speed. Their rounded hulls show a modest V, and they are about 18 feet long. They are another medium-volume canoe.

• *Wilderness-tripping* canoes are also about 18 feet long, but they are wider than cruising canoes and thus have greater volume. Their bottoms tend to be rounded with a slight V; they can handle rough water, but they are not whitewater craft.

• *Whitewater* canoes are the real play boats of the rapids and roily rock-garden waters, built with extreme rocker, high sides to keep out the water, and flat bottoms for maneuverability. Solo models may be only 13 feet long, and tandem models are up to 16 feet.

• *Decked* canoes are also known as C-1 or C-2 models, depending on whether they carry one or two passengers. Used for whitewater and slalom racing, they look much like kayaks since they, too, have a covering that is an integral part of the canoe with openings for each paddler. Kayakers sit on the deck, or bottom, of the kayak, however, whereas paddlers in decked canoes either kneel or sit on seats.

• *Competition-cruising* canoes are made to go fast, fast, fast; speed is the top priority, so the profile is long, slim, and low. They may be up to 18½ feet long and are for highly skilled paddlers only.

• *Downriver* canoes, also built for fast paddling, are sometimes used by experienced racers. Usually 17 feet long, they have vertical ends.

• *Sportsman* models are wide, stable craft, sometimes with flotation bars along the outwales. Designed chiefly for fishermen and hunters, they are sometimes built with square sterns to hold a small motor.

• *Sport* canoes are akin to the weekenders. They offer a compromise between tracking and maneuverability and usually measure between 15 and 16 feet. They are best suited for easy trips, and for

(A) A modern development is the canoe designed chiefly for serious, solo whitewater canoeing. It is wide, short, and has an extreme rocker, which is clearly visible in the photograph. (B) The canoe is designed to carry two sturdy flotation bags at bow and stern, with space for the paddler midships.

The flat bottom with only a slight rocker marks this canoe as a typical river cruising model. It is very stable and easy to turn, yet it will hold a steady course.

simply having a pleasant time on flat water.

• *Freighter* canoes (yes, they still make a few for wilderness travel) are behemoths of the waterways that can be 20 to 30 feet long and carry up to 5,000 pounds of equipment, plus the paddlers.

• *Specialty* canoes don't fit into any specific category. The outdoor writer Nessmuk had a canoe once made for him that weighed a mere 16 pounds, and it was all wood. It would carry little more than a paddler and a few pounds of gear.

Canoe Materials

Birchbark, Wood, and Canvas

All wood canoes are made much the same way today as they have been for generations. First a keel is laid. Then wood strips are steamed and curved to form ribs that are fastened to the keel and to wooden gunwales. Finally, the outside of the ribs is covered with wood planks, and the seats, thwarts, and other essential parts are added.

If the planks are sheets of specially cut and seasoned birchbark, the result is a birchbark canoe. These are still produced on a limited scale by a few skilled craftspersons. On the other hand, if the planks are covered with canvas, the result is the famous wood-canvas canoe, which was the standard model for many years, having superseded the birchbark, and only began to become scarce after

The once universal wood-and-canvas canoe is now either an antique or a custom-made specialty item for affluent canoeists. Note how carefully each rib is installed in this beautiful example.

World War II. If the planks are made of attractive wood and are masterfully finished and fitted, the result is the all-wood canoe.

In all three instances the outer covering is given a special treatment both to protect it from scrapes and bangs and to preserve it against the disintegrating effect of water. Birchbark canoes are usually coated with spar varnish, or they may be covered with a clear fiberglass. Wood canoes with decorative planking may be covered with clear fiberglass, spar varnish, or high-density polyurethane. Canoes with canvas-covered planking go through a more elaborate process. The canvas is coated with a silica-based liquid, then cured under heat for several weeks. It is then sanded to a satin-smooth finish and coated with spar varnish or polyurethane.

Wooden canoes are superbly useful. They can sustain a great deal of punishment. They can be repaired if injured and, if properly cared for, will last for decades.

Aluminum

There is nothing extraordinarily difficult about manufacturing an aluminum canoe. A sheet of corrosion-resistant aluminum is placed over a mold and pressed into shape at a pressure of around 3,000 pounds per square inch. The same mold is used to press both halves. The half shells are cleaned, trimmed, and drilled so that they can be riveted together. Then they are heated to a T-6 temper, which makes the aluminum about 35 percent stronger than the original sheets.

After that, the two halves are riveted together. Rivets generally are anodized alumilite, with the heads set flush to minimize damage in an accident.

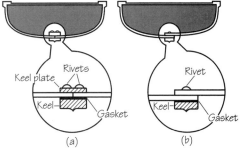

Figure 6

The most complex part of the assembly is fastening the keel. The keel is not needed on a canoe for directional stability (as it is on a sailboat), but it is essential for structural strength. The most satisfactory method of assembly is to place a gasket atop the keel, put the hull halves together on top of the gasket, butting each other, place another plate over the halves, and rivet all the parts together. A less satisfactory method is simply to overlap the halves and rivet them to the keel (fig. 6).

Grumman, which pioneered the aluminum canoe and gave the world canoeing as a whitewater sport, once produced nine different aluminum models, from 13-foot solo to 19-footers for professional guides. Though, the company no longer makes aluminum canoes, there are thousands still bouncing around on rivers and lakes and will be for decades to come. Aluminum canoes have one distinct advantage over the plastics that have replaced them: They never wear out.

But, aluminum canoes do have their drawbacks. They tend to be noisy, slapping against the water and resounding when a paddle shaft hits the outwale. If your craft bumps a rock, everyone in your party will hear the boom. Aluminum canoes also hang up on rocks that canoes made of synthetics will slide off. And they often seem either too hot or too cold. The fact is, they get no hotter or colder than canoes made of any other material, but they do heat up and cool off faster.

In addition, aluminum craft will dent and bend with sufficient

The American Indian, skilled in the ways of the wilderness on land and water, developed the most versatile of all river craft—the canoe. The Grumman company, seeking to make use of aluminum left over from World War II, in 1946 put the first metal canoe on water. The result: Canoeing exploded into a sport for playing in whitewater, challenging rapids, and frolicking where the waters run swift and deep.

impact. The dents remain until they are removed in a shop (or are stomped on with heavy shoes). Serious tears and cracks are not so easy to mend; they need a patch of aluminum riveted over the break. But if you don't wrap your aluminum canoe around a rock somewhere, and you give it only the most casual care, your grandchildren will be paddling it someday.

Fiberglass

Fiberglass, a product of World War II research, emerged as a canoe material not long after Grumman began stamping out aluminum craft. The material used is polyester plastic reinforced with glass fibers. Making a fiberglass canoe is a hands-on project, and you can get a kit if you want to make one in your own basement—though be sure you can get it out when it is finished. The vast majority are professionally fashioned.

The process begins with a "plug," a wooden mold that is really a wooden canoe with all the external features the fiberglass canoe will have. The plug is coated with a gel that, in turn, is coated with a couple of thin layers of resin-soaked fiberglass to produce a "female" mold. When thoroughly set, the female mold is removed from the plug and checked on the inside to make certain there are no blemishes.

The inside of the female mold is coated first with a special wax and then a gel, which will become the *outside* of the fiberglass canoe. Next, glass cloth is placed inside the female mold and wetted with a laminating resin, then smoothed by hand with a brush and roller. Varying thicknesses of glass cloth may be used—perhaps three layers of 10-ounce cloth and one of 6-ounce cloth; the formulas vary.

After the basic layers of cloth are laid, additional strips of fiberglass are added to strengthen the bilges and stiffen critical areas.

In a less expensive method, a "chopper gun" is used to spray a mixture of short glass fibers and resin onto a mold. The chopper canoes are considerably cheaper than hand-laid fiberglass, but they are heavier and less serviceable.

In both hand-laid and chopper canoes, the thwarts, gunwales, seats, and decks are added after the fiberglass has thoroughly cured. These canoes are easily repaired using kits that include fiberglass cloth and the impregnating resins.

ABS

Modern plastic canoes, made of ABS (acrylonitrile-butadiene-styrene), can best be described as sandwiches. The outer layer might be a vinyl skin to protect the craft from ultraviolet rays, then two layers of ABS, three layers of foam, two layers of ABS, and a final vinyl layer.

The ABS resists penetration by sharp objects but is too rubbery to make a sturdy canoe hull. The foam adds stiffness, and the final sandwich is not only rigid, but unusually durable and reasonably light.

When a canoe is made, sheets of the ABS sandwich are heated to around 305 degrees F and pushed into a female canoe mold, either by hydraulic rams or by suction. As the sandwich is heated, the layer of foam expands. Its millions of air bubbles make the canoe somewhat buoyant; to make it more so, flotation blocks are often added under the seats or the bow and stern decks.

There is one danger with seats with flotation blocks: Some come so close to the bottom of the canoe that a paddler's feet can get wedged under the seat, a deadly prospect if the canoe capsizes.

ABS canoes are unusually durable, and the plastic slides easily off rocks. The canoes can withstand the most shocking treatment. I have seen an ABS canoe wrapped around a rock like a horseshoe and then spring back to its original shape once it was pulled free—wrinkled, but otherwise undamaged. The wrinkles can be removed by heat, but removal should be done by an expert, not a garage mechanic with a blowtorch.

Within the industry some ABS canoes are known as Royalex.

Polyethylene

Polyethylene canoes are made of a plastic resin blended with heat stabilizers and ultraviolet inhibitors. The material is tough, resists impacts, and has a "memory" so that the canoe will bounce back to its original shape after a major bending on a rock. Indeed, Old Town demonstrates the toughness of its Discovery canoe, made of a specially formulated polyethylene, by crushing it against a wall with a truck in reverse; the canoe returns to its original shape. Still, even these canoes can be cracked and broken under extreme circumstances.

Polyethylene is popular for both canoes and kayaks because it can be molded more precisely than ABS—an especially important factor in whitewater and racing craft. Polyethylene is also more flexible than ABS, making it somewhat easier to handle in shallow water and rock gardens.

Polyethylene canoes are made much as ABS canoes are—sheets of the material are heated and molded. After cooling, the hull is completed with the necessary hardware.

Kevlar

Kevlar 49 is the material of the future. Pound for pound, it is five times as strong as steel. A canoe fashioned from Kevlar is both lighter and stronger than one made from any other widely used material. A 16½-foot cruising canoe made of Kevlar weighs about 45 pounds, as opposed to about 72 pounds for one made of ABS or aluminum. Now, pile that on your shoulders on your next portage.

Kevlar is a golden-yellow fiber originally developed by DuPont in the late 1960s to replace steel cord on huge aircraft tires. It is woven into fabric much the same way fiberglass is, and almost the same techniques are used in making Kevlar canoes as in making fiberglass canoes. Since the material is more expensive than fiberglass and more difficult to work with, a Kevlar canoe may cost two or three times as much as a fiberglass canoe of equal quality.

The Allagash

Half legend. Half history. Half lake. Half challenging white water. Meld these together and the result is a tremendous canoe experience—paddling the fabled Allagash Wilderness Waterway weaving its way through the great forests of Northern Maine.

Established by the state in 1966 to protect a 92-mile long "ribbon of lakes, ponds, rivers, and streams" the Allagash became the first of the country's National Wild and Scenic rivers in 1970.

Although it is not a true wilderness, canoeing its waters through a 2-mile-wide band of forested hills and mountains is a true wilderness experience. Fortunately there are occasional campsites chopped out of the rich forests. We found them a pleasure on a recent week's trip.

Moose munch on underwater grasses as you paddle by. Deer leap from the banks. Eagles and egrets keep you company.

It is possible to take only short trips on lakes, but for those who would paddle the entire waterway, previous canoe and camping experience is strongly recommended.

The area appears as remote today as it did when Henry David Thoreau penetrated its deep forests in the mid 1800s and wrote:

"In wilderness is the preservation of the world."

Kevlar also is used to reinforce crucial areas of fiberglass and ABS canoes.

Even Kevlar may not be the last word in canoe materials. Scientists are developing new types of plastics that are even stronger and lighter. Some, though, are simply too difficult to work and are far more expensive than Kevlar. But one of these days we'll all hear of yet another newest miracle material for a canoe, lighter and stronger than anything yet paddled on the world's waterways.

Proprietary Lay-up

This material might best be described as a secret. What the name refers to is the combination of fabrics and resins used by a specific manufacturer for its canoes. The combination is not always revealed.

Transporting a Canoe

Hauling a canoe is a problem that private canoe owners eventually seem to resolve to their satisfaction. On the other hand, paddlers who rent canoes may find it a complicated problem to haul their craft to the river or lake of their choice.

Obviously, if there is no room inside the car, and you are not driving a pick-up truck, that leaves the car top as the only solution. Never worry. There is a better way to use the roof than to cover it with a heavy blanket and try to tie the canoe down on top of it. A roof rack. But roof racks and cars come in so many different shapes and sizes that fitting the right rack to the right car for a canoe may seem like an insolvable problem. It is not. Here are a couple tips when buying—or renting—a roof rack that will carry one to three canoes.

Manufacturers make roof racks in two different styles, those for cars with traditional rain gutters or drip rails, and those that fit gutterless cars. If buying a rack, consult the manufacturer's roofrack guide to find the one that fits your car.

Next, check out the new multipurpose roof rack systems then buy the specific accessory to attach to it. There are accessories designed to carry bicycles, skies, kayaks, or luggage. Generally, accessories are rack ready so they can be put on or taken off the rack without removing the rack from the car.

The proper way to secure and transport a canoe.

Some accessories are equipped with locks. If yours has a lock, you won't have to sit by an open window keeping an eye on your canoe when you go into a road-side fast food restaurant for a relaxing snack en route to that distant river. Cable locks that can go around a thwart and the rack are excellent.

Canoes not only must be securely tied to the rack, but both the bow and stern must be tied to the bumpers so that in an abrupt stop the canoe does not go flipping over the engine, nor slide to the back of the car at high speed. Adjust the tension on the bow and stern ropes with tautline hitches (see page 56).

When two canoes are tied to the racks, they are placed upside down and side by side. A third canoe also can be carried—placed top up and between the two inverted canoes. Thus:

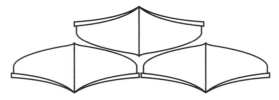

Bon voyage!

Paddles

A paddle is not an oar, even though both are roughly the same general shape. There are significant differences. An oar is almost always longer. It is inserted into an oarlock that serves as a fulcrum; the oar acts as a long lever, with the rower's hands on one end and the blade on the other. The blade always moves in the opposite direction of the force applied to the other end of the lever by the hands; therefore, rowers usually face away from where they're going, since they can get more power that way.

A paddle is unattached and is held in both hands. The blade can move in the same direction as both hands—one of which is on the grip, the other on the throat. Or the lower hand can act more as a fulcrum while the other applies the force. A paddler normally faces forward and

The rounded pear-shaped grip, on the left, is for cruising and touring; the T, on the right, is for whitewater maneuvering. The middle grip is a compromise between the two.

moves the canoe forward.

Now, never call a paddle an oar again.

Basic Design

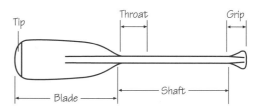

Figure 7

All single paddles (that is, those with only one blade) are similar in design (fig.7), though they differ in details. For instance:

• The *grip* may be either pear-shaped or T-shaped.

• The *shaft* is straight but may be either round or oval in cross section.

• *Blades* are made in three general shapes: beavertail, tulip, and whitewater.

• *Material:* Paddles are made of solid wood, wood laminates, aluminum, or synthetic materials.

What the Shapes Mean

Let's start with the grip. The pear shape is comfortable in the hand and is widely used for general paddling. The T gives the paddler the ability to hold on more firmly than the pear and is favored by whitewater paddlers, who frequently use considerable vigor in fast maneuvers.

Next, consider the shaft. Is there any reason to select an oval-shaped shaft over a round one? It's purely a matter of which feels better in your hand. Manufacturers usually produce the shape they have found to be most comfortable.

Blade shape is a more complicated matter. Originally all paddles made of a single piece of wood had long, narrow blades for a very basic reason: It was easier to find a flawless piece of wood in a narrow width; wider pieces often con-

The three most popular paddle blades, from right: beavertail, round-tip or tulip (for cruising), and square-tip or whitewater (for cruising and whitewater).

Today's superior wooden paddles are laminates of several types of wood. Each wood is chosen for properties of strength, flexibility, or light weight. Better paddles have special tip guards, either internal, external, or both. Note the bent paddle, increasingly popular for touring.

tained flaws, which could crack and break under pressure. A long and narrow blade is shaped somewhat like a beaver's tail, hence the name.

At present, beavertail blades are usually 5 to 7 inches wide and 14 to 20 inches long. Most beavertail paddles are still made from a single piece of wood. The beavertail shape is the easiest blade for a novice canoeist to handle.

The tulip shape is wider and longer than the beavertail—that is, 8 to 10 inches wide and 20 to 24 inches long. The tip of the blade has rounded corners. The blade moves a greater volume of water than the narrower beavertail and is the most popular shape used by modern canoeists.

The whitewater blade usually has about the same dimensions as the tulip. The major difference is that the corners of the whitewater blade are square, not rounded. The reason is important: In whitewater, paddlers frequently make important maneuvers by jamming the paddle into rocks and the bottom of the swift water, and the square tips hold better than the rounded tips. Whitewater paddles usually have T grips.

Bent Paddles

In addition to the standard straight paddles, the newest design is a paddle with the blade fastened to the shaft at an angle of 5 degrees to 15 degrees. In flat water or easy river paddling, where maneuvering is less important than distance, the bent blade is more efficient at propelling the canoe forward with each stroke. Here's why: As a straight paddle is driven backward through the water, the greatest forward pressure comes at the moment the blade is at the bottom of the arc. Forward pressure decreases as the blade continues its backward course. When the blade is attached to the shaft at an angle, the blade continues to exert more pressure on the water on the final quarter of the arc, and therefore a paddler gets more distance from each stroke. The paddler must remember to hold the paddle with the blade at a forward angle.

Bent paddles have one important drawback. They are not as efficient in maneuvering through rough water. So, if you're racing a friend across a lake, use a bent paddle; if you're challenging rock gardens and lots of crisscrossing currents, use a straight paddle.

Paddle Materials

As mentioned before, paddles are made from a variety of materials as time-honored as solid woods and as newfangled as complex synthetics.

The solid wood paddles generally are made of ash, highly favored by generations of paddlers because it is flexible, sturdy wood, yet not overly heavy. In New England a once-common expression among paddlers was, "Lay 'er to the ash." (Translation: Pour on the steam, pal; let's get this canoe moving.) Wooden paddles have also been made from solid maple and cherry, which, like ash, are strong, flexible, and straight grained.

Today's finest wooden paddles are made of laminates of wood. Through lamination several kinds of wood can be combined to bring together all the qualities necessary for a fine paddle: toughness, light weight, springiness, and the tendency not to warp. For example, paddles made by McCann Paddles of Cornell, Wisconsin, are made of butternut, white cedar, sitka spruce, and black walnut.

Fine wood-laminate paddles are treated to protect the wood and strengthen the tip of the blade. Grey Owl Paddle Company of Cambridge, Ontario, tips its blades with urethane and coats the entire paddle with a high-impact varnish, epoxy, and linseed oil.

Paddles made from modern synthetics are lighter and stronger than wood. Among them are Kevlar, graphite, foam core plastics, and ABS, as well as thermoplastic and fiberglass. Aluminum is also used. One company, for example, makes an ABS blade fastened to an aircraft-grade aluminum shaft; another makes a graphite-reinforced fiberglass blade with a foam core that is fastened to an aluminum shaft. Yet another makes a foam core inside a wooden skin of unidirectional graphite, Kevlar, and fiberglass. The least expensive models generally are an ABS blade on an aluminum shaft or an all-aluminum paddle.

Paddle Care and Costs

Synthetic paddles need little attention. Wooden paddles, whether solid wood or laminates, require a more careful approach. Even the toughest epoxy or varnish coating can crack. After each use a wooden paddle must be carefully inspected for any signs of damage that would permit water to seep into the inner wood. Usually a bit of sanding and a light touch of oil or polyurethane can take care of the problem.

Solid wood paddles are far more easily damaged than wood laminates. Unless they are specifically reinforced, their tips can be chewed into a thin strip of mush by constant banging and pushing against rocks and sand. To reinforce the tips, cover them with an inch-wide "bandage" of fiberglass, easily obtainable in fiberglass repair kits at automotive, boat, and hardware stores.

All blades, regardless of the materials they are made of, can be reinforced in the same way, but, as a rule, this is not necessary in any but the all-wood paddles. Should a blade crack, you can mend it with fiberglass regardless of the material of the blade.

Broken shafts are more difficult to repair permanently. The best on-the-spot solution is to glue the two halves together with a water-resistant glue and wrap a fiberglass bandage around the mended section. Replace the paddle before your next trip.

All paddles should be stored upright in a dark, cool place. Synthetic materials will, in time, deteriorate under the sun's ultraviolet rays, and aluminum will oxidize.

Choosing a Paddle

I would guess that nearly every canoe enthusiast, whether paddling flat water or challenging roaring rapids, eventually will buy a paddle of his or her own. Before making such a purchase, first decide what kind of canoeing you are most likely to do. If you anticipate chiefly recreational canoeing on flat water, consider a tulip blade and a straight shaft, or perhaps a blade bent at a modest 5 degrees. If you anticipate cruising the wilderness on long trips, you might consider a shaft with a greater bend, say of 10 degrees. If you are involved in both light rapids and river cruising, look at the whitewater paddles with straight shafts. If you are eager to get into whitewater playing, then a square-tipped whitewater blade is a must.

With the upper hand holding the grip at a position between the shoulder and the tip of the nose and the lower arm fully extended toward the water with the hand on the lower shaft, the blade should be fully immersed.

Next, consider the weight of the paddle. The more expensive the paddle, says the rule of thumb, the lighter and stronger it will be. If you think a few ounces are unimportant, try to image what those few ounces will feel like as you swing them back and forth a couple of thousand times a day.

Proper length is the next consideration. Begin by rejecting all of the following myths:

• *Myth 1:* Stretch your arms sideways as far as you can reach and hold the paddle parallel to the ground across your chest. You should just barely be able to close your fingers over the blade and grip for the right length.

• *Myth 2:* Rest the tip of the paddle on the floor and measure the height of the paddle against your own height. The grip should be somewhere between your chin and your forehead as you hold the paddle vertically in front of you.

• *Myth 3:* The fellow tossing around canoes at the livery knows the size you need.

The right way to select the correct length for you is to sit in a canoe and measure the distance (roughly) from the height of your nose to the water line. This measurement should be used as the length of the shaft from the grip to the *top* of the blade. Add to that the length of the blade you are most comfortable using. The sum of those two lengths is the right length for your paddle, subject only to such minor variations as you might acquire as you become a veteran with specific preferences.

If you favor a bent paddle, deduct approximately two inches from the total length. If you always paddle the bow, you can choose a paddle a bit longer than the sum of the two lengths. If you always paddle the stern, you can choose one a little shorter. If, like me, you paddle bow as well as stern and also from time to time stand up in the stern to check out what's ahead while still paddling, you might opt for a slightly longer paddle.

Most paddle manufacturers make adult paddles in lengths from 46 to 60 inches, but only in two-inch increments. Some manufacturers make paddles shorter and longer than the usual range; another half-dozen manufacturers make them to order at any length you choose.

Finally, consider the aesthetics of the paddles you see. As for myself, I want only a beautiful wood laminate.

Making the Purchase

Unfortunately, few sporting or canoe sports stores stock a large variety of paddles. Unless you are aware of the great variety available and spend some time looking for your first choice, you may find yourself buying a paddle just because it's in stock. Chances are you'll be disappointed you did. Shop around before you buy.

Current prices range from around $15 to $20 for aluminum cheapies to as high as $100 to $200 for superb, handcrafted synthetics and wood laminates.

Personal Flotation Devices

No one goes canoeing to drown.

I assume everyone will agree with this statement. So, if you are off to enjoy some paddling, personal safety has to be your number one priority. Accidents can happen. When an accident on the water becomes a tragedy, the odds are hundreds to one that the victim was not wearing a life jacket.

Types of PFDs

To the Coast Guard, life jackets are Personal Flotation Devices, or PFDs, of which there are five categories:

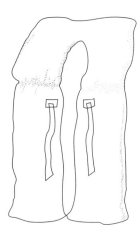

Figure 8

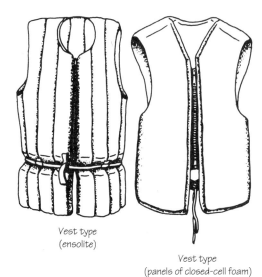

Vest type
(ensolite)

Vest type
(panels of closed-cell foam)

Figure 9

• *Type I:* These are big, bulky affairs, worn like a vest, with most of the flotation material in front so that an unconscious person will float face up. They weigh around 35 pounds. They are best suited for seagoing sailors, not canoeists.

• *Type II:* These PFDs (fig. 8) are shaped like horse collars that fit over the head, with some support material around the back of the neck and the rest across the front of the canoeist. Although popular with liveries, they are uncomfortable. As with Type I, they will float an unconscious person face up. They are not considered suitable in rough water.

• *Type III:* These are vest-type PFDs that look much like down vests (fig. 9). The better jackets are made with ensolite tubes sewn inside a nylon fabric; others are made from panels of ensolite (closed-cell foam), with the largest panels across the chest to help paddlers float head up. Since these require some effort by the wearer to remain upright, the Coast Guard says they are not life jackets but "buoyancy aids." Type IIIs are the most comfortable PFDs and the type most paddlers now wear.

• *Type IV:* Not to be worn, these are boat cushions and the doughnut rings popular at swimming pools. They are not recommended for canoeists, though some liveries will offer seat cushions instead of life jackets, especially if they rent only for use on flat water.

• *Type V:* Hybrids. These range from flotation belts for sailboarders and water-skiers to bulky PFDs similar to Type I, for commercial rafting and boat operators.

A couple of other configurations have not yet won final Coast Guard approval. One is a small PFD that can be inflated to improve its flotation capacity. The other is a "rescue jacket" for whitewater paddlers. It offers special features such as pockets and,

For more than an hour as we paddled easily down a wide, pleasant stretch of the Delaware River, flowing between New York and Pennsylvania, a small, single engine plane kept plying up and down the section we were on. This was the first, but by no means the only, time I ever saw an aircraft hunting for a drowning victim.

When we reached our take out at the Kittatinny canoe livery, I asked the young and muscular fellow who tossed out canoes onto a portable rack if the pilot had been searching for someone.

"Yup. Found the body 'bout an hour ago. That's the canoe he fell out of," he said and pointed to a canoe on the bank of the river.

Curious, several of us walked over to take a look. What startled me was to see, lying on the bottom of the canoe, the PFD he had NOT been wearing still tied around a six-pack.

on the back, a D-ring that can be used in a swimming rescue.

Sizes of PFDs

PFDs come in several sizes, though the size does *not* change the minimum Coast Guard flotation standards. Devices marked 0 (or one size) fit all adults with chest sizes between 30 and 52 inches. Those marked M (or adult, multiple) include small for a 32- to 37-inch chest, medium for a 38- to 41-inch chest, and large for a 42- to 52-inch chest. Children's sizes are marked with a C and come in two sizes: small for chest sizes between 19 and 23 inches and medium for chest sizes from 24 to 29 inches. It is essential that a small child wear only a PFD that has the major flotation material on the chest so that the child's head will stay out of the water in the event of an accident.

Old PFDs

Look with suspicion upon any old life jacket that shows obvious signs of deterioration, torn fabric, ripped safety cords, or corroded zippers. To test an older PFD that appears normal, the authors of *River Rescue* (Appalachian Mountain Club, 1984) suggest that you put it on and jump into the water. If your nose is underwater, toss it out.

Never, *never* wear an old-style PFD that uses kapok sealed inside plastic for flotation. Any tear in the plastic seal renders the life jacket useless.

Buying a PFD

PFDs are widely available in boating and marine supply stores.

Before buying try on several kinds or styles. Remember, you will be wearing it paddling a canoe, not roaring down a river in a speedboat. Is it comfortable? Sit down on a chair in the store and, with a paddle or broom in hand, mimic paddling. Does it bind? Does it bunch up awkwardly across your lap while you're sitting and stroking? It's too long if it does. If it is made with large panels of flotation foam, do you think you will be comfortable wearing it on a hot, sultry day, or would you prefer one with the flotation foam in strips inside a nylon fabric?

Although the Coast Guard does not require it, a child's PFD should have crotch straps that loop between the legs to prevent the life jacket from floating over a child's head. Crotch straps are also recommended for adult nonswimmers.

Though PFDs come in a variety of colors, go for the luminescent dazzle. The brighter and livelier colors give you a certain river chic, but more important, they are easier to spot in the water in the event of an emergency.

Wearing a PFD

Let's be reasonable about wearing a PFD. Must it be worn at all times? Not absolutely. On flat water with low currents—for instance, on a lake on a calm day when the weather is enticingly warm and the sun is shining brightly—keeping it on may not be essential for the average adult canoeist who also has some swimming ability. Children, however, in any situation should *always* wear a PFD. In any case, when not worn, the PFD should *at all times* be quickly accessible. Do *not* tie it to a thwart or hide it under other gear. When you need it, you may need it quickly.

When you're not familiar with a river and the possibility exists of a rock garden appearing unexpectedly around a bend, well, keep it on.

In more than twenty years of paddling, I've known of only two confirmed cases in which a person wearing a PFD drowned. One involved a fisherman wearing waist-high waders. His canoe flipped in a fast current, and the weight of the water in his waders was too much for his life jacket. The other case involved a sturdy, 6-foot nonswimmer who had been given a child's life jacket by a careless livery attendant. A novice paddler, he did not realize his too-tight life jacket could not support him. Every other canoe fatality I have known of involved a person *not* wearing a life jacket.

Accessories

As with any sport, the accessories for canoeing range from those that are essential to those that are merely convenient. And, as with most sports, these accessories range from items cleverly selected from household discards to expensive paraphernalia sold at canoe and sporting goods stores. Your ingenuity and your pocketbook will decide which accessories you choose.

Necessary Gear

The following items should be part of every canoe trip, short or long. They help you perform the most basic tasks of the sport and, especially in the case of fast water, are important to your safety.

• *Bailer and sponge.* Keeping a canoe clean and dry is important. Even an inch of water sloshing inside your craft will affect your ability to maneuver. If you can't bail it out quickly, put ashore and dump the water out. The two essentials for drying and cleaning are a bailer and a sponge (fig. 10). A large sponge is handy for mopping up water that splashes over the gunwales or drips into the canoe when you climb in and out. It's also amazingly effective for wiping up the mud and sand that collects in the bottom of every canoe. A bailer is necessary to scoop out larger amounts of water that splash into the canoe and gather quickly in a rain. For a highly useful bailer, cut the bottom from a 2-quart plastic bottle, but leave the cap on. An empty chlorine bleach bottle with a handle is especially easy to use.

• *Painter.* Every canoe should also be equipped with a painter, which is the canoeist's term for the 15- to 20-foot length of rope fastened to the bow for use as a tie rope, a rescue line, and so on. While canoeing, the painter is usually kept coiled and is placed on the deck in front of the bow paddler. A heavy rubber band will keep the rope from uncoiling (fig. 11). On most short, easy

Figure 10

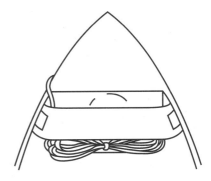

Figure 11

Don't underestimate the importance of a painter on a canoe trip in the wilderness. When not used in the canoe, it has multiple good uses ashore.

trips a light rope makes a satisfactory painter, but when there is a likelihood that the painter may be used for rescue work, a sturdy rope is essential.

A ⅜-inch soft-braid, floating polypropylene rope with a breaking strength of at least 2,500 pounds is the best choice. A canoe filled with water can weigh more than a half ton. A sturdy rope, indeed, is necessary to haul such a load in an emergency. In addition to its own dead weight, a canoe is subject to the drag of the current, which adds to the load. Painters have other important uses in addition to rescue work. They are used to tie your canoe ashore and are highly useful around camp for such tasks as supporting an overhead tarp and serving as a clothesline.

• *Water.* Unless you are certain of the quality of the water available on your route for drinking, always bring your own. A 2½ gallon plastic water jug is excellent for a small group of canoeists. Such jugs also come in 5-gallon sizes, but if you believe you will need more than 2½ gallons of water I would recommend that you bring two of the smaller size jugs; the weight of a full 5-gallon container is difficult to handle and cannot be distributed, of course, between two canoes or two portagers.

Essential Extras

These items are part of your basic equipment, but you should always take along extras of each for emergencies or accidental loss.

• *Paddles.* Though they shouldn't, paddles get lost. They can also break. Thus, even on an easy water tour, it makes good sense to take along one extra paddle for every three or four canoes. If you are paddling rough water, an extra paddle is an essential in *each* canoe.

• *PFDs.* You should also take along an extra PFD for each group of paddlers. Why? You may need the extra for the canoeist who left his ashore where you stopped for lunch or for the paddler whose PFD was left behind in the confusion and clutter of a wilderness portage, when canoeists are stepping over and around each other in thick brush, unloading and carrying equipment from the take-out to the next put-in.

• *Waterproof Bags.* Even on short and pleasant trips you should put everything you want to keep dry into some kind of waterproof packing. On pleasant day trips, heavy-duty plastic garbage bags are excellent. When the trip is longer and the likelihood of your gear getting wet increases, the waterproof bags must be sturdier than plastic trash bags. Excellent rubberized or plastic bags specifically made for canoeists are available at sporting goods stores and outfitters that specialize in such equipment.

One of the outstanding waterproof bags is Dacron-coated with PVC. Made by Northwest River Supplies of Moscow, Idaho, the bags have shoulder straps that make them easy to carry into camp or on a portage. They also feature a short strap handle that makes the bag easy to haul around in a canoe or on shore. A bag with a capacity of at least 2 cubic feet is fine for one person. A bag of approximately 4 cubic feet will provide enough room for the gear of two paddlers. Midway between plastic bags and the PVC gear bags are nylon stuff bags popular with backpackers. Insert a tough plastic inner bag to make them waterproof.

Gear for Comfort and Convenience

This equipment is not essential, but it will add to the ease and pleasure of short or long trips.

• *Solid Containers.* Used primarily to carry food on short trips, two types of solid containers are highly popular with casual canoeists. The first is a small ice chest, which fits easily into the canoe and can be tied by its handles to a thwart. The second is a plastic 5-gallon joint compound or paint drum with a secure plastic lid and a sturdy handle that can be tied to a thwart. On longer trips experienced paddlers usually carry all gear, including food, in waterproof packs with shoulder straps.

• *Thwart Bags.* It's always pleasant to have within easy reach a small waterproof bag in which to store little items like a comb, hand lotion, binoculars, lip salve, compass, or anything else you may want to use without having to dig into a large, waterproof bag.

You can fashion such a bag from a small nylon stuff sack with an inner plastic liner (such as a Ziploc bag) that can be sealed to keep out water. You can also purchase small PVC-coated nylon or Dacron bags from canoe sporting goods shops; these can be sealed against water and usually include a strap for hanging from a thwart.

• *Air Bags.* A fairly recently developed item for whitewater canoeists is the canoeing air bag, a large plastic inflatable bag held inside a canoe by tying it to the thwarts. The idea is to replace empty space with an inflated bag to keep water from swamping the canoe. Such bags are used almost exclusively by whitewater canoeists tackling Class III or Class IV rapids. As a matter of fact, an open canoe cannot paddle Class IV waters unless it is equipped with such bags.

• *Poncho.* This item is *not* recommended as rain gear. (Feet can become tangled in the loose fabric of a poncho in the event of an upset, seriously interfering with one's ability to swim or maneuver in the water.) The poncho makes an excellent ground cloth for lunch and a great cover for gear in a canoe should the weather turn rainy. A poncho also can be used as a ground cloth under a tent or a protective cover for a woodpile or camp supplies. It also makes an excellent temporary sail while canoeing, but more about that later.

• *Knee Pads or an Ensolite Pad.* These items have an obvious use: They offer comfort when you kneel while paddling. You can purchase knee pads in any sporting goods store, or you can buy a ¼-inch thick, closed-cell ensolite pad about 6 inches wide and 3 feet long.

• *Portable Seats.* Light seats usually made of a simple aluminum frame with nylon webbing are a comfort on easy trips and are available in two styles. One is basically a backrest that can be affixed to a canoe seat. The other is a portable seat that can be used as a backrest while canoeing and then brought ashore for use as a low camp seat. Anglers who do more casting than paddling are especially fond of the backrest style.

• *Wet Suits and Dry Suits.* Wet suits like those used by scuba divers are widely worn by experienced canoeists who paddle in cold weather. Usually made of neoprene or sponge rubber, the suits trap a thin layer of water next to the skin to retain body heat. Outfitters frequently provide the suits for clients taking major rafting trips in chilly waters. Originally designed to be worn in cold weather over a paddler's clothing, dry suites are also used as rain gear. They come in two styles: a one-piece outfit or jacket and pants. The fabric is either coated with polyurethane or a breathable material, such as Gore-Tex or Exeat, which blocks out water but permits sweat to escape. The garments have neck, wrist, and ankle gussets that can be worn loose or wrapped firmly. In some styles the chest may be opened with a zipper for comfort when the weather permits.

Odds and Ends

Need an anchor? A strong nylon mesh bag filled with rocks and tied to the painter makes an excellent one.

If you bring a camera, either keep it in a waterproof camera container (widely available at camera shops) or wrap it in a Ziploc plastic bag.

You really won't need a map for a short river trip, but good maps of the river—often available at the livery where you rent your canoe—will have interesting details and information about the river and countryside. They also make fine mementoes of a trip.

If you're interested in bird life, by all means take one of the pocket-sized bird identification guides for the unusual waterfowl you will see. A pair of 7- or 8-power binoculars are handy.

Plan on a bit of fishing? Be certain you have the appropriate license. Fish and game wardens are highly suspicious of canoeists with fishing tackle.

Bugs usually are not a problem once you are waterborne. A good

Want to find out about outdoor equipment before you buy it? For the most honest, and unbiased, information, check the annual gear reviews now published by *Backpacker* and *Outside* magazines. *Consumer Reports* also, from time to time, publishes excellent reviews on such things as boots, tents, and sleeping bags.

repellent, however, will come in handy when you're walking or camping along the water's edge.

To protect your eyes from sun glare, wear sunglasses with a high UV factor. Protect your skin from the sun's burning rays with a sunscreen with a factor of 15 or higher.

The Bottom Line

So, what do you need for a pleasant day trip? Not much. A bailer, a sponge, and a painter. A waterproof bag for your gear. A small ice chest or 5-gallon plastic bucket for breakables and food and a plastic jug with clean drinking water. That's it. The livery provides the canoe, paddles, and PFDs. Fancy comes later.

CHAPTER TWO

PADDLING

Basics for All Paddlers

The first time you climb into a canoe and pick up a paddle it's painfully apparent that propelling your craft in the direction you want isn't quite as easy as an experienced paddler makes it look. Stroke. Your canoe sort of wanders away from where it should be heading. Stroke. Stroke. Your canoe is now turning in a sloppy circle, pointing the wrong way. Whose fault? If you are in a tandem canoe, the fault obviously lies with your partner. So, try again.

Without guidance even the most awkward beginners learn to paddle a couple of strokes on one side, switch hands, paddle a couple on the other. By constantly switching back and forth or calling stern warnings to a tandem partner, beginners can eventually move from point A to point B on a reasonably calm lake or slow-moving river.

With some instruction and some practice, you will quickly—far more quickly than you might believe—become adept at using the key strokes to go precisely where you want under generally calm conditions. Handling difficult currents or any class of whitewater, or fighting tides and winds, will require more knowledge of a canoe and paddling strokes.

Step One: Relax

To learn to canoe, learn to relax. You can neither learn nor paddle when you are tense, worried, or ill at ease. *Relax. Let go.* Before you step into your canoe, stretch and warm up. Flex your muscles. Bend and twist. Swing your arms. Breathe deeply. These exercises won't strengthen you. They will give you an outlet for unnecessary tension. In a canoe you must be emotionally nimble and flow with the currents. You control a canoe by working with it, not against it—by becoming one with the currents and the wind.

T'ai chi ch'uan, the ancient Chinese discipline of meditative movements, teaches as its first principle a flexible yielding natural to a child but usually lost to adults. T'ai chi enunciates an unconscious awareness of the down-flowing of the body, a flowing balance from the navel into the earth. When you sit in a canoe, practice the first principle of t'ai chi—let your mind and body flow into the water. Become a fish. The water is your medium. Do not soar above it as a bird. You are not reaching for the sky. Flow with the river as a fish does.

Skilled canoeists have this concept ingrained into their nature. New canoeists learn it only by letting go of apprehension and fears and accepting the medium of a canoe in water.

Making Basic Moves

Getting In. Though there is no particularly right way to get into a canoe, the usual method is to push the canoe well into the water with only its stern touching the bank. In a tandem canoe, the stern paddler locks the end of the canoe between his or her legs while the

With bow partner and guest safely seated, the stern paddler pushes away from the bank, one foot in the canoe, then climbs all the way in as the canoe moves forward.

bow paddler steps aboard and, with one hand on each gunwale, walks directly down the middle of the canoe and steps into the bow seat. The stern paddler, holding one hand on each gunwale, puts one foot on the deck forward of the stern seat and shoves away from the bank with the other, climbing into the canoe as it becomes waterborne. The solo canoeist boards much as the stern paddler in a tandem canoe does, grasping both gunwales, putting one foot inside the canoe, shoving off, and then getting all the way in as the canoe moves away.

It is embarrassing, but not at all uncommon, for novice paddlers to flip a canoe over while climbing in. The mistake is putting *both* hands and all of one's weight on the same side. Splash.

Getting Out. As there is no one right way to get in, so there is no one right way of getting out. In the days of wood-canvas canoes, the great sin in getting out was to paddle into the bank before the bow paddler jumped out, thus letting the bottom of the bow scrape

Courtesy and stability are good reasons for the bow paddler to step out and brace the canoe so that the stern paddler can come ashore.

against the sandy shore. With tough, modern materials, this method is no longer sinful. (Be careful, though. Don't smash into rocks or scrape harshly against sand or gravel.) It is usual to drive the bow gently onto the shore so that the bow paddler can step out onto dry land and pull the canoe farther up the shore; that paddler then turns and holds the bow between his or her legs while the stern paddler puts one hand on each gunwale and walks down the canoe and steps ashore.

Sitting and Kneeling. As for sitting in a canoe, sit any way in which you are comfortable: feet tucked under, or feet spread out, or one under the seat and one stretched ahead. In a new canoe make certain that when you push your feet under the seat they are not wedged in if the seat is exceptionally close to the deck.

When maximum control is important, such as when you are canoeing in a stiff wind or moving through heavy currents or rock gardens, then you kneel. Spread your knees wide apart and lock your fanny against the edge of the seat. This position gives you far greater control over the canoe than sitting does.

Some old-timers believe the greater control is a result of lowering your center of gravity. Nonsense. If that's all it takes to improve control, you might as well toss a 10-pound sack of sand in the canoe and all will be well. Alas, it won't change a thing. When you kneel, what really happens is that your knees and fanny are locked more firmly into the canoe than is possible in the nor-

A. *In easy water sit any way you're comfortable, legs extended, if you wish.* B. *When sturdy control is essential, in wind or fast currents, drop onto your knees, lock them into the bilges, and brace your fanny against the seat.*

Sure, it's okay to stand—in the correct position. A. Keep legs spread wide, feet locked against the bilges, knees slightly bent. B. Most important, keep one calf lightly touching the seat so that the body knows where to sit when the need arises.

mal sitting position, and so each stroke becomes more powerful and the canoe more responsive.

To test for yourself the dramatic difference a kneeling position offers, try a little experiment. First, sit on the seat, hold your paddle over your head with both hands, and rock the canoe from side to side with your hips. Then, drop to your knees, still holding the paddle over your head, and rock the canoe from side to side. You will discover that you are able to rock the canoe at a far greater lean in each direction in the kneeling position.

Paddlers who own their

One paddler walks to the middle of the canoe and crouches down, and the other paddler walks over the partner. A hand on each gunwale during this maneuver is important—the water could be cold.

own canoes often install thigh straps, one on each side of the canoe, just in front of their seat so they can thrust their knees through the straps for even greater control.

Standing Up. There is a popular saying in summer camp: Never stand up in a canoe. More nonsense. Standing is perfectly permis-

The Russian

Paddling the Russian River near Healdsburg is a sobering experience. Indeed, if canoeing the quiet waters flowing through the California countryside of the great wine region north of San Francisco is too sobering, end your trip the way we did. At the end of a pleasant one-day journey, we slipped out of our PFDs and into our car, then headed for a nearby winery for delicious free samples of the liquid wares made from its grapes. Our preference, a local dry white.

For those who may have forgotten their history, the Russian river once was paddled by Russian settlers who claimed the area before it became American territory.

sible and in fact should be practiced. Canoeists often need to stand to check out an obscure obstacle ahead without paddling ashore and getting out for a better look. On easy water the bow paddler may want to stand and spread out a poncho for a sail in a brisk tail wind. Some advanced paddlers enjoy the challenge of standing through light rapids, just as a good skier enjoys the thrill of racing down a black diamond drop.

The proper way to stand is to spread the feet so that each one is wedged against the bilge. Place one foot slightly ahead of the other. Bend the knees a bit to achieve better balance than a stiff-legged stance. Place the calf of the rear leg lightly against the edge of the seat so that you will be constantly aware of the exact location of the seat in case you must drop quickly into a sitting position.

It should be emphasized that the stern paddler should never stand without keeping the paddle in his hands in case there's a need for a quick maneuver to avoid a problem. When standing, practice paddling. Learn the feel of the strokes, performed in approximately the same manner as sitting, but there will be less power in the strokes.

Changing Positions. When bow and stern paddlers want to shift places in the canoe, it can be done in mid-river without paddling over to the shore. Here's how: Bow turns, facing the stern, stands up, and, keeping one hand on each gunwale, walks forward, stepping over the center thwart, then drops into a kneel on the deck, head down. Stern then stands up and, keeping a hand on each gunwale, walks forward, stepping over the kneeling bow partner, to the bow seat. Once the paddler is seated in the bow, the kneeling partner stands carefully, of course, keeping a hand on each gunwale, and moves to the stern seat (see photographs on page 42).

Paddle Position

First understand that canoeists refer to the terms *inside* and *offside* of the paddler. The inside of the paddler is the side on which he or she is paddling. The offside is the other side. Thus, if you paddle on your left, the left is the inside and the right is the offside.

Now you're ready to learn how to handle your paddle properly.

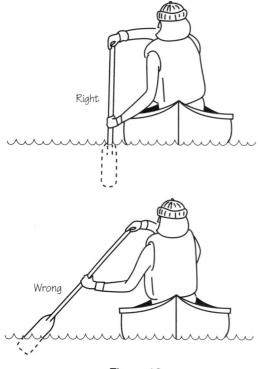

Right

Wrong

Figure 12

The offside hand grips the top of the paddle. To start the basic stroke, hand and forearm are level, about the height of your nose, and the hand extends over the gunwale. When the blade is fully immersed, the inside hand holds the paddle by the throat, as far above or close to the blade as you are comfortable. In the normal stroke the paddle is held as vertical as possible to the water. As the upper hand pushes down on the paddle, the lower hand pulls the paddle backward (fig. 12).

It will help to understand the basic forward stroke if you visualize that you are not so much pulling the paddle backward as you are pushing the canoe forward, almost as though the tip of the blade were pushing against the sandy bottom of the river, rather than merely traveling through water.

Bow and stern paddlers use the same vertical paddle position for maximum efficiency.

As you learn various paddle strokes, you should understand that a canoe has a central pivot point, like a weathervane. Thus, if you push the stern to the right, the bow will move to the left (fig. 13). If you pull the stern to the left, the bow will swing toward the right. In the bow, however, the canoe will move in the direction of the force. Thus, if your paddle pushes the bow to the left, the canoe will swing to the left. If the paddle moves the bow to the right through a pull stroke, the canoe will swing to the right. (See fig. 14.) The words *push* and *pull* have equivalents in canoe terminology. A push stroke is either a sweep or pry, and a pull stroke is a draw, or reverse sweep. But more about that later.

Without any knowledge of canoe strokes, beginners will strug-

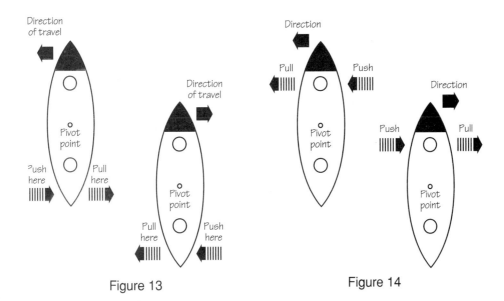

Figure 13   Figure 14

gle to keep the canoe in a straight line or make necessary turns by paddling first on one side, then on the other. By learning key strokes, paddlers can maneuver the canoe without changing the hands that hold the paddle.

As you study the following descriptions of strokes and what they do, it might be helpful to interpret what you are reading with a few props. Grab a chair and a long-han-

The basic forward stroke is properly executed with the upper hand slightly over the gunwale so that the paddle is vertical to the water.

Vertical paddle position is used by both bow and stern paddlers.

dled broom. Sit yourself down. As you read about each stroke, try it out with your broom as the paddle. Keep it clearly in your focus as you practice the strokes that each one is performed by paddling with vigor—spelled V-I-G-O-R. The paddlers of the world are divided into two classes: the Little Dippers and the Big Dippers. It's easy to separate them: Big Dippers stick that paddle straight and deep into the water and pull, pry, push, or sweep with V-I-G-O-R. Little Dippers poke their blades out at about a 45-degree angle, swish them lightly, then complain that the canoe just doesn't seem to respond.

Tandem Paddling

The bow and stern strokes described on the following pages are used by paddlers in a tandem canoe.

Bow Strokes

It is important to realize that all the bow strokes described here, with the exception of the cross draw, are done on *one* side of the canoe. And *all* the strokes are done without changing the position of the hands on the paddle.

Forward Bow Stroke. The bow paddler—who *always* paddles on the side opposite the stern, except in special circumstances—achieves forward momentum by placing the blade in the water well forward and pulling it straight back, keeping the path of the blade as parallel to the keel line as possible. That's all. Reach and pull. Reach and pull. (See fig. 15a.) If the stroke is sloppy, it will affect the direction of the bow (fig. 15b).

As the blade reaches the maximum back motion, lift it out of the water and turn it so that its face is parallel to the water. Keeping the blade close to the water in a horizontal position, bring it forward to the point where you want to put it back in the water for the next stroke. Now raise the paddle to a vertical position and begin your stroke. This applies to both bow and stern.

Bow Back Stroke. When a car gets in trouble, the first reaction

As I tell our beginner canoeists when discussing and demonstrating paddling techniques and strokes ashore prior to putting into the water for a weekend of basic canoeing, "Before we get started, I want too remind all of you that there is only one absolute in learning how to paddle tandem. If something goes wrong, it's always your partner's fault."

is to put on the brakes. Canoeists have a brake. It is called the back stroke. Jamming on a car's brakes is almost instinctive. Not so with the back stroke. Most novices forget they have this source of braking power and fail to use it. Don't minimize its importance.

For the back stroke, thrust the blade well back, drop it into the water, and drive it forward. It's simply the reverse of a forward stroke (fig. 16). This stroke gives you a moment to draw a deep breath and figure out what is going wrong and how to set it right.

Bow Sweep. The sweep is a stroke that moves your canoe away from the side you are paddling on as well as moving it forward. It's usually referred to as a quarter or half sweep. Reach well forward, keeping the face of the blade vertical to the water. Drop the blade into the water and sweep vigorously away from the canoe in an arc. The more vigorous the sweep and the greater the arc, the faster the bow will respond. (See fig. 17.)

Bow Cross Draw. The same movement of driving the bow away from the paddler can be achieved with a cross draw. Although tricky to learn, it is more efficient than the sweep. In this stroke, without changing the position of the hands on the paddle, pivot in your seat toward the offside of the canoe, reach forward on the side opposite to where you were paddling, keep the blade vertical to the water, and pull the blade in toward the canoe. Quick, strong strokes will work wonders in moving the bow swiftly. (See fig. 18.)

Bow Draw. Reach out at a 90-

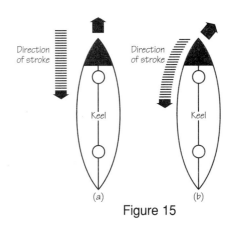

Forward Bow Stroke

Figure 15

When the paddle is brought forward, keep the blade low and parallel to the water until it reaches the maximum forward point where the paddle is shifted to a vertical position and a new stroke begins.

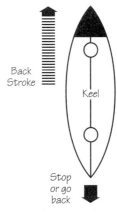

Bow Back Stroke

Figure 16

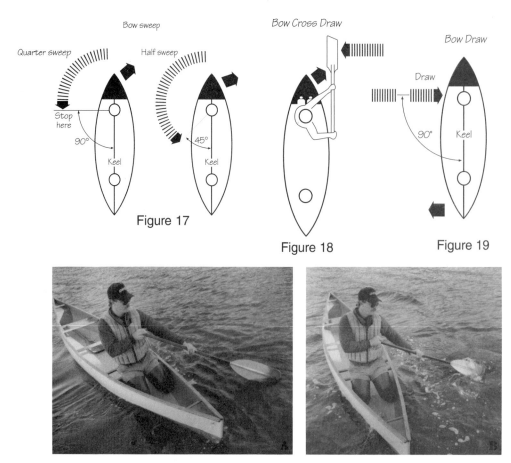

Figure 17

Figure 18

Figure 19

When executing a sweep stroke in the bow, (A) reach well forward to start the stroke and (B) sweep in a wide arc away from the canoe.

The draw is similar to the high brace. In both strokes the paddler leans out, holds the paddle as vertical to the water as possible, and pulls the blade toward the canoe. The vigor used in performing the stroke is the only major difference between the two strokes.

degree angle to the keel line and, holding the paddle as vertical to the water as possible, pull the blade toward the canoe. Just before the blade touches the canoe, sweep the blade backward and pull it out of the water (fig. 19). *Note:* When performed with maximum vigor, this stroke becomes a high brace, which is described later.

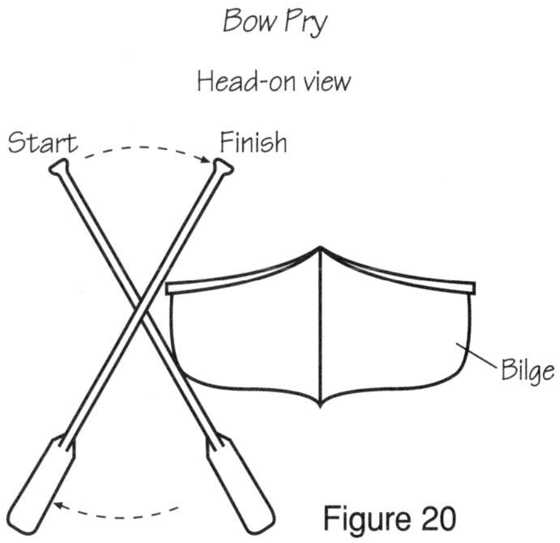

Bow Reverse Sweep. The reverse sweep is the opposite of the sweep. Extend the blade at a right angle to the canoe and sweep it forward in an arc. The bow is then pulled toward the inside of the paddler. At the same time the forward momentum of the canoe is slowed down.

Bow Pry. The pry stroke is achieved by dropping the paddle directly into the water and, using the gunwale itself as the fulcrum, literally prying the blade away from the canoe by pulling down on the grip. Pull with vigor. The pry is a powerful stroke and useful to avoid an immediate problem in troublesome currents or waves. (See fig. 20.)

Bow Jam. This is a stationary stroke. The paddle is held vertical, the blade is at right angles to the canoe, and it is jammed into the water. It is used chiefly in a quick pivot where the power of the pivot is provided by the current or the stern paddler.

Bow Rudder. Want to turn the canoe without effort? Use the stationary rudder stroke. To turn the bow to the inside, place the paddle in the water well forward and, keeping the face vertical, hold the paddle firm at a 45-degree angle. A moving canoe will move toward the inside. The cross rudder, like the cross draw, is achieved by pivoting toward the offside, putting the blade in the water well forward of the paddler, and holding it at an outward angle of 45 degrees. (See fig. 21.)

Bow Pry

Head-on view

Start - - - - - Finish

Bilge

Figure 20

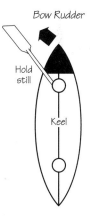

Bow Rudder

Hold still

Keel

Figure 21

Stern Strokes

Let's change seats now and move to the stern. In the stern you are the captain of the ship, the paddler with the greatest power. The bow paddles the side opposite you.

As we have discussed, the canoe moves on a pivot point. Look what happens when the stern is paddling alone. If the paddler were using only a straight, forward power stroke, the result would be akin to what would have happened to a Mississippi side-wheeler if it had had only one working paddle wheel. Look at figure 22.

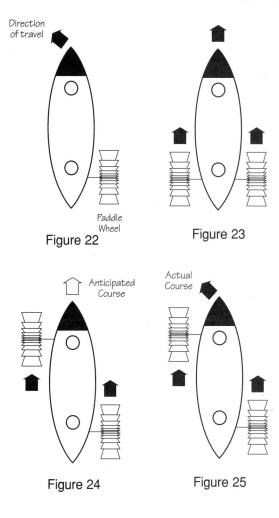

Figure 22

Figure 23

Figure 24

Figure 25

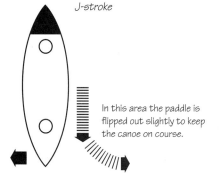

Figure 26

The force of the single paddle rotating through the waters would push the bow in the opposite direction.

To correct this veering off in one direction, the second paddle wheel could be added, as in figure 23. A rowboat achieves this by having the oars opposite each other. A bright inventor might decide, however, to place one paddle wheel toward the stern, the other toward the bow. If each moves at the same speed, exactly parallel to the keel and the same distance forward or backward from the center of the boat, the side-wheeler would move straight ahead. (See fig. 24.)

What would happen, however, if the forward paddle wheel was well back of the bow and the rear paddle wheel closer to the stern? The boat would move in an angle opposite the push of the rear paddle (fig. 25). So it is in a canoe. In other words, the stern paddler cannot simply use a straight, forward–back–forward–back stroke to propel the canoe; the canoe would be pushed to the offside of the paddler with every stroke. This is true to a lesser degree even when the bow is paddling. Thus, a corrective stroke is necessary.

J-stroke. This stroke is the equivalent of the bow's forward stroke. It is designed to push the canoe forward with the all-important and critical adjustment necessary at the end of the stroke to keep the bow in a straight line. Look at figure 26. The paddle is drawn back until, toward the end of the stroke, the blade, now basically vertical in the water, is pushed away from the paddler.

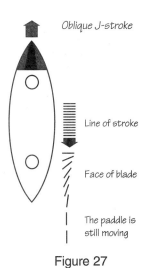

Oblique J-stroke

Line of stroke

Face of blade

The paddle is still moving

Figure 27

In the standard J-stroke, the paddler's thumb is in an upright position.

When this is done on the left side, the pattern of the blade in the water is the letter J. Hence, the name J-stroke. It is the push-away moment of the moving blade that corrects the tendency of the canoe to swing off course during the part of the draw that is parallel to the keel line. In the normal J-stroke the thumb gradually rotates to an upright position.

Oblique J-stroke. This form of the J-stroke also is given several different names, such as the pitch stroke or the modified J-stroke. As the paddle is pulled backward, the working face of the blade is gradually turned to the outside (see photographs). The paddler ends the stroke with the blade vertical and the thumb on the grip pointing down. The two forces of the oblique J—moving backward and at an angle—help the canoe maintain a straight course (fig. 27). If a subsequent adjustment is necessary, it is a push-away movement, precisely the same as in the regular J-stroke.

Stern Rudder. It is elementary for the stern to use the paddle only as a rudder, yet many novices have difficulty doing so simply because they do not hold the blade deep in the water. For the stern to move the canoe to his or her inside, the paddle must be held at a 45-degree angle out from the stern. By pivoting backward and holding the paddle at a reverse angle, the bow of the moving canoe will move to the offside of the stern paddler (see fig. 28).

Stern Pry and Draw. Pry and draw strokes are performed the same way in the stern as in the bow. If the pry is used far to the rear of the stern, it will push the canoe's stern away from the paddle, forcing the bow in the opposite direction. If the pry is used well forward of the paddler, it will have a tendency to push the entire canoe away from the paddle. The same is true with the stern draw.

For the oblique J-stroke: (A) The paddler places the blade well forward and close to the gunwale; (B) as the blade moves backward, it starts the movement at right angles to the keel line; (C) the blade begins to turn at an angle as it moves backward until (D) it is parallel to the keel line, and (E) the stroke ends as the blade moves outward in a slight J-shaped motion.

If it is used far in back of the stern, it will pull the stern toward the paddle and shift the bow in the opposite direction. If it is performed well forward of the stern, it will have a tendency to pull the entire canoe toward the paddle. Essentially, pry and draw are static strokes since they have no effect on the forward momentum of your craft. Look at figure 29.

Stern Sweep. The sweep stroke is a dynamic force, adding to the canoe's forward momentum as well as shifting the paddling angle. It is used to move the bow in a curve opposite the side on which the sweep is applied. The stern paddler places the blade in the water, reaching far forward and sweeping it back in an outward arc until it almost slaps the side of the canoe to the rear of the paddler. The greater the vigor applied, the more positive the results (fig. 30).

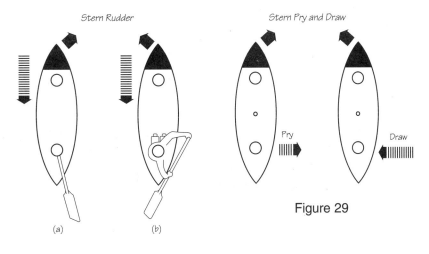

Figure 28

Figure 29

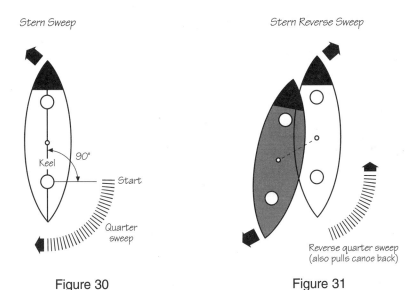

Figure 30

Figure 31

Stern Reverse Sweep. The reverse sweep is used to curve the bow to the same side on which the stroke is applied. It also will slow the forward momentum of the canoe (fig. 31.). The secret to a successful reverse sweep is to place the blade as far back as possible, immerse it completely, and sweep it vigorously in a forward curve. A half-submerged blade or a gentle forward arc produces minimal results.

Stern Jam. The jam is completely static. Drop the blade in the water at right angles to the canoe and hold it still. It will produce a slight arc by the bow on the same side on which the jam is applied.

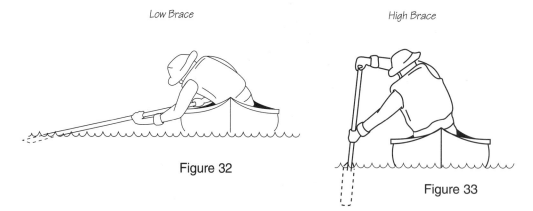

Low Brace

High Brace

Figure 32

Figure 33

High and Low Brace. Though your paddling goal may not be to run the thunderous currents that foam in whitewater channels, two of the key strokes that make whitewater canoeing possible are equally important for all canoeists: the low brace and the high brace. Why? Because they are the recovery strokes that rescue you from trouble when your canoe is in danger of tipping over because of whitewater currents, strong wind, the wake of a passing speedboat, or bumping into an unexpected rock on a moderate river.

Let's look at what happens when your canoe is in danger of tipping over on the side of the paddler. The gunwale dips toward the water. Once water splashes over the gunwale, the chances of rolling completely over are, well, let's say only 99 percent. So if the gunwale starts to drop, don't panic; throw a low brace. This is done by extending the paddle as far out as possible on the tilting side, slapping down on the water hard, and pushing down vigorously to keep the gunwale above the water line. At the same time, throw your hips (not your torso) to the offside to push the gunwale above the threatening water. It is this vigorous thrust of the hips into an upright position, along with the pressure of the paddle on the water, that straightens the canoe. (See fig. 32.)

The high brace is comparable to the draw, but is done with maximum vigor. It is put into action when the canoe tilts toward the offside of the paddler. To keep the gunwale from dropping into the water, the paddler leans way out, reaching as far as possible, and slices the blade down into the water, instantly pulling it toward the canoe in a vigorous draw. The paddler keeps the lean toward the paddle, exerting weight on the gunwale to force it down. (See fig. 33.)

The high and low brace strokes cannot be casually whipped out of the canoeist's repertoire of half-remembered strokes. They are effectively performed only when they are practiced, practiced, practiced long before they are needed.

For the low brace: (A) Paddler reaches well out and slaps down hard, (B) pushing the blade into the water swiftly; (C) when the low brace is used as an outrigger for canoeing whitewater, the blade is simply held steady at a slight upward angle to the water.

Practice

It's most helpful to have an observer along when practicing paddle strokes. Tandem paddlers have a great advantage—they can help each other in the same canoe. Seated in the correct positions, the stern can easily give the bow guidance. For the bow to help the stern, the bow turns around in the seat and faces the stern to observe the stern's movements.

Two paddlers new to canoeing can face each other and practice stern strokes one at a time without changing seats or position.

Paddling Solo

Yes, solo paddling is different from tandem paddling. First, when something goes wrong, you can't blame your partner. Second,

The buddy system is an excellent way for two canoeists to help each other learn. In this instance the bow paddler turns around and faces the stern. Each watches and coaches the partner in the proper strokes used by a stern paddler, from the correct J to backpaddling and all the strokes in between.

reread the previous sentence.

There are also other differences. Solo canoeists can use smaller, lighter canoes than tandem paddlers, so it is far easier for them to pick up the canoe, lash it to the car, toss a paddle inside, and head off for a day of paddling. Once on the water, there is an extra measure of quiet beauty to solo paddling. You select your own pace. You stop when and where you want for whatever purpose you have in mind—whether to cast a line and bring in bass or to set up an appealing camera shot. You set your own level of challenge if you want to play in whitewater and your own level of cruising comfort if you want to paddle a gentle stretch of a remote river.

Two experienced paddlers do it the right way. Paddles are almost straight, upper arms are parallel to the water, blades are well immersed. These guys are Big Dippers, getting maximum efficiency from each stroke.

The downside of solo paddling is the danger the canoeist may have to face alone. Where can the solo paddler turn for assistance? Many canoeists solve the problem by paddling in company with other solo enthusiasts. On one of my Sierra Club trips, a friendly couple of paddlers showed up with two canoes. Hers was a Mad River "Twister" model, his was an Old Town H2PRO. Both canoes are designed for whitewater and swift currents, but their owners were just as happy to paddle them on our trip through relatively tame Class II rapids. The woman told us, "We just love canoeing. It's our sport. But we can't share a canoe with each other, so we canoe alone—but with others."

Solo Position

Let's look at where the solo paddler sits. In tandem canoeing there is a bow paddler and a stern paddler at each end of the canoe. To approach the same level of control that two paddlers have, the solo paddler sits closer to the center of the canoe—in fact, just behind the center of the craft.

Specially built solo canoes are designed to place the paddler in this position; if, however, a solo paddler is using a tandem canoe, it is helpful if he or she reverses the position of the canoe, and sits in the bow seat *facing* the stern or kneels against the stern thwart. If the solo paddler tilts the canoe to one side, he or she reduces the contact of the hull with the water, thereby lowering the friction and raising the efficiency of the strokes.

Solo canoes generally are about 11 to 13 feet long. Tandem canoes for cruising, weekend trips, wilderness paddling, or even whitewater work, range from 16 to 18 feet. The solo paddler uses a shorter canoe for one important reason: It is easier to maneuver on whitewater as well as on a quiet lake.

Solo Strokes

The descriptions of strokes under Tandem Paddling apply to solo paddling as well. A pry is a pry, for example, and a draw is a draw. It is critical, however, for the solo paddler to remember that every stroke to adjust the course of the canoe must be executed with vigor, since no other paddler can assist in the maneuver.

Solo paddlers need to be close to the center of a tandem canoe. One way to do this is to kneel against the stern thwart or sit on it.

Tilting the canoe to one side when solo paddling puts the smallest amount of hull in contact with the water, thus reducing friction and increasing efficiency.

The solo paddler uses the same technique for a cross draw as does the bow paddler in a tandem canoe.

Forward Stroke. The stern paddler in a tandem canoe uses a modified J-stroke to keep the canoe on a straight course. In solo paddling the J-stroke is further modified into a stroke more or less resembling a C. The paddle is extended forward and slightly out from the gunwale, then brought back in a sort of inward sweep, ending in an outward J (or C). In this stroke the thumb on the grip points outward at the start of the curve and downward at the end of the stroke in a manner reminiscent of the oblique J of the tandem stern.

Sweep Strokes. The regular sweep stroke begins as it does in a tandem canoe. The paddler reaches well forward, beginning the stroke with the blade next to the gunwale and sweeping it outward in a quarter or half circle. The stroke pushes the canoe both forward and to the offside of the paddler. The reverse sweep is begun by the paddler dropping the blade well behind him and then sweeping it forward in a quarter or half circle. The power here pushes the stern to the offside and the bow to the inside; at the same time it slows the forward momentum of the craft. When the C, or forward, stroke begins in a power draw, the canoe will move forward and the bow will swing to the paddler's inside. If, on the other hand, the C ends in a vigorous outward movement, the effect is precisely the same as in the reverse sweep.

Draw and Pry. To push the canoe to the offside of the paddler, use a strong pry. If the pry is initiated forward of the paddler, the effect is to shift the entire canoe to the offside. If the pry is initiated behind the paddler, the effect is to put the greater motion into the stern, with the bow moving in the opposite direction or to the side of the paddler. A full sweep also pushes the bow to the offside of the paddler, but with forward momentum.

Cross Draw. By pivoting the body to the opposite side, but without changing the positions of the hands on the paddle, the blade can be used in a cross draw to swing the bow away from the paddler. For example, if the paddler is paddling on his left and uses the cross draw to reach to the right side of the canoe, the drive of the bow will be to the right.

Jam. Using a jam or simply planting the blade directly in the water and holding it motionless will cause the canoe to pivot toward the jam when the stroke is executed forward of the canoeist. The canoe will pivot more rapidly on the side of the paddler when the blade is jammed toward the stern.

Backstroke. The solo canoeist must understand and use the backstroke to avoid trouble in much the same way as tandem canoeists. The backstroke can be achieved in various positions relative to the center of the canoe. Practice will illustrate whether the backstroke should be done by reaching forward or to the back of the paddler and what effect each placement will have on the canoe.

High and Low Brace. The high and low brace are as important for the solo paddler as they are for the tandem canoeists. The high brace is not only a recovery stroke that pulls the canoe upright when the opposite gunwale is dropping swiftly into the water because of a haystack (high turbulent wave), rock, broach, or wind. It is also tremendously useful as a power stroke to make a swift inside turn such as an eddy turn. It can be used going into an eddy as well as going out of one.

The low brace has one chief function: to force up a gunwale dropping into the water. Use it for recovery with force. Slam the blade hard, working face down, to push up on the canoe.

The Double Paddle

A final note on solo paddling. Many who paddle alone prefer a double-blade, kayak-style paddle. A popular style is the "breakdown" paddle, which unscrews in the center. If you are new to solo paddling, you will become a better paddler quicker if you start with a single-blade paddle.

Paddling with Disabilities

It was a tiny flotilla—three canoes and one small four-person raft—casually paddling an interesting stretch of the Delaware River with some easy whitewater sections, fast water, and flat water. But there was something special about this group. Everyone was unusually cheerful, laughing, splashing one another, and impressively enjoying what they were doing.

Two persons on the raft and one in each canoe were paddling for the first time in their lives, discovering that even though they had major physical disabilities, canoeing was a sport in which they could have as many thrills as the guides who were taking them on a two-day trip that included a night ashore in tents.

Of the three in the canoes, a cheerful man in his mid-twenties had only one arm, another had lost a full leg, the third had lost a leg below the knee and had only two fingers on one hand. One woman and one man in the raft had lost the use of their legs because of spinal injuries.

At present special programs, all manned by volunteers, are bringing self-propelled water sports to people who are physically challenged. The specially trained Delaware trip leader, a warm and friendly man with eyes as blue as the sky, in his late thirties, told me later that there was something "beautiful about people who are involved in bringing outdoor pleasure to the disabled." He emphasized that those who volunteered recognized the work involved—and were willing to do it.

Regardless of the type of disability, there is almost no limit on the canoe, kayak, and raft activities available for the disabled, no matter how serious the physical problems. A number of organizations nationwide have special programs for the handicapped, with qualified and trained instructors. They include the following:

Cooperative Wilderness Handicapped Outdoors Group, Attention: C. W. Hog, Director; Idaho State University, Box 8118, Pocatello, ID 83209; (208) 236–3912. University-based adventure programs, including paddling.

Challenge Alaska, P.O. Box 11065, Anchorage, AK 99511; (907) 563–2658. Sea-kayaking trips.

Environmental Traveling Companions, Fort Mason Center, Landmark Building C, San Francisco, CA 94123; (415) 474–7662. Day and overnight trips in the San Francisco area.

Jumping Mouse Camp, Attention: Jeff Aronson, 215 West Bonita Street, Flagstaff, AZ 86001; (602) 774–9608.

Maui Sea Kayaking, Attention: Ron Bass, P.O. Box 106, Puunene, HI 96784. Sea-kayaking and canoe trips.

Nantahala Outdoor Center, IS19W, Box 41, Bryson City, NC 28713; (704) 488–2175. Trips and instruction.

Northeast Passage, P.O. Box 127, Durham, NH 03824-0127. Canoeing and sea-kayaking.

Norumbega Outfitters, 58 Four Street, Portland, ME 04112; (207) 773–0910. Sea-kayaking trips.

SOAR (Shared Outdoor Adventure Recreation), P.O. Box 14583, Portland, OR 97214. Oregon river tours in August and September.

S'Plore (Special Populations Learning Outdoor Recreation and Education), 699 East South Temple, Suite 120, Salt Lake City, UT 84102; (801) 363–7130. Flat-water canoeing and river rafting.

Wilderness Inquiry, 1313 Fifth Street SE, Box 84, Minneapolis, MN 55414-1546; (800) 728–0719. Canoeing and sea-kayaking trips nationally and internationally.

For additional information: The American Canoe Association has a Disabled Paddlers Committee that lists organizations offering disabled paddling programs, instructors with training in working with the disabled, and a schedule of Disabled Paddler Endorsement Instructor Training courses. Special information is offered by Ergosport Inc., Attention: Colin Twitchell, RD 2, Box 25M, Brattleboro, VT 05301; (802) 257–4926. An instruction manual, *Canoeing and Kayaking for Persons with Disabilities,* is available from the ACA for $16.95.

CHAPTER THREE

GETTING UNDERWAY

Classification of Rapids, Water Level, and Canoeists

Part of the planning of a canoe trip entails knowing what to expect on your trip. This is not so difficult to figure out when you are canoeing on a lake. For canoeing on a river, however, you should learn about the ratings given to rapids, water level, and even canoeists.

Rapids

A skier is aware that a black diamond run is a lot steeper and more difficult than a green circle slope. Rapids, like ski slopes, vary in their intensity. The International Rating system classifies rapids as follows:

• *Class A:* Lake water. Still. No perceptible movement.

• *Class I:* Easy. Smooth water; light riffles; clear passages, occasional sand banks and gentle curves. The most difficult problems might arise when paddling around bridges and other obvious obstructions.

• *Class II:* Moderate. Medium-quick water; rapids with regular waves; clear and open passages between rocks and ledges. Maneuvering required. Best handled by intermediates who can maneuver canoes and read water.

• *Class III:* Moderately difficult. Numerous high and irregular waves; rocks and eddies with passages clear but narrow and requiring experience to run. Visual inspection required if rapids are unknown. Open canoes without flotation bags will have difficulty. These rapids are best left to canoeists with expert skills.

• *Class IV:* Difficult. Long and powerful rapids and standing waves; souse holes and boiling eddies. Powerful and precise maneuvering required. Visual inspection mandatory. *Cannot be run in canoes* unless the craft is decked or properly equipped with flotation bags. Advance preparations for possible rescue work important.

Skill test number one: Paddle a light set of rapids, maybe a Class 1.5, while standing stern. Keep your PFD on.

• *Class V:* Extremely difficult. Long and violent rapids that follow each other almost without interruption. River filled with obstructions. Big drops and violent currents. Extremely steep gradient. Even reconnoitering may be difficult. Rescue preparations mandatory. Can be run only by top experts in specially equipped whitewater canoes, decked craft, and kayaks.

• *Class VI:* Extraordinarily difficult. Paddlers face constant threat of death because of extreme danger. Navigable only when water levels and conditions are favorable. This violent whitewater should be left to paddlers of Olympic ability. Every safety precaution must be taken.

Water Level

The characteristics of a river can change remarkably as the water level rises or falls. As you might expect, a set of Class II rapids can become raging Class IV when the water is abnormally high following spring runoff or heavy storms. Conversely, a Class IV can turn into a shallow pussycat when the water level is low in the late summer. Even normally calm stretches become turbulent and dangerous at flood stage, because the force of currents slammed this way and that by rocks and obstructions creates powerful and dangerous surface conditions.

An International Rating system has also been devised to describe river flow. The classification for a specific river may change from season to season; the following letter designations are used to describe water level and rate of flow:

• *L,* or *Low.* Below-normal levels for the river. Below-normal depth may interfere with good paddling. Shallows may turn into dry banks and low areas become muddy sandbars.

• *M,* or *Medium.* Normal river flow. Medium water generally is used to describe good water for rivers with slight gradients and enough depth for passage on the steeper sections.

• *MH,* or *Medium High.* Higher than normal. Faster flow on gentle gradients. The best flow for more difficult river sections with enough water for passage over low ledges and through rock gardens.

• *H,* or *High.* Water is becoming difficult to handle. The river is well above normal stage. Canoeists may refer to the strong currents as "heavy." Small debris may come floating by, a warning that the river is dangerous and better left to skilled kayakers or canoeists whose craft are supported by flotation bags.

• *HH,* or *High-High.* Very heavy water. Hydraulics are complex. Even slight gradients become treacherous. Debris frequent. Only for experts.

• *F,* or *Flood.* Abnormally high water, overflowing the banks; current extremely violent; low-lying areas underwater. TV crews show up to shoot tape for the evening news. Not for any boaters except those with appropriate equipment on dangerous rescue missions.

Canoeists

The Appalachian Mountain Club rates canoeists on a scale of I through V. Check your competence against their ratings:

• *Class I: Beginner.* Is familiar with basic strokes and can handle a tandem canoe competently from the bow or stern in flat water; solo canoeist is familiar with basic strokes.

• *Class II: Novice.* Can handle more advanced whitewater strokes solo or in either bow or stern of a tandem canoe. Knows how to read water; can negotiate easy and regular rapids with assurance.

• *Class III: Intermediate.* Can negotiate rapids requiring linked sequence of maneuvers; understands and can use eddy turns and basic bow-upstream techniques; is skilled in either bow or stern of a tandem canoe; can paddle Class II rapids in a solo canoe or kayak.

• *Class IV: Expert.* Has established ability to run difficult (Class III and Class IV) rapids in bow or stern of a tandem craft; can paddle solo in a properly equipped canoe or kayak; understands and can maneuver in heavy (Class H) water.

• *Class V: Leader.* Is an expert canoeist; possesses the experience, judgment, and training to lead a group of any degree of skill on any navigable waterway and in the wilderness.

To the preceding list I would add a "Class A" to describe one who has virtually no familiarity with canoes or canoeing.

Should You Paddle That River?

Three elements must be evaluated before you are competent to judge your ability to handle a river: (1) your ability; (2) the class of rapids; and (3) the river flow level. You should have no trouble deciding whether you should paddle an unknown 12-mile stretch of the Foamy River when a friend tells you:

"The first couple of miles are sort of flat, but then you'll run into five or six sets of Class II rapids just after you pass the old covered bridge on Route 6. There's a rock garden after the river swings past the only island you'll find on your trip. After that it's clear sailing, but the river normally runs pretty fast for the last 2 miles.

Of course, you gotta keep in mind we've had a lot of rain the past two weeks, and I know before that the river was running maybe a little below Medium, but it could be Medium-High right now. If it is, you can run a set of ledges to the left of the island. Otherwise, stick to the right. And that rock garden might be a Class III set of rapids, a helluva lot of fun—it's usually just a lot of maneuvering."

A helluva lot of fun is right, that is, if you and your partner have the experience to handle this kind of water.

The moral: Know what to expect from a technical description of a river and your own skill at the class of rapids and expected water level. Don't put yourself and your partners at risk. If in doubt, personally inspect the river first, or don't run it.

Canoe livery operators are excellent sources of information about the rivers they service and usually are quick to warn customers about any unusual situations. When the waters are dangerous because of high levels or unusual cold temperatures, most operators will cancel all rentals. The better ones will give out rain checks. Even if you have your own canoe, operators will be as ready to warn you about dangerous conditions as they are their own customers.

On-Shore Activities

There are various activities you need to undertake on shore before you actually set out.

Checking the Canoe and Equipment

Before you actually begin paddling on any trip, whether solo or tandem, make a careful survey of your canoe and equipment. Is everything properly lashed to a thwart? Is the painter tied to the bow? Have you forgotten any equipment on shore? Have you checked everyone's PFD? Do you have all the food, water, clothing, or equipment you will need? Taking the time to make these last-minute checks is well worth it; your comfort, convenience, and safety may depend on just a few minutes of caution.

Checking Weight and Balance

Once aboard, check the trim—the horizontal position of the canoe relative to the water. Canoes are designed to perform best when level. Skilled paddlers may deliberately choose to ride with the bow slightly up or down because of the wind or for technical reasons in whitewater, but unless you have a specific reason for changing trim, keep the canoe level. In addition, make sure your gear is centered as much as possible to make it easier to maneuver your craft. Do *not*, however, stack gear higher than the gunwales;

this will create genuine problems in a stiff breeze.

Lastly, check the freeboard—that is, the height of the gunwale above the waterline. It should be at least 6 inches out of the water. If the freeboard is less than 6 inches, your canoe is overloaded.

Tying Knots

Before you canoe it's a good idea to acquire some basic proficiency in tying knots. The knowledge is useful on portages, in camp, and on the trip to and from your canoe route. If you need to tie two ropes together, use a sheet bend or fisherman's knot (fig. 34). If using nylon or Dacron rope, tie either knot with an extra-long end to make it easier to untie; the knot will jam tightly under heavy loads, and the long end will help you work the knot loose.

When a long strain is not involved and you just want to make one end fast, use two half hitches (fig. 35). This knot is good for tying a canoe ashore or for tying one end of a camp clothesline. A

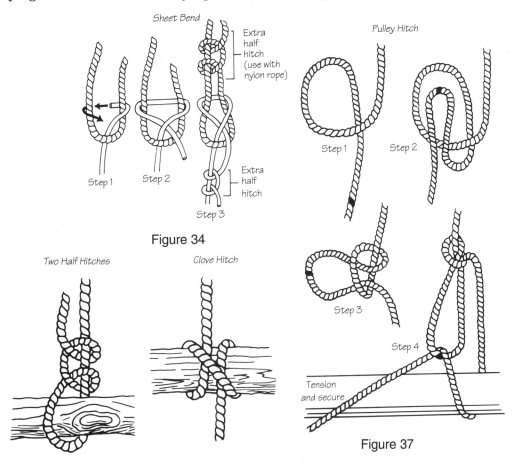

Sheet Bend

Extra half hitch (use with nylon rope)

Pulley Hitch

Step 1   Step 2

Step 1   Step 2   Step 3

Extra half hitch

Figure 34

Step 3

Two Half Hitches   Clove Hitch

Step 4

Tension and secure

Figure 37

Figure 35   **Figure 36**

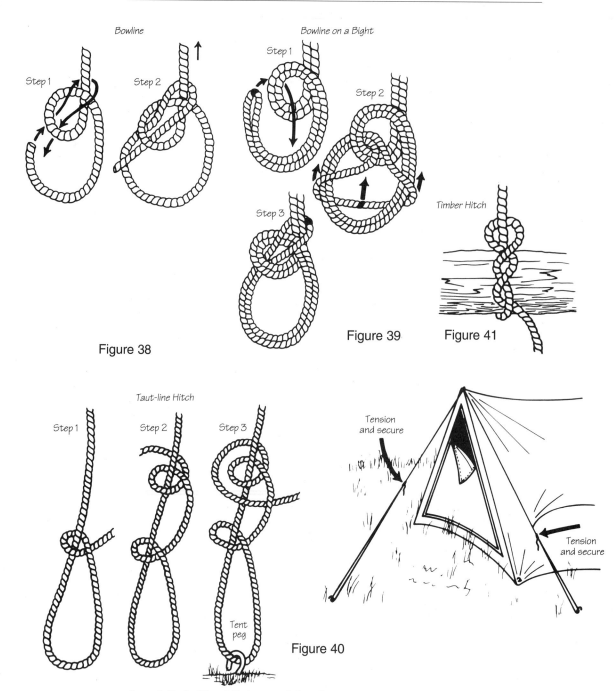

Bowline

Step 1

Step 2

Bowline on a Bight

Step 1

Step 2

Step 3

Figure 38

Figure 39

Timber Hitch

Figure 41

Taut-line Hitch

Step 1

Step 2

Step 3

Tent
peg

Tension
and secure

Tension
and secure

Figure 40

clove hitch (fig. 36) is used for the same purposes.

When you need to tie down a load and make it secure (such as putting a canoe atop a car), use a pulley hitch (fig. 37). The hitch doubles the force of pulling on a straight rope. Use caution as you pull the rope tight because you can apply far greater pressure than you would ordinarily.

For an excellent nonslip loop, tie the bowline knot, perhaps the most useful type you will have in your tying repertoire. A bowline may be tied in a single loop or in a double loop, which is known as a bowline on a bight. Bowlines may be tied anywhere on a rope—in the middle or at the ends, depending only on where you want to place the loop or loops (figs. 38 and 39). It is belaboring the obvious to warn you that you must secure your painter to the canoe with a sturdy knot. A bowline is excellent for this purpose.

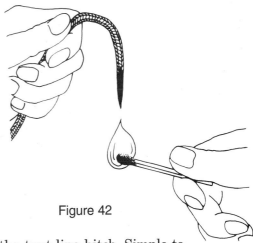

Figure 42

To adjust tension on a rope, use the taut-line hitch. Simple to tie, it can be moved up or down a rope until the proper tension is reached (fig. 40).

Lastly, the timber hitch you learned as a Boy or Girl Scout is still useful for hauling a load of firewood to camp (fig. 41).

To keep a synthetic-fiber rope from unraveling, melt the end with a match. As soon as the fibers begin to melt, wipe the tip of the rope quickly with a heavy cloth. This will pull the end into a ravel-proof thin strand instead of a melted glob larger than the diameter of the rope (fig. 42).

For more information on knots, visit your favorite outdoor equipment store. Virtually all such stores have books or pamphlets on knots and ropes. Learning how to tie complex knots is an enjoyable pastime when you're sitting out a terrible rainstorm in your tent.

Communicating with Your Partners

Communication between paddlers is essential at all times. Even before you begin paddling, talk to your partner or group. Let me tell you a grim story about not communicating.

My partner and I were canoeing an easy stretch of the beautiful Housatonic River, and we neared the only set of rapids for 10 miles. We had shot these rapids before, always taking a course to the left of an old concrete pillar in the middle of the river. As we paddled toward the rapids I thought it would be interesting to try the channel to the right. Did I tell my partner? No. I swung the bow to the right. My partner immediately swung to the left. Not realizing she was trying to correct for what she perceived as my error, I dug in my paddle and swung the bow swiftly to the right. Again it swung back. The next moment the canoe was caught on the pillar squarely midships. Smash. As I fought to hold the upstream gunwale out of the water, the power of the rushing river cracked the canoe and pinned it to the pillar, the bow on the left, the stern on the right. My carelessness about communication cost me hundreds of dollars for canoe repairs and a ruined afternoon.

Communicate. Communicate. You can talk about the weather and the birds, but make sure you also talk about your canoeing:

"Look—big rock at eleven o'clock."

"There's a better course to the right. See the V at two o'clock?"

"Hey, let's pull over for lunch near those two maples at one o'clock."

On the Water

When you're on the water, your attention is required for staying on course, anticipating upcoming currents or obstacles, and making the moves that allow you to negotiate the route.

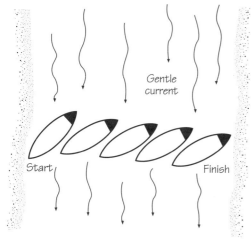

Figure 43

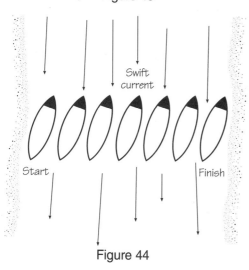

Figure 44

Learning to Handle the Craft

• *Putting In.* As has been previously explained in Chapter 2, when putting in, slide the canoe well into the water with the stern close to or touching the bank. The stern paddler locks the stern between his or her legs while the bow partner gets in, walking balanced in the center of the canoe, a hand on each gunwale, to the bow seat. After the bow paddler is seated, the stern paddler puts one foot into the canoe, shoves off, then climbs all the way in as the canoe moves forward (see photograph on p. 36).

• *Ferrying.* Crossing from one side of a current to the other in a straight line is achieved by a process known as "ferrying" or "setting." To ferry across in a straight line from bank to bank, point the bow upstream and paddle at an angle. The degree of

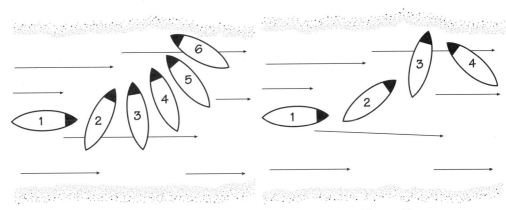

Figure 45

Figure 46

angle will be proportional to the speed of the current (figs. 43 and 44). A downstream ferry is achieved by backpaddling at an angle, a much more difficult maneuver, but an essential one for paddlers who challenge whitewater.

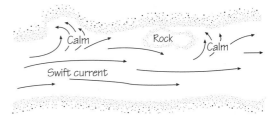

Figure 47

• *Taking Out.* In quiet water it's simple to paddle up to the shore so that the bow noses onto the bank.

When taking out in a current, however, swing the bow upstream and nose into shore at an upstream angle (fig. 45). If you attempt to paddle ashore at right angles, you may find that the current will simply push the canoe back out (fig. 46). In a strong current look for any kind of obstruction jutting out from the bank or a curve in the shoreland. Downstream of the obstruction will be a back eddy of calm water for landing (fig. 47).

Adjusting Your Course

Even the most experienced team makes constant minor adjustments to maintain course. If the canoe begins to shift from its intended path, an almost undetected change in a paddle stroke by bow or stern can return the canoe to its proper course.

This delicate art requires practice. Novices should learn to make small corrections early. Do not wait for the bow to swing so far to the right or left that it takes a major effort to return it to its course (fig. 48). A minor correction can be made, for example, by the stern the moment a change in course is detected. Simply hold the blade in the water at the end of a power stroke and use it as a rudder to put the bow on course (fig. 49).

Beginning paddlers need to master minor adjustment strokes

This is what happens to the tandem paddlers who overcorrect each off-course movement.

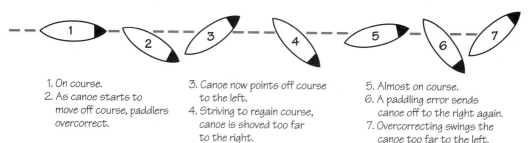

1. On course.
2. As canoe starts to move off course, paddlers overcorrect.
3. Canoe now points off course to the left.
4. Striving to regain course, canoe is shoved too far to the right.
5. Almost on course.
6. A paddling error sends canoe off to the right again.
7. Overcorrecting swings the canoe too far to the left.

Figure 48

Compare the novice erratic swings to right and left in figure 48 with the course by an experienced team. Each movement, from 1 through 5, shows how the canoe is maintained on course with almost imperceptible adjustments made at the end of each stroke.

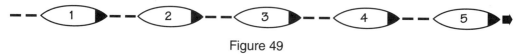

Figure 49

and overcome the rookie's tendency to watch only one's paddle, ignoring important directional aids like the horizon, the water, and the shoreline.

Shifting currents, the play of the wind upon the canoe, and the movement of waves and ripples all affect one's sense of direction. Beginners and novices have to learn to "read" the signs correctly to assess speed and direction. For example, what happens when a pleasant tail wind is helping the canoe move along? If you watch the water, you may get the sensation of traveling slower than you really are because the tail wind pushes ripples ahead of you faster than the canoe is moving. A light head wind will seem to be stronger than it is as you see waves rippling quickly past your canoe.

To avoid losing your sense of speed and direction, keep your eye on the nearest shore *and* a place on the horizon (a tall tree or a hill, for instance). You will quickly judge your rate of speed by the rate at which your canoe is moving along the shoreline. When you are trying to make some headway against a strong breeze, a glance at the shore will help you realize (frustratingly) that you're scarcely moving. You will use the point on the horizon as an "aiming stake." Keep the bow aligned with the aiming stake so that you know you are on your planned course. On a river with frequent curves, you will have to change your horizon point frequently. You may intend to follow a near bank for the shortest curve around a bend. It won't happen if

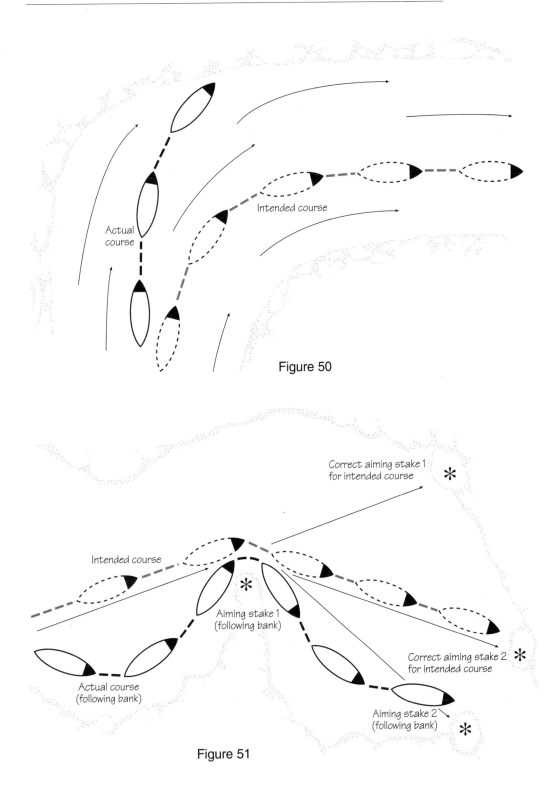

Figure 50

Figure 51

you pick out an aiming stake that leads you away from your intended course because of a steadily shifting direction (fig. 50).

On a large body of water, a very wide river, or a lake, the aiming stake is very important. Most beginning canoeists tend to stay parallel to the bank. The mistake of moving in and out of every little bend in the shore becomes quickly obvious on a small or narrow body of water, but not nearly so obvious when you are a very small canoe on a very large body of water (fig. 51).

Reading Water

Even if your only goal in canoeing is to enjoy the pleasure of paddling quiet waters through scenic countryside or in distant wilderness, it is important to know how to read the water. Every canoeist will eventually face light currents and rock gardens, both of which can be maneuvered safely and easily if the paddler knows what the wave configurations mean.

If your long-range goal is to paddle roaring Class II and Class III rapids, learning to read water is absolutely essential. Canoeists interested in advanced techniques need on-the-water training by skilled paddlers; souse holes and haystacks are beyond the scope of this book. All paddlers, however, will benefit from a short course here on reading waves and sizing up other water formations for the information they reveal.

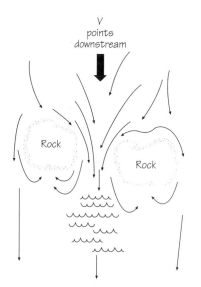

"U" formed by water flowing around an almost submerged rock, such as the rock on the right, means trouble.

Figure 52

• *Waves and V Formations.* River waves are different from ocean waves. Ocean waves move, and the water stands still. River waves stand still, but the water moves. Ocean waves are formed by the pull of the moon and the pressure of the winds. River waves are formed by the movement of water over and around rocks. They are also formed by underwater obstructions and the angle of the gradient of the river bottom.

The single most important formation to look for in rough water is a V, a smooth tongue of water shaped like a V pouring between the rocks (see fig. 52). The V means: Come this way; no rocks; no obstructions.

The size of a V depends on the depth of the water and the strength of the current. When the water is only deep enough for a canoe to

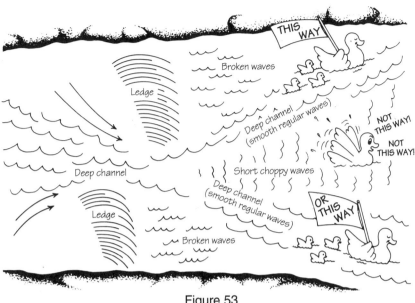

Figure 53

remain afloat and the current is gentle, a V may be quite small. In fast and heavy water, a V will stand out like a road sign.

Vs always point downstream. Beware when you approach a U, with the base of the U upstream. This is formed when water pours around a low rock, but you may not see the rock. Believe me—it is there.

As you emerge from a V, you will notice the water break up in various wave patterns. A choppy pattern means more rocks, seen or unseen, below the V. When the V flows into a series of regular, scalloped waves, this indicates a clear channel. Follow the scalloped waves for the safe route through (fig. 53). The size of the scalloped wave pattern does not indicate the degree of safety, but the regularity of the formation does. The more regular the pattern, the smoother the passage.

• *Standing Waves.* Waves formed by a drop in the river bottom are created by an inflexible law of motion: The amount of water passing a given point will be equal both on the surface and at the bottom. When the river bottom slopes, the water pouring over the sand and gravel on the bottom will be slowed by the variation in the patterns of the rocks and sand and also by friction. To compensate for the slower movement of the bottom water, the surface will form waves to maintain the same volume of water passing a given point.

Waves formed by the gradient of the river are a canoeist's delight. The more regular or scalloped they are in formation, the fewer the obstructions to harass or impede the paddler. On a fairly steep drop, the first waves can be huge; on a small drop, the scalloped waves may be very small. (See fig. 54.)

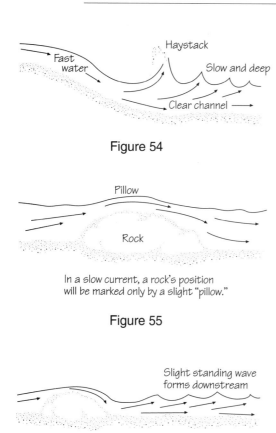

Figure 54

In a slow current, a rock's position
will be marked only by a slight "pillow."

Figure 55

In a faster current, there will be
greater turbulence.

Figure 56

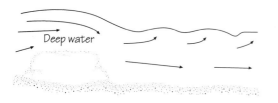

Figure 57

• *Submerged Rocks.* Look for two types of submerged rocks: the big, lazy rockopotamus and the mean, nasty rockagator. The rockopotamus tends to be found most frequently sleeping just below the surface of a gentle waterway. How do you know it's there? Its presence is indicated by a "pillow" of water. When you see a slight upswelling of water in front of the canoe, draw or pry your way to one side. (A failure to do so is usually not hazardous to your health. The canoe slides atop the bulging rock and stops.) Rockagators occur in faster, rougher water. The pillow they form is more of a small standing wave or a sudden foamy patch. Hitting one of these in a swift current is often a prelude to an unexpected dunking.

Study figures 55, 56, and 57 for an understanding of how the depth of the water affects the formation of pillows. You can see that rocks in deep water are easiest to pass over safely and cause the least surface disturbance. Rocks in shallow water cause more obvious pillows and subsequent waves and should be avoided.

• *Quiet Pools.* You are paddling merrily along and as you round a bend you see a turbulent stretch of water. You cannot see any rocks, but the broken formation of the water indicates a submerged rock garden. In the middle of the turbulence is a quiet stretch of water. Don't head for it. At the head of the quiet stretch is a submerged rock, large enough to create a back eddy (a reverse current below the rock) on the river, and trouble if you crash into it.

Looking Back

Rock gardens and wave formations appear differently when you

The Delaware

The Delaware River, where it forms the border between the forested hills of New York and Pennsylvania, is one of the country's all-too-few rivers protected as a scenic canoeing-rafting waterway by the National Wild and Scenic River system. The 75 miles of protected waters range from the wide and flat to fast waters splashing through rock gardens.

Enjoy spotting the slowly returning Peregrine Falcons and soaring Bald Eagles circling overhead but beware the Mongaup. Here the small Mongaup River joins the Delaware. The result—a rousing couple hundred yards of three-foot standing waves where kayakers love to practice the Eskimo roll and unwary canoeists learn how laborious it is to drag a flipped canoe ashore. Keep that PFD on.

Trips range from a few hours to five days, with camping limited to well-maintained waterfront livery campgrounds.

approach them than when you pass them. Once you've maneuvered through a difficult section, look back. How do the formations appear as you paddle away from them rather than toward them? This glance backward is an excellent lesson in reading the water.

Looking Ahead

What happens when you see some rapids ahead and you haven't the vaguest idea how strong or long they are? They may look quite mild; you may see only little edges of whitewater above the lip of the drop in the river where they begin. Before you proceed, though, follow the absolute "Rule of the Unknown Rapid"; it's the same for canoeists of every class:

Inspect *first*.

Paddle over to the shore. Get out. Walk down the bank. Walk to the very end of the rapids. Scout them well. Easy? You can run them? Fine. You've seen for yourself. Not certain you can manage when your canoe starts bouncing its way through? Then line down or portage around (see pages 115–119).

Canoeists sometimes are fooled into not inspecting the waters when a river is split by an island and one channel looks rough and mean, the other smooth and gentle. Remember—both channels join together at the same level again. The channel that starts easy has to make its plunge somewhere. Check *both* channels first.

One of the most dangerous obstructions is the low dam or ledge that crosses a river that otherwise is absolutely placid. It looks about as frightening as a thin rope crossing the entire river, but below it may be a drop of 2 or 3 feet. This drop forms a wave parallel to the ledge that curls back toward the ledge. The back flow can trap the unwary canoeist in a deadly roll almost impossible to escape.

Inspect *first*.

Coping with Wind

Few moments in canoeing are more blessed than when, after a long and wearing day, the wind suddenly comes to life, pushing steadily at your back, easing your work, saving wear and tear on the muscles. But for each such moment comes another not quite so blessed. The wind is head-on, slowing your swift progress to an aching fight against uncooperative elements or blasting your canoe to one side or the other, stubbornly challenging you to use all your skills to maintain directional control.

Light breezes are no particular problem in either lake or river canoeing. A breeze from the stern is actually helpful, and even a head-on breeze is only a slight nuisance. Beam winds, on the other hand, require more pry and draw strokes. Strong breezes on a wide river or lake can become a big problem. This section offers guidance for dealing with the hazards caused by wind and waves.

Makeshift Sails

Let's study the fun stuff first. Stronger breezes and light winds from the stern can be wonderful if the water is reasonably calm and you rig up a temporary sail to let the air speed you on your way. (Unfortunately, only tandem paddlers can do this; solo canoeists would need special rigging.) For the tandem team, the sail is rigged in the bow and can be achieved by one of two methods. In the first the bow partner dons a poncho and stands with arms outspread; the bottom of the poncho is firmly held between the sides of the legs and the gunwales. In the second method paddlers slip the arms of one or two sweaters or jackets onto the handles of two paddles or poles. The bow partner sits on the bow seat and holds this "sail" aloft. When under sail, directional control is maintained by the stern through the lazy technique of lying back and using the paddle as a rudder.

The Canoe Catamaran

If you are lake canoeing, you can lash two canoes together and erect a poncho sail between them. The canoes are tied catamaran-style with a long pole fore, a second aft, and the canoes spaced so

One can never be certain of summer weather in the wilderness of the North Country. On one two-week August trip in the wilds of Canada, the morning of our put-in the sun was glorious. The next seven days and nights—mist and showers and rain without let-up.

The early morning of the eighth day I awoke to find my tent ablaze with the morning sun. Ah. Heavenly blue skies. I popped my head outside, took one look, and groaned. The scattered pools of water were, but of course, pools of ice.

that the bows are 3 to 4 feet apart and sterns 5 to 6 feet apart. The spacing keeps water from piling up between the two canoes. The two bow paddlers jury-rig a sail (anything that works; ponchos held aloft by the two bow paddlers are excellent). The stern paddlers? Relax and steer.

Trimming the Canoe

On an open body of water, it makes sense to adjust the placement of gear so that the bow sets slightly higher in a tail wind and slightly lower in a head wind. In no case, of course, should the bow or stern be balanced to ride high out of the water. This is an invitation for the wind to push and shove your canoe around. On a river keep the canoe trimmed so that it rides reasonably level. Currents shift suddenly, the winds changes direction at each curve, and you must control your way through rock gardens and even mild whitewater. Under these changing conditions a level canoe is least vulnerable to the wind. In both situations gear should be stowed so that as little as possible is above the gunwale to catch the wind.

Tail Winds

Running before a breeze is a breeze, except when the tail wind is strong enough to start piling up high, mean waves. A tail wind then becomes a menace to your safety. In a sturdy tail wind, both the wind and the waves outrace the canoe. As the waves racing up behind the canoe grow bigger, a high wave rolling forward underneath the canoe can push the bow so high that the stern slides backward and the next onrushing wave overruns the stern, pouring water into the canoe. In such a situation a quartering maneuver is usually the one maneuver you can use to ease yourself out of danger. Swing the canoe so that it rides at an angle across the waves. Be careful, though—in a quartering swing, the wind is coming at you from an angle. Such a wind can push the canoe at right angles, so the craft is parallel to the waves and at risk of broaching and overturning in the troughs. As a general rule, paddlers do not have to change sides to keep a canoe on course in a tail wind. Canoeists can get some assistance by fashioning a sea anchor and tossing it over the stern. The drag will keep the canoe from being swung broadside in heavy seas. A sea anchor can be a large pot or kettle tied to the stern painter. A word of warning: If possible, tie the painter to the towing link on the stern bang plate. If the painter is fastened too high, such as on a thwart, it may pull the canoe into the water instead of stabilizing it.

Light Head Winds

When paddling into a head wind with no shifts in the direction of travel, the canoe offers the smallest possible target to the wind. The slightest movement off-course, however, will allow the wind to push the canoe broadside. To avoid this, paddlers must stay alert to the constant need to face directly into the wind. This is not terribly difficult on open water, but river paddlers may have more trouble staying centered when every curve means a shift in wind direction. The best solution in this situation may be to paddle to shore until the winds subside.

Moderate Port and Starboard Winds

Paddling at an angle to the wind may require a shift in the side you are paddling on to maintain a course with the least amount of increased effort. For example, if a wind is from the port (left) front, the bow should be paddling on the left with the stern on the right. Usually if the bow converts a power stroke to a modified draw and the stern simply uses a sweep instead of a straight power stroke, the canoe will remain on course. If the wind, however, is from the starboard (right) front, it may be easier if the stern switches to his or her left, so both bow and stern are paddling on the same side. Remember, the force of the wind is constantly attempting to push the canoe at a right angle to the direction of the wind; this is the force that must be neutralized. On the other hand, if the force of the wind increases, it makes good sense for the stern *always* to paddle on the windward side so that he or she is in a good position to throw a quick recovery stroke if the blast is strong enough to threaten the stability of the craft. (Don't forget that in any type of threatening wind situation, both bow and stern should give up the comfort of their seats and paddle from a kneeling position.)

Strong Head Winds

Danger from a powerful head wind sweeping up a long reach of open lake is comparable to the danger from a strong tail wind. When waves pile up to 3 or more feet in height, the bow rides high as the wave crest hits the canoe, then drops swiftly as the crest passes under the stern. If the waves are powerful, the bow can drop into the trough as the next wave sweeps against the uptilted canoe, breaks over the bow, and swamps the canoe. The obvious solution in this situation is to deliberately quarter the canoe, riding the waves at an angle. (See fig. 58.)

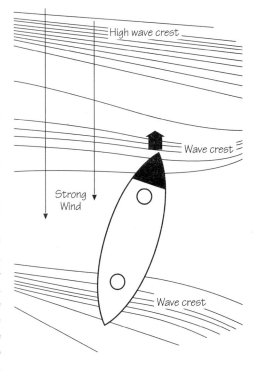

Figure 58

When the waves are high and the canoe is quartering, two problems can arise. First, the canoe can be swept into a broach and rolled over by an oncoming wave. Second, the canoe may veer sharply off-course when the bow rides onto an approaching wave at one angle and the stern drops into the wave at the opposite angle. In either situation the bow must be prepared to throw a brace and to maintain a strong forward momentum, relying on the ability of the stern to keep the canoe from swinging into the trough.

Paddling into a head wind or struggling with a loaded canoe in a tail wind is enough to make any canoeist, novice or veteran, cautious about crossing a wide lake. As long as you and your partner can handle a canoe with sufficient skill to keep the waves from crashing over the bow or leaping into the stern, you should feel confident you will arrive safely at your destination.

Beam Seas and Crosswinds

A beam sea (when the waves are crashing into the canoe parallel to the keel line) creates another set of hazards, enough to make any paddler question the wisdom of paddling when the wind is blasting the canoe from the port or starboard side. In the face of these crosswinds, frail craft may seem very frail, indeed.

An empty canoe on a beam sea will stay at right angles to the wind and will rise on the wave as the wave sweeps against it. It will lean to the opposite side of the wave, hold firmly erect for a brief moment as the wave crest passes, then slide down the passing wave, leaning again in the direction opposite to the movement of the wave.

When two canoeists and all their gear are aboard, this slight rocking as the wave passes beneath the canoe is sharply magnified because of weight added to the craft above the waterline. In this situation the canoeists must relax and become as flexible and fluid as a downhill skier. While the skis edge and shift constantly, the skier maintains a fluid balance. If the skier becomes rigid, so do the skis, and disaster results. In a beam sea the paddlers face real trouble if they forget to relax and remain fluid.

Two wave patterns cause particular problems in a crosswind. In the first pattern the crests of the waves are twice the width of the canoe's waterline. The time period between waves is short, and the canoe rides up crests and down troughs so quickly that the paddlers have trouble adjusting to the rate of the roll. The second challenge involves breaking waves. In this situation the canoe is hit by water falling from the crest of the wave as it starts to ride up the lee side of the wave. The canoe can fill with water in this way *very quickly*.

In these patterns, only one solution is practical: Quarter the canoe into or away from the wind and head for the nearest shoreline.

On the other hand, if the waves are manageable, you may be able to control the situation by bracing to the lee side. A solo canoeist can achieve this by leaning the canoe slightly to the lee side and paddling on that side. In a tandem canoe the stern paddler should be on the lee side and the bow paddler on the windward, since the stern paddler's brace stroke is more effective than the bow's. The bow also can either sweep or draw to maintain the canoe's balance as it slides up to the crest and slips into the moving trough.

Adjusting Your Course

When canoeing a beam sea with all your attention focused on keeping your balance at each wave, remember that you probably are being swept off the course you'd be paddling in a calm sea. To maintain your course you have to quarter into the wind and waves. Shorter waves should pose no particular difficulty; you slice at an angle across them. Longer waves appear more challenging, but they offer a maneuver not possible in a short wave pattern—ride in the trough briefly, then quarter upwind to adjust your course. In breaking waves, however, you'll find it impossible to ride a trough because the foaming crest to windward will add enough water to your boat to swamp it, whether you're paddling solo or tandem. In such a case you have no alternative but to alter your intended course simply to stay afloat. There will be time later to return to your planned course of travel.

Time to Stay Ashore

Now and again, no matter what the canoeists' skill or experience, prudence dictates: *Get off the water; it's too rough for your safety.* As a general rule, it is easier to make your way to shore by running with the wind rather than paddling against it. As you search for a take-out, avoid a shore battered by oncoming wind; the waves near shore will become higher and meaner. Stay clear of waves breaking on shore until you can paddle to the security of the lee side of any land projection.

When the winds are playing rough and you are still ashore, *stay ashore.* You may reach your final take-out a day late, but you and your party will be safe.

Advanced Paddling

Even though this book is not a manual for handling a canoe in Class III whitewater, intermediate paddlers may find much in these next pages to help them avoid trouble and have fun on rivers more challenging than Class I water.

Follow the Current

The first and most important lesson in running rock gardens (navigable waterways filled with rocks) and strong, shifting currents is to keep your canoe aligned with the current and

Veteran paddlers maneuver skillfully through the rocks on a Class II stretch of river in Ottawa's wilderness Parc de la Verendrye.

always lean downstream. Since the current does not always flow parallel to the bank in rough water, you must keep an eye on the water as well as the shoreline. If your canoe swings sideways to the current (a movement known as broaching), it is in immediate danger of lodging on a rock. If the current is strong enough and the canoe hits the rock midships, the power of the water can literally wrap a canoe around the rock. I've seen aluminum canoes bent into a horseshoe shape.

Broaching may also cause the canoe to flip over. When this happens, the canoe rolls *upstream*. The rock has stopped the canoe, and the water sweeping under the canoe is like a rug being pulled swiftly out from under a standing person—the canoe rolls opposite to the current.

If your canoe broaches and lands against a rock, you must act immediately to keep the upstream gunwale *above the water*. The upstream paddler throws a hard, low brace, pushing the gunwale up. The downstream paddler hangs a high brace, pulling down with full vigor on the downstream gunwale. Once a canoe is stabilized, then the paddlers can study the options for getting the canoe moving downstream without swamping it.

Control, Control, Control

Obviously, it is much drier and more pleasant to sweep through the rock garden without broaching or slamming against a rock. Without realizing their error, novice canoeists often predetermine a capsized canoe by paddling incorrectly. For example, beginners tend to paddle faster and harder in the rapids, as though they believe speed will guarantee safety. Nonsense. They are moving fast enough toward trouble without doubling their paddling speed so that they approach a difficult passage at a breakneck pace. Slow down. Backpaddle!

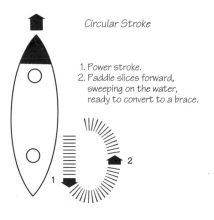

Figure 59

If there is one secret to successfully navigating a rough stretch, it is *control*. Not speed—*control*.

You know the backstroke. Both bow and stern should use it to give them time to figure out what lies ahead. Each paddler can use the low brace stroke as an outrigger to maintain balance. In the outrigger position tilt the face of the blade upward on the water. Refer to the photograph about the low brace in

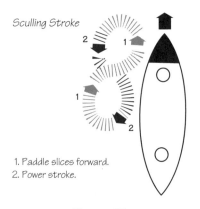

Figure 60

the tandem paddling section.

Two strokes are especially useful in a rough-water situation. In the *circular stroke,* best used in the stern, the paddle never really leaves the water. The paddler starts with a regular forward or power stroke, but as the paddle reaches the end of the stroke, the blade is *not* lifted from the water; rather, it is swung forward in the water, the blade feathered to ride almost as a moving outrigger. (See fig. 59.)

In the *sculling stroke* the blade rotates through a figure-eight motion (fig. 60); here too, the blade never really leaves the water. It usually is used in the bow where it can be converted almost instantly into a draw, brace, or backstroke to hold the canoe on course.

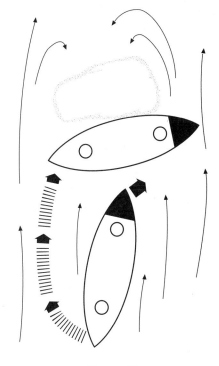

Figure 61

Avoiding Obstacles

When a monstrous rock looms in front of the bow, the bow paddler often reacts nearly automatically with a quick sweep stroke or draw, depending on which direction he or she hopes to take to avoid the rock. The immediate result of this stroke is that the bow curves away from the rock, but the stern is thrown right up against the rock—just as the back end of a heavy truck is swept in a wide arc as the driver turns the front of the cab (fig. 61).

The better response is to edge the bow slightly past the rock so that if

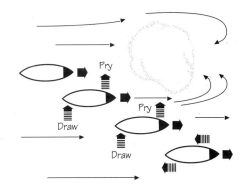

Figure 62

the canoe hits the obstruction, it will do so aft of the center thwart. As the bow edges away from the rock, the stern, depending on which side he or she is paddling, will use either a pry, or a draw to help pull the canoe away from trouble (fig. 62).

Backpaddling Downstream

Despite your best intentions, one day your canoe may be literally pivoted around by a rock and started on a backward ride through the rapids. Your first reaction may be to attempt to swing the canoe downstream, bow first. Resist it. First, both bow and stern should pivot in their seats so that they face the rear of the canoe and take a clear look at what lies downriver. The stern can control the direction of the canoe, aided by the bow; simply paddle backward through the water until it is safe to turn the canoe around.

Indeed, it is a splendid idea for inexperienced canoeists to practice paddling backward on quiet water so that if the need arises in turbulent water, they will realize how effectively they can maneuver in this position.

Eddy Turns

If you've ever paddled down a swift river and seen a canoe sitting just below a rock, its

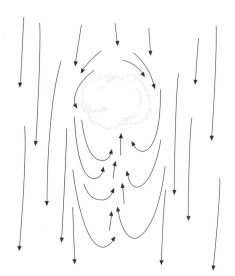

Figure 63

Backpaddling may be a necessity at any time for solo or tandem paddlers on lively waters. Pivot, face the rear, and paddle backward until it is safe to turn around.

Figure 64

bow pointed upstream, its paddlers relaxed and watching everyone go past, you've seen a canoe that has performed an eddy turn. An eddy turn is an advanced canoeist's friend. It also can be a fun maneuver for advanced beginners who want to try a new move. With the eddy turn you can whip your canoe behind almost any rock to wait for slower canoes or simply to rest before resuming your paddling.

Downstream of every obstruction in the water (a point of land jutting out from the shore or a rock in the middle of the river) lies an eddy, a phenomenon where the water flows upstream below the obstruction and downstream on either side (fig. 63). Now look at figure 64. It shows how an eddy turn is achieved. Use the eddy to maneuver your canoe below the rock and into the upstream flow. Note that the bow passes close to the rock (3), almost sliding against it as the canoe swings into the upstream eddy (4), bow upstream. Once turned, sit with the bow against the obstruction (5).

When attempting an eddy turn, lean the canoe toward the inside of the turn. As the bow cuts into the upstream flow, the bow paddler uses a vigorous draw or cross draw (depending on the side the bow normally paddles on) to reach toward the rock and pull the bow into the rock.

The stern will start with a vigorous draw or quarter sweep, again depending on which side of the craft the stern is paddling, to swing the stern into a direct line below the rock simultaneously with the bow's maneuver to nose into the rock. Now both paddle, as necessary, to edge the nose into the rock itself.

An eddy turn takes some practice, of course. Begin in easy currents. Try to avoid these mistakes as you practice:

1. not slicing the bow close enough to the rock at the beginning of the eddy;
2. having the bow begin the draw while the canoe is still in the downstream current (instead of pulling the canoe into the eddy, this will push the canoe downstream);
3. not turning quickly enough; the canoe will enter the eddy so far downstream from the rock that the paddlers may or may not be able to drive upstream into the eddy current;
4. in very swift current, not approaching the eddy line with enough force to drive well across it;
5. not leaning into the turn.

Leaving the Eddy

Leaving the security of an eddy requires an equal amount of judgment and control as entering one. First, backpaddle slightly. Then, both paddlers drive vigorously forward, swinging the canoe broadside to the current as it pivots, nose downstream, with the bow using either a sweep or draw and the stern, of course, doing the reverse of the bow.

It is important to lean into the turn when you are going *into* the eddy, but it is absolutely critical when leaving an eddy. Lean downstream in the exit maneuver. If not, the penalty is severe. The downstream current, acting like a rug being pulled out from under you, may easily tilt the canoe upstream. Result: wet, uncomfortable paddler with no canoe.

Note: I've used the word *vigorously* several times. This is not dropped in merely as a colorful adjective, but as a literal directive: *Vigorously* means *paddle with all the muscle at your command.*

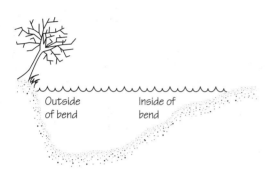

Outside of bend   Inside of bend

Figure 65

Paddling Around Bends

Paddling around a bend in a swift current on an unknown river may lead to problems. Remember, the outside of the bend (fig. 65) is where the deepest water will be found. In swift currents, the outside of the bend will be swift *and* dangerous. Stay to the inside.

Obviously far more can be said about canoeing techniques. Those interested in pursuing technical skills for tandem or solo paddlers should read some of the excellent books available through the book service of the American Canoe Association. The ACA also offers some superb videocassettes that demonstrate paddling techniques for easy flat water as well as for Class III, IV, and V rapids. The tapes feature open and closed canoes and one-person craft with air-bag support.

There are a number of outstanding canoe and kayak schools in the United States and Canada that teach everything from basics to classes for advanced experts. They are listed in the appendix.

Challenging Whitewater

On a warm, early spring day, when the river was still racing along at a moderately high level from snow runoff and a few days of heavy rain, I stood on a bank checking out a familiar set of rapids. My concern was whether my weekend group of eight canoeists, all basically advanced beginners or low intermediates, would have any special problems in the waves smashing over the rocks, and slicing into Vs, or would we have to portage around this moment of turbulence?

Only a few canoeists were on the river. As I stood making note

The first whitewater Olympic slalom competition was in Munich in 1972. The second in Barcelona in 1992, and the third in the United States in 1996. The Olympic Committee will drop the events for the game in 2000 because of the heavy cost of building a whitewater course. 2004?

of the water, two canoes paddled around a distant bend, heading toward the rapids.

One canoe swung off to the far left where the water was fast, but with only a few rocks, almost a Class II stretch. The second arrowed itself directly toward the most tumultuous currents and bounced skillfully through a run that was a rough Class III.

Once through the rapids, both canoes paddled over to the shore where I stood watching, pulled up their canoes, and stepped out. Suddenly, I recognized one of the paddlers in the canoe who had so expertly raced through the wild Class III water.

We waved to each other.

"Hey, Eddie," I congratulated him. "You made it look so easy."

"Oh, come on," he laughed, "It wasn't that rough."

"No? Well, that far side is Class III in this water." I turned to his companion, a slender girl with wide eyes that seemed to still reflect the roaring water she had just canoed through. "I think your friend was just starting canoeing when I met him on this river only two years ago," I said to her.

Eddie grinned and said: "Actually, that was the first time I'd ever been in a canoe."

The girl glared at him. "You told me you were an expert. Good heavens, I'd never have gotten into your canoe if I'd known you'd only started paddling a couple years ago." Then her glare turned into a smile.

"Let me make just one observation: He came through as an expert. Believe me, he must have gotten a lot of experience in two years."

I urged Eddie to give me a call when we all got back to our civilized city life, thinking of asking whether he might want to consider working with the local Sierra Club as a potential canoe leader. We waved goodbye.

I took my group through the channel on the left.

Moving Up

Learning to hop, skip, and splash through moderate Class II rapids is a goal that can often be reached with no more guidance than a solid understanding of appropriate strokes and maneuvers, and practice. A lot of practice. Of course, it's far more exciting and fun practicing on easy rapids when you are joined by friends as intrigued with the sport as you are—with at least one expert paddling along.

On the other hand, the skills to negotiate extreme Class II water and the roaring noise of all Class III water (the maximum rough water an open canoe, without flotation bags, can survive), are best learned from the experts.

The two most convenient sources of such experts are paddling schools and paddling clubs found throughout the United States.

For a fee, paddling schools do it all: food, housing, canoes, everything, plus great leaders who are eager to help you achieve the highest level of excitement you personally can handle, both through technique and mentally, on whitewater.

Among the nation's hundreds of canoe clubs, about one hundred are members of the American Whitewater Affiliation and playing whitewater is one of their major activities. Want to meet up with a new bunch of men and women who have canoed the roughest and toughest, and are willing to help you move into the glowing circle of experts? Join one of them—they all hold out their hands to welcome newcomers.

For information on these clubs, as well as subscribing to *American Whitewater,* the nation's only magazine devoted to whitewater maniacs, whether canoe or kayak, solo or tandem, write: American Whitewater Affiliation, P.O. Box 636, Margaretville, NY 12455.

Certification

The various divisions of the American Canoe Association all offer special training in basic and advanced paddling. This is the training routine, by way of example, for the Atlantic Division: Part I: Introduction for new paddlers covering basic tandem skills and self rescue; Part II: Solo skills, sophisticated maneuvers, rescue of others. Completion of both parts makes a paddler eligible for a Red Cross Fundamentals of Canoeing certificate.

For information contact the ACA, 8580 Cinderbed Road, Suite 1900, P.O. Box 1190, Newington, VA 22122.

Equipment

Canoe clubs that are involved in whitewater generally have the distinctive canoes and paddles suited to strenuous waterways for members who do not have their own.

As a usual rule, advanced paddlers are expected to have their own top-quality whitewater PFD, as well as the practical clothing, packs, gloves, and wet or dry suites, among other items, that the well-equipped enthusiast requires. Increasingly, lightweight helmets are worn when paddling whitewater, a sensible precaution to protect the head from those hard rocks if a canoe or kayak should flip. Most canoe clubs today require helmets for whitewater adventurers.

Emergency Procedures

Occasionally you'll be called on to react quickly to an unexpected mishap. The following techniques are probably all you'll ever need for recreational canoeing, but a refresher course in first aid or CPR may be useful, too.

Capsizing

It happens to the best of paddlers and to novices. It happens in Class III water and in quiet ponds. But no matter where or why a canoe capsizes, the first law of the water is to look to the safety of the paddlers. Canoes, gear, food, a six-pack—all can be recovered later. Rescue paddlers first.

If your canoe flips in fast current, move *instantly* to the up-stream side of the canoe and grab hold of the craft, holding on until you're in calm water. *Never* hold onto the downstream side of a swamped canoe. If it crushes you against a rock, the result can be disastrous.

If you're thrown clear of the canoe, turn onto your back and float downstream with your feet ahead of you to fend off rocks. Do not try to swim. You cannot swim in a swift current, and trying will only compound a difficult situation.

The only time it makes sense to abandon a canoe is if the water is cold, or the stretch of rapids is long, and/or you are in danger of suffering from hypothermia or exhaustion. Make a quick value judgment. Can you reach safety more quickly if you let go of the canoe?

Recovery Techniques

A capsized canoe is not an unusual circumstance. The following scenarios are paired with situations that will get you back in your canoe again.

• *Scenario 1.* The canoe is upside down and lodged against a rock. This almost inevitably means it has filled with water that is held inside the canoe by air pressure. *Solution:* If the current is not too swift, one canoeist moves to the bow, the other to the stern. At a given signal one canoeist lifts his end at the same time the other is depressing hers. This will break the seal of pressure holding water in the canoe. As the water pours out, flip the canoe back upright. (In a strong current one end of the empty canoe will start to swing downstream, so be prepared.)

• *Scenario 2.* The canoe is half-swamped from a heavy wave but is still upright. *Solution:* Paddle immediately to a shallow point where you can get out and tilt the canoe to empty it, or head for the nearest shore, pull the canoe up on the bank, and roll it over.

• *Scenario 3.* The canoe is upright but is stuck atop a monstrous rockopotamus sleeping under a pillow. *Solution:* First, rock the canoe from side to side to edge it into the current. If that doesn't work, put a foot over the edge and try to shove the craft off the rock. If *that* doesn't work, step out of the canoe and push it off the rock while holding onto the gunwale or the painter so that the canoe does not go bouncing off without you.

• *Scenario 4.* The canoe is badly wedged into rocks or other obstructions and cannot be jiggled, joggled, or maneuvered loose. *Solution:* Use ropes to haul it free.

One of the obvious ways—and one that usually works—is to tie a rope to the canoe and have everyone pull to get it free after first, of course, emptying any water that can be removed in any method you choose. Rolling the canoe with a rope lashed around the beams is often the most effective for those who have learned the technique through advanced rescue training. When pulling directly on a rope attached to a canoe with sheer muscle power does not work, add a 2:1 mechanical advantage through the use of carabiners, also known as snap links, carried by mountain climbers.

Here's how:

Step 1. Tie a carabiner (of course you have one with you!) to the canoe.

Step 2. Tie one end of the rescue rope to a tree, or other shore anchor.

Step 3. Loop the free end of the rescue rope through the carabiner tied to the canoe, and haul it back to shore.

Step 4. Stand on shore and pull on the rescue rope.

This method also can be used for dragging a canoe up a steep bank.

Rescue Equipment

On every canoe adventure that involves any degree of whitewater, even maneuvering through a Class 1.5, whether on a familiar river or distant wilderness, one canoe should be equipped with a "rescue pack." The pack should contain:

1. Two or three carabiners or snap links. These can be used as pulleys.

2. A throw bag. This is a small bag with 50 to 75 feet of ⅜-inch polypropylene rope stuffed inside it. Such rope floats and does not absorb water. In an emergency, the rescuer holds on to the end of

the rope sticking out of the bag and, literally, throws the bagged rope to a victim in need of help. Before the need arises, rescuers new to throwing bags should go into the backyard, or amble down to the nearest park, and practice throwing the bag—with a sweeping underhand motion. The rope is *STUFFED* back into the bag. Do not carefully coil it in.

Keep in mind that if you are tossing the rope to someone being swept swiftly down the water, aim directly toward the victim. The rope landing behind or in front of the struggling paddler will float at her same speed—and remain behind or in front of her.

The bagged rope also can be used for other rescue purposes.

3. A small folding "hand" saw 6- to 10-inches long, or a sturdy, sharp knife to cut rope instantly if necessary.

The rescue pack should be fastened independently to a thwart, where it is easily available, and not hidden inside a food or equipment bag.

Other techniques for rescuing canoes in more difficult situations are best learned from competent instructors.

Person-to-Person Rescue

If it is necessary to wade into heavy currents to help a paddler in trouble, use a tri- or quad-formation. In the tri-formation three canoeists move out together with linked arms, balancing one another against the current. In more severe currents, use a quad-formation. Four canoeists form a square, facing one another and holding tightly to arms or PFDs. The quad moves in slow circles toward the victim.

National Canoe Safety Patrol

Novice paddlers will be reassured to know about the existence of the National Canoe Safety Patrol. Patterned after the National Ski Patrol, the NCSP is made up of volunteers whose job is to patrol difficult rapids on popular canoeing waters and to come to the aid of any canoeists in trouble. On the Delaware River's Wild and Scenic section, the patrol members work along with the National Park Service in offering aid to paddlers. All members have exceptional paddling skills, special training in rescue operations, and basic first aid and CPR training.

For more information contact the National Canoe Safety Patrol at 6 Katherine Road, Rockaway, NJ 07866, or call (201) 627–5416.

"Lifting the Veil"

Every sport has its arcane skills, techniques only known to the experts and jealously kept from casual participants. Canoeing is no exception.

There are those special strokes and important body positions, for example, that lurk in the canoeing repertory of every instructor but are never taught in canoeing school.

Regardless of consequences, I feel it is time to lift the veil, to disclose those clandestine strokes and secret maneuvers for all paddlers, even the most nervous beginners, so that they can put them into play at the appropriate moment, with a sense of accomplishment over using them successfully. Here are some of the truly important ones:

Gunnel Grasp

The gunnel grasp is initiated when a canoe paddles into an unexpected stretch of difficult water, with souse holes and haystacks looming ahead.

A. Paddlers simultaneously gasp, even scream, to indicate instant awareness of the situation;

B. Each paddler grasps gunwales while, simultaneously, (1) holding the paddle shaft in an iron grip with the little and fourth fingers of the lower hand or (2) locking the paddle into an unbreakable vise between the knees.

C. Once initiated, the gunnel grasp should be rigidly maintained until (1) the canoe bounces into calm water, or (2) the canoe rotates on beam's end into a reverse mode.

Note: Novices should practice the gunnel grasp in calm water. Failure to execute the grasp properly may result in a paddle flying overboard.

Sun Stroke

Although seldom referred to by name, the sun stroke is widely used and highly popular with experts and even novice paddlers, who may not be aware that they are using it. It is executed in the following manner:

A. PC (Pleasant Companion) in bow initiates stroke with comment on sun, warmth of day, and the joy of paddling.

B. BDB (Big Dumb Brute) in stern agrees.

C. PC leans far backward in an appropriate horizontal position, with face upward and eyes closed, placing paddle across stomach at a right angle to the axis of the torso and the flow of the current.

D. BDB smiles, a mandatory response, while maintaining canoe's forward motion.

Reverse Bow Pivot

The reverse bow pivot is initiated during a conversation

between bow and stern when stern says: "What? I can't hear you." At this signal a skilled bow paddler:

A. slides paddle, blade down, into the canoe, with the shaft projecting forward at a 45-degree angle above the dow deck;

B. simultaneously pivots in a torso spin, placing the shoulders in a reverse stance to the feet, which remain projected toward the bow; and

C. maintains this position while resuming conversation with stern.

Abbreviated Reverse Bow Pivot

The abbreviated reverse bow pivot is simply a short version of the reverse bow pivot. In the abbreviated reverse bow pivot, when the bow's counter torso twist reaches its maximum configuration, it is held only long enough for an appropriate and vigorous comment from the stern. *Note:* This hidden maneuver is frequently practiced between expert spouses paddling tandem.

Stern Commendation Rudder Stroke

This difficult maneuver is initiated by an accomplished stern offering the bow fulsome compliments on the bow's capacity to maintain a constant power stroke throughout the day while stern concurrently sets the paddle in a stationary rudder stroke position.

Stern must be prepared to convert the stationary rudder stroke into an active power stroke at the first indication that the bow may be initiating a reverse head position.

Headlong Express

The headlong express maneuver is especially effective when the canoe enters an unknown stretch of high waves and rocks. By mutual agreement both canoeists paddle with major force, increasing the power of their strokes as the bow plunges up and down, as expressed in the equation $(FS \times PF \times MP) + RV = ID$, where FS equals Forward Speed, PF equals Paddling Force, MP equals Muscles Power, and RV equals River Velocity, which converts into ID, or Instant Disaster factor.

High Air Brace

The high air brace is one of the most technically difficult of all arcane strokes. It is performed in fast water as the canoe bears down hard on an almost invisible rock. The maneuver is performed in the following sequence:

A. Bow and stern individually initiate a series of linked pries, draws, cross draws, and reverse sweeps, which instantly places the longitudinal axis of the canoe at a 90-degree angle to the current. If timed carefully, the angle is assumed simultaneously with the keel coming to a brief rest amidships on the obstruction.

B. In the brief halt the current sweeps under the keel, tilting the upstream gunnel toward the water. The downstream paddler immediately activates the high air brace. If properly thrown, the tip of the blade stops at a distance of no more than 2 inches above the level of the river.

C. Downstream paddler pulls the airborne blade vigorously toward the canoe as the upstream gunnel drops below the current level.

Note: When correctly performed, the downstream paddle will curve gracefully in a 90-degree arc toward the sky as the craft rotates into the foaming water.

CHAPTER FOUR

LIVERIES AND OUTFITTERS

Most of the millions of Americans and Canadians who canoe rent equipment from liveries and outfitters. An estimated 2,500 such enterprises operate in the two countries and range from backwater Mom and Pop ventures to highly sophisticated businesses.

The line separating liveries and outfitters is not clearly defined. In general, liveries rent canoes or small rafts for use on local rivers and lakes by the hour, the day, or the weekend. If the river is wide and gentle and the course winds through charming countryside, rentals are likely to be provided by a livery. Outfitters, on the other hand, are best known for offering packaged commercial trips on heavy-duty rafts, with guides, on major rivers with massive sets of rapids. These trips range from one-day outings to those lasting a week or longer, with everything included—food, tents, rafts, and a handy-dandy cook.

Liveries

Liveries are, for canoeing enthusiasts, the equivalent of ski resorts for those bound for the slopes. Geared to make your trip a "destination" experience as well as a lot of fun, their facilities offer a lot more than rows of canoes stacked in a field. Take a peek at what the Kittatinny Canoe livery offers to Delaware River paddlers:

• 1,200 canoes, 300 family rafts, and 100 kayaks;

• five canoe bases spread over 75 miles (canoes can be rented at any one of them and dropped off at a downriver base or a designated spot arranged in advance by paddlers);

• three major campgrounds that include shower facilities, latrines, washrooms, tent and RV sites, and bundles of prechopped firewood for your camp fire;

• a few sites equipped with open-front Adirondack-type shelters and others with two-bedroom cabins;

• well-equipped stores that sell almost anything a canoeist might need, from outdoor supplies to canoes, paddles, camp gear, and PFDs;

John Mitchell, writing in the *National Geographic*, says by the year 2000, National Forest–based recreation "is expected to pump $100 billion in to the U.S economy, compared with $3.5 billion in timber sales."

- a coffee shop at one base;
- a swimming pool at one base.

General Livery Services

Many liveries operate their own campgrounds. Those that do not offer campgrounds usually can direct clients to nearby public or private camp facilities.

Well-run liveries brief new paddlers on their river. They can tell you what to expect from put-in to take-out and can give advice on any problems you might face (such as a sand bar or a bank that may require getting out and walking the canoe to a navigable spot). They usually provide a simple map of the area. You may find mileage from point to point printed on the map without any indication of how long it takes to paddle from point A to point B. Ask about paddle time in *hours,* not in *miles.* Make notes on your map.

Be sure to talk to the livery folks about where you may pull ashore to rest, sunbathe, stop for a swim, or have lunch. Most shoreline property throughout the nation is privately owned. Some owners welcome canoeists but expect them, of course, to leave the area as clean or cleaner than it was on their arrival. The livery should be able to tell you where you are welcome. On some trips you can go ashore only where public launch sites or state or national lands abut the water.

Liveries usually offer transportation to the put-in, if it is not near the main base, or from your take-out back to the main base. Some liveries offer transportation as a free service; others charge an extra fee. Inquire in advance about haulage costs and determine if the transportation is suited to your needs.

At a canoe livery, an attendant secures canoes on the trailer before it is hooked onto a bus and taken to the put-in for a day of fun on the water.

Safety Tips

Before their paddlers put in, a well-run livery offers a few safety reminders, such as keeping your PFD on at all times or at least never using it as a seat cushion or tying it to a thwart. Most liveries also make sure you know what to do if you capsize. If you've heard it before, be patient. If not, take heed.

Weather can pose problems for canoeists. If the water temperature is at or below 50 degrees F, many canoe liveries do not rent canoes, or they insist that paddlers have wet or dry suits to prevent hypothermia in the event of a spill.

The livery personnel should also apprise paddlers of the level of the water and its suitability for canoeing; that is, you should be told if the water level is so low you may have to get out frequently and walk your canoe over sandbars and shallows or if recent rains have raised the level to a point difficult or dangerous for paddling.

Canoeing Instruction

Few liveries offer canoeing instruction for novice or beginning paddlers. Occasionally an attendant will toss out some casual advice, but this is not meant as instruction, and beginners should not think such advice is sufficient preparation for a day on the water. In fact, many liveries seem unaware of your inexperience or are reluctant to tell you that what you are doing is wrong or inefficient. Essentially, then, beyond their basic safety reminders, liveries are simply renting equipment—you are at your own risk.

You may find a livery that offers an occasional paddle class. If you think you might benefit from it (believe me, you will), then enroll. A few liveries provide such classes at no charge; others levy a fee. Some liveries, especially the larger ones, have qualified personnel who provide private one-on-one or group instruction for a fee.

Release Forms and Insurance

It is standard within the canoe livery industry to ask clients to sign a release before leaping into the canoe and paddling off downriver. This custom prevails in most industries where risk is involved; the ski industry, for example, has perfected a subtle approach to the issue. Have you ever read the small print on your ticket about accepting responsibility for whatever happens to you on the mountain? Basically it tells you that you are at your own risk. Canoe liveries do not issue tickets, but they do ask you to sign a release in case of accident or injury of any kind and for whatever reason. The release, from the liveries' point of view, serves to make sure that paddlers know that canoeing can present inherent and unpredictable dangers. The fact that you sign the form does not in any way release the livery from a possible lawsuit if it turns out that an accident or injury is caused by the livery's negligence or carelessness.

It also is a common practice to offer clients insurance to cover the loss of or damage to any of the rental equipment. The cost currently ranges from $1 to $5 per person. You decide. If you have any experience and you are paddling flat water, it may not be worth the price. If there are rapids and therefore more chance that a canoe could be seriously damaged, then insurance might be advisable.

A relatively new practice in some liveries is to ask the canoeists to sign a credit-card slip authorizing payment of up to $300 to cover any damages or losses. The credit slip is torn up when all the equipment is returned in good shape.

Costs

Weekend rental costs generally are higher per day than mid-week costs. Some liveries on popular rivers will rent canoes by the single day during the week but only for two days on weekends.

For paddlers spending a night or two in a livery's campground or at its lodging, discount packages often are available, and group reductions usually can be obtained for canoeing and/or lodging. If you are paddling with one friend, you will pay top dollar. If you are bringing together a group of friends—let's say ten or more—ask for a group discount.

Long gone are the days when renting was only a cash-on-the-barrelhead proposition. Some liveries do not accept checks, but almost all accept credit cards as well as cash. Call in advance if you want to charge your outing.

It is especially important to know the payment policy when renting from small liveries and outfitters in remote towns and from liveries in Canada. Canadian liveries accept American and Canadian currency, but some do not take credit cards. Others take traveler's checks but do not offer the discount that comes from converting American to Canadian dollars.

Know what is included in your rental costs at all liveries. Sophisticated and well-run liveries include paddles and PFDs for

When renting a PFD from a livery, make certain you have fastened it properly. If you are not certain how to fasten it, ask an attendant to help you.

each person, along with the canoes. They usually do not stock bailers, sponges, or painters. If visiting an unknown livery, especially those that are not members of the Professional Paddlesports Association, check on their equipment. Are the canoes well maintained? Most liveries sell off their older canoes at the end of each season and replace them with new equipment. If the livery gives you a canoe that is heavily patched or appears to have taken some hard knocks, you have every right to put it in the water and paddle for a few minutes to make sure there are no leaks. It's somewhat disconcerting to discover water leaking into your canoe ten minutes after you put in and 15 miles to go to your take-out.

Do not accept cracked or broken paddles or ones that are the wrong size. Generally liveries have paddles of three sizes: a child's length and two adult lengths, one too large, the other too small. If in doubt, use a slightly longer paddle in the bow and a shorter paddle in the stern. If the livery has only one paddle size, however, drive down the road to the next livery.

And, if the livery employee tossing your canoes around like matchsticks carries your equipment down to the water and forgets to include an extra paddle for you, ask him to provide one—you may need it.

Never accept ancient PFDs filled with kapok or PFDs that are obviously too small for an adult or much too large for a child. A child can slip out of a PFD that does not fit securely.

Refunds and Rain Checks

Liveries in general have no set policy regarding refunds or rain checks. If you've sent in a deposit and the weather turns brutal, canceling every activity on the river, some liveries will return your deposit, some will give you a rain check, and some will stick the money in the cash register and bid you farewell. Ask about refunds and rain checks before you send in a deposit.

Outfitters

If your ambition is to ride a raft through the tumultuous rapids of the Colorado, the Snake, the Salmon, or the West rivers, you will be contacting an outfitter. Outfitters offer a variety of trips from a few hours through a major set of rapids to a week or two for longer journeys. Generally they provide all the equipment and food necessary for such trips. For instance, you will be given lunch on the one-day runs and all your meals, tents, and even a portable cocktail bar, on the long junkets.

Some outfitters provide services more akin to those of liveries than to raft-trip packagers. They rent canoes and all the equipment you may need for wilderness trips of varying durations. Most also can provide the services of a competent guide to take you into unknown waters or simply to help you catch the fish you've been thinking about all winter long.

If you do not know the outfitter with whom you want to make arrangements, ask the questions you would ask an unknown livery. What are the costs and what do they include? Do they give rain checks or rebates? What, specifically, do they provide in the way of food? Can you bring your own food? What kinds of tents and gear do they have?

If you are planning a wilderness trip with an outfitter from which you will be using the services of a guide, ask lots of specific questions. Some guides are all gung ho: "Hey, let's get up and start moving." They want to move out at daybreak and quit just before sunset. It never seems to occur to these guys that while they paddle every day, you don't. Thus, it is critical to emphasize, when planning a trip through an outfitter, that the hours per day as well as the miles per day must meet *your* idea of a great trip, not anyone else's. Set firm limits in advance, considering both your ability and physical condition and the ability of those paddling with you.

A few outfitters may answer your queries with evasive phrases such as "Now, don't worry about that" and "We'll take care of it." Stuff and nonsense. You are entitled to know exactly how they will take care of your concerns before you book your trip. Insist that they answer your questions, or make arrangements elsewhere.

References, Please

Despite the preceding advice, you will probably have difficulty finding any recreation industry more concerned with the welfare of its clients than the liveries and outfitters. Again, however, you should be on guard against those few operators who will take casual advantage of new customers. You can verify the quality of liveries and outfitters by some tried-and-true methods before you even see them or do business with them. The first, and probably the most important, information to gather is the operation's reputation among those who have dealt with them. Get the recommendation of a friend or other reliable source before committing to any tour.

Another excellent indication of the quality of an operation is its membership in any of several organizations with high standards. The best-known national group is the Professional Paddlesports Association (PPA). Members must adhere to PPA standards, which insist on the provision of "safe, high quality service and equipment to the canoeing public" and "education, to the best of their ability and within the scope of their specific operations, in regard to safety, canoeing skills, and conservation practices." To maintain status

The Housatonic

Take two days to paddle the Housatonic in the northwest corner of Connecticut. Practice canoe strokes on the quiet water upstream from Falls Village the first day. Then put your skills to work the second paddling the sometimes tumultuous waters below Falls Village for the next 12 miles.

Dead in the middle of a bouncy set of class IIs is one of those prides of an earlier New England, a traditional one-lane-for-cars-or-wagons covered bridge at Cornwall. After you run the rapids, beach your canoe, take pictures and stroll through the adjacent small town. It's as traditional as the bridge.

as an accredited member of PPA, liveries and outfitters are subject to periodic inspections by teams of their peers.

Active membership in various state livery associations is also an excellent indication that a livery offers quality service. The equivalent organization to PPA among outfitters is America Outdoors, formed in 1990 when two outfitter associations, the Eastern Professional River Outfitters and the Western River Guide Association, merged. For information and a list of current members, write to America Outdoors at 360 South Monroe, Suite 300, Denver, CO 80209, or call (303) 377–4811.

Locating Liveries and Outfitters

More than 400 Professional Paddlesports Association (PPA) liveries and outfitters are located in the United States. For information and a list of current members, write to the PPA at P.O. Box 249, Butler, KY 41006-9674, or call (606) 472–2205.

Both liveries and outfitters often run ads in various outdoor magazines, especially in *Canoe & Kayak* magazine, *Paddler* magazine, and *Sport* magazine. As a rule, all of them have some type of printed information that they will be happy to send you on request.

Hardware stores and sporting-goods outlets in towns along canoeing rivers are another source of information. The folks inside can usually tell you where the nearest liveries are—as well as something about their reputation.

If you are camping, ask your camp operators about liveries in their area. Liveries usually work in close association with campgrounds. Indeed, a substantial number of liveries and outfitters operate their own campgrounds.

State Sources

Almost all states have agencies that provide information about river trips, points of interest to canoeists, and names of liveries and outfitters. Call or write to ask for the information available. Many state agencies have special recreation or canoeing publications they will send free or at a small charge. The following list of state agencies includes the titles of the pamphlets available at this writing. Bear in mind that economic problems in many states have caused cutbacks in the agencies dealing with recreational resources. Some materials may no longer be in print when you request them.

Alaska
U.S. Forest Service, Alaska Region, P.O. Box 1628, Juneau, AK 99802. Ask for *Alaska Travel Index.*

Arizona
Arizona Office of Tourism, 307 North Central Avenue, Suite 506, Phoenix, AZ 85012. Ask for *Canoe Trips.*

Arkansas
Arkansas Department of Parks and Tourism, One Capitol Mall, Little Rock, AR 72201. Ask for *Float Streams of Arkansas* pamphlet and others on canoe rentals.

California
Department of Boating and Waterways, 1629 S Street, Sacramento, CA 95814; (916) 445–6281. The state publishes a number of pamphlets and maps on canoeing in California.

Colorado
Colorado Division of Wildlife, Department of Natural Resources, 6060 Broadway, Denver, CO 80216. Provides pamphlets listing canoe routes, campgrounds, guides, and outfitters.

Colorado Division of Parks and Recreation, Centennial Building, Room 618, 1313 Sherman Street, Denver, CO 80203. Publishes a *Guide to Colorado Parks and Recreation Areas.*

Connecticut
Department of Environmental Protection, State Office Building, Hartford, CT 06115. Publishes a booklet describing the state's four river systems.

Delaware
Division of Economic Development, 630 State College Road, Dover, DE 19901. Ask for newsletter with general information about canoeing in the state.

Florida

Florida Department of Natural Resources, Crown Building, 202 Blount Street, Tallahassee, FL 32304. Ask for the *Guide to Canoeing Florida Rivers.*

Georgia

Chamber of Commerce, P.O. Box 756, Folkston, GA 31537. Publishes a pamphlet, *Canoe Outpost,* listing liveries.

Georgia Canoeing Association, P.O. Box 7023, Atlanta, GA 30357. Ask for the association booklet on canoeing Georgia.

Idaho

Idaho Department of Parks and Recreation, Statehouse Mall, 2177 Warm Springs, Boise, ID 83720. Publishes *River Runner's Guide to Idaho.*

Illinois

Department of Conservation, Lincoln Tower Plaza, 524 South Second Street, Springfield, IL 62706. The *Illinois Canoeing Guide* lists river routes throughout the state.

Indiana

Department of Natural Resources, Division of Outdoor Recreation, 612 State Office Building, Indianapolis, IN 46204. *Indiana Canoe Guide* is filled with canoeing information.

Iowa

Iowa Conservation Commission, Wallace State Office Building, Des Moines, IA 50319. Ask for *Iowa Canoe Trips.*

Kansas

Department of Economic Development, Travel and Tourism, 503 Kansas, 6th floor, Topeka, KS 66603. (913) 296–2006. General outdoor recreation information.

Kansas Canoe Association, Box 2285, Wichita, KS 67201. Contact them for specific information.

Kentucky

Kentucky Department of Tourism, Capitol Plaza Tower, Frankfort, KY 40601. Ask for *Oh, Kentucky Outdoors,* for information on paddle sports.

Louisiana

Louisiana Office of Tourism, P.O. Box 44291, Baton Rouge, LA 70804. Ask for *River Trails, Bayous, and Back Roads.*

Maine

Department of Conservation, Bureau of Parks and Recreation, State House, Station No. 19, Augusta, ME 04333. Send for booklet *Maine Canoeing*.

Maine State Development Office, State House, Augusta, ME 04333. Send for pamphlet *Canoe Rentals*.

Maryland

Department of Natural Resources, Tawes State Office Building, Annapolis, MD 21401. Check on the newsletter *Access* for information on eleven rivers.

Massachusetts

Best source: Appalachian Mountain Club, 5 Joy Street, Boston, MA 02108. Booklet *Canoeing Information Resources* lists sources of canoeing information throughout New England.

Minnesota

Department of Economic Development, 480 Cedar Street, Saint Paul, MN 55101. Send for *Minnesota Canoe Trails* brochure.

Department of Natural Resources, Centennial Office Building, Saint Paul, MN 55155. Its *DNR report* describes canoeable rivers.

Mississippi

Department of Natural Resources, Bureau of Recreation and Parks, P.O. Box 10600, Jackson, MS 39209. Brochure *Mississippi Rivers and Streams* lists canoeing waters.

Missouri

Department of Natural Resources, P.O. Box 176, Jefferson City, MO 65101. Brochure listing parks, canoeing, and camping facilities.

Montana

U.S. Department of Agriculture, Forest Service, P.O. Box 7669, Missoula, MT 59807. *The Floater's Guide* has general information on Montana waters.

Nebraska

Games and Parks Commission, P.O. Box 30370, Lincoln, NE 68503. Publishes *Nebraska Canoe Trails*.

Nevada

Department of Tourism, Capitol Complex, Carson City, NV 89710; (707) 885–4322. Ask for information on canoeing facilities.

New Hampshire

New Hampshire Office of Vacation Travel, P.O. Box 856, Concord, NH 03301. Send for *About Stream Canoeing in New Hampshire.*

New Jersey

Department of Environmental Protection, Division of Fish, Game and Wildlife CN400, Trenton, NJ 08625. Will send *Canoeing the Pinelands Rivers.*

New Mexico

Natural Resource Department, Parks and Recreation, P.O. Box 1147, Santa Fe, NM 87504; (505) 827–7465. Ask for canoeing information.

New York

State Department of Environmental Conservation, Albany, NY 12233. Send for *Adirondack Canoe Routes* and the *I Love New York Travel Guide.*

North Carolina

Division of Travel and Tourism, Department of Commerce, Raleigh, NC 27611. Request the *North Carolina Camping and Outdoor Directory.*

North Dakota

U.S. Bureau of Land Management, P.O. Box 1220, Dickinson, ND 58601. Publishes *North Dakota Canoeing Waters.*

Ohio

Department of Natural Resources, Division of Parks and Recreation, Fountain Square, Building C, Columbus, OH 43224. Two fine pamphlets: *Canoe Livery Association Directory* and *Explore Ohio by Canoe.*

Oklahoma

Oklahoma Tourism and Recreation Department, 500 Will Rogers Building, Oklahoma City, OK 73105. Ask for *Oklahoma Canoe Trails.*

Oregon

Department of Transportation, Transportation Building, Salem, OR 97310. Publishes *Popular Drifting, Canoeing Streams in Oregon.*

Pennsylvania
Pennsylvania Fish Commission, P.O. Box 1673, Harrisburg, PA 17120. Send for *Canoe Country Pennsylvania Style.*

Rhode Island
Rhode Island Department of Economic Development, Tourism Promotion Division, 7 Jackson Walkway, Providence, RI 02903; (401) 277–2601. Best publication: *Boating in Rhode Island.*

South Carolina
South Carolina Department of Parks, Recreation, and Tourism, P.O. Box 167, Columbia, SC 29202. Ask for *South Carolina River Trails.*

South Dakota
State Department of Game, Fish and Parks, 221 South Central, Pierre, SD 57501. Send for *South Dakota Canoeing Guide.*

Tennessee
Tennessee Wildlife Resources Agency, P.O. Box 40747, Nashville, TN 37204. Send for *Canoeing in Tennessee.*

Texas
Texas Parks and Wildlife, 4200 Smith School Road, Austin, TX 78744. Send for *Floating Texas Whitewaters.*

Utah
Western River Guide Association, 994 Denver Street, Salt Lake City, UT 84111. For information on Utah and other states.

Vermont
Department of Forest, Parks and Recreation, Agency of Environmental Conservation, Montpelier, VT 05602. Send for lists of canoe trips and names of liveries.

Virginia
Virginia Department of Conservation and Economic Development, 1201 Washington Building, Richmond, VA 23219; (804) 786–2132. Publishes *A Great Place to Canoe.*

Washington
No state agency handles canoe information.

West Virginia
U.S. Forest Service, Monongahela National Forest, P.O. Box 1548, Elkins, WV 26241. Ask for lists of river trips, outfitters, and liveries.

Wisconsin
Wisconsin Department of Tourism, Department of Business Development, P.O. Box 7606, Madison, WI 53707. Booklet on all outdoor activities.

Wyoming
Wyoming Travel Commission, Frank Norris, Jr. Travel Center, Cheyenne, WY 82002. Send for *Family Water Sports, Big Wyoming.*

Canoeing Canada

Canoe liveries can be found in all of the major provincial parks. For information, contact the park officials for the names and locations of liveries that they service.

An important source of information for all outdoor activities are the tourist offices of the separate provinces. Write or call for names of liveries and canoe outfitters. If they do not have specific names, they can generally provide sources that will help you locate a canoe rental service.

Most liveries will accept credit cards. Some will not. Check in advance for their payment policies. If possible, pay in Canadian dollars. Some liveries will accept U.S. dollars at a premium below the official rate. Others will accept U.S. dollars at the official rate.

Provincial Tourist Offices

Alberta
Travel Alberta Vacation Counselling, 15th floor, 10025 Jasper Avenue, Edmonton, Alberta T5J 3Z3; (800) 661–8888.

British Columbia
Tourism British Columbia, Parliament Buildings, Victoria, British Columbia V8V 1X4; (800) 663–6000.

Manitoba
Travel Manitoba, Dept. 9020, 7th floor, 155 Carlton Street, Winnipeg, Manitoba R3C 3H8; (800) 665–0040, ext. 20.

New Brunswick
Tourism New Brunswick, P.O. Box 12345, Fredericton, New Brunswick E3B 5C3; (800) 561–0123.

Newfoundland and Labrador
Department of Development and Tourism, P.O. Box 2016, St. John's, Newfoundland A1C 5R8; (800) 563–6353.

Northwest Territories
TravelArctic, Yellowknife, Northwest Territories, X1A 2L9; (800) 661–0788.

Nova Scotia
Department of Tourism, P.O. Box 456, Halifax, Nova Scotia, B3J 2R5; (800) 565–7105.

Ontario
Ontario Travel, Queen's Park, Toronto, Ontario M7A 2E5; (800) ONTARIO.

Prince Edward Island
Department of Tourism and Parks, Visitor Services Division, P.O. Box 940, Charlottetown, Prince Edward Island C1A 7M5; (800) 565–9060 (east of the Mississippi).

Quebec
Tourisme Quebec, CP 20,000, Quebec G1K 7X2; (800) 443–7000 (from the eastern United States).

Saskatchewan
Tourism Saskatchewan, 1919 Saskatchewan Drive, Regina, Saskatchewan S4P 3V7; (800) 667–7191.

Yukon
Tourism Yukon, P.O. Box 2703, Whitehorse, Yukon Y1A 2C6; (403) 667–5340.

CHAPTER FIVE

SHORT TRIPS

One- or two-day weekend jaunts are the most popular types of canoe trips. Planning for such trips is no more complicated than planning one- or two-day outings for a ski holiday or a trip to the shore.

The First Trip

For the novice paddler the first canoe journey should be limited to one day on the river. What do you need? Start with a canoe livery located on the river where you want to canoe. Will it involve you and a friend? A group? No problem there. Talk to the livery for some sound advice about your plans. Tell them precisely your experience (or lack of it) and other essential details like the number of people involved and—this is important—the length of time you expect to travel in terms of hours. Ask them if they provide transportation to or from the river, or both, and for what fee, if any.

Remember, other than canoes, paddles, and PFDs, everything else is your responsibility. See Chapter 1 to remind yourself about other equipment needed.

Personal Basics

For that first day trip, let's look at your personal needs:

Clothing: Two sets of everything. One to wear in the canoe, one to wear when anything gets wet. Windbreaker or sweater if the day is chilly.

Shoes: One pair of old tie-on shoes, such as tennis shoes.

Broad-brimmed hat.

Gloves: Optional, depending on the weather.

Rain gear: Even if the weather promises to be warm and sunny, bring it. First choice, a rain suit with jacket and pants; second choice, a raincoat. Last choice (and not recommended) a poncho. An accidental spill in the water could prove a problem if you are wearing a poncho because your legs could get entangled in the garment.

Swim gear: Optional. Some folks wear their paddling shorts; some go skinny-dipping.

Towel: Large. Handy for everything from sunbathing on shore to wiping off after a swim.

Glasses: Sunglasses that protect the eyes against UV rays. Polarized UV glasses are excellent. They not only protect the eyes but also help cut the glare of the sun reflecting off the water. If you wear prescription glasses, use an elastic band to hold them on.

Sunscreen lotions: Some dermatologists now recommend a sunscreen with a protection factor of no less than 20 to 30, both to prevent sunburn and to protect against the long-range problem of skin cancer.

Waterproof watch (only if you must reach a take-out point before a specific time).

Do not bring money, wallet, jewelry, credit cards, or car keys. Canoe liveries generally will keep these items for you.

Everything important that you bring, from extra clothing items to a camera, should be kept in a waterproof container and tied to a thwart in case of an accident. The handiest waterproof pack is a plastic garbage bag.

Tips on Food and Drinks

Packing a picnic lunch for an afternoon drive is quite different from packing a lunch that will sit in an open canoe until you pull into shore to relax and eat. For at least a few hours the food will be sitting in a container on which the sun is beating down. Even if the day is cool and the water chilly, the contents of a closed container will warm up.

Foods that can spoil easily, especially meats, should be packed into a portable ice chest with ice or dry ice. You can also partially or completely freeze the food at home and pop it into an insulated chest where it will stay cold until you take it out for lunch.

If you don't have access to a water source that is proven safe, bring along your own water in an insulated plastic jug. Fruit juices and carbonated drinks are safe bets, too, but water may be the best thirst-quencher.

It would be hypocritical of me to say that you should not drink alcohol on a canoe trip; we usually have a chilled white wine for lunch on our day trips. Each of us drinks only in very modest quantities, however. Those adults who prefer beer, for instance, drink only one. The key point here is moderation. One glass of wine or one beer and *no* hard liquor. Remember this one terrible, brutal

The small campfire had diminished to a glowing spark. One by one, we headed toward our tents, pitched on the shore of a lac in northern Quebec. It had been a tiring day, 10 miles of river with a head wind and a ½-mile portage over rocky terrain. Sometime around 10:00 P.M. I made a last check of the canoes and camp. The night sky, touched by the ever constant glow of the Northern Lights on the horizon, seemed brighter than usual. But I ached to crawl into my tent and snuggle into my sleeping bag.

Around midnight I heard a tent zipper. Then I heard a loud voice.

"Hey. You gotta see this. Anyone awake? Take a look."

I stuck my head outside. The northern sky was ablaze. In a moment, everyone had crawled out to observe the splendiferous sight. The Northern Lights had burst into glory. Great folds of glowing curtain descended from outer space. The light faded and flared. The spectacle was awesome.

We could not tear ourselves away from the most glorious Aurora Borealis any of us had ever seen. For hours we were hypnotized by the folding and unfolding of drapes of light reaching into infinity. Morning could wait, tonight belonged to the heavens.

fact: The statistics show that almost all canoeists who drown are guilty of one, or both, deadly sins: (1) not wearing a PFD, and (2) drinking while paddling. Don't become a statistic.

Summing Up

Your first canoe adventure is most likely to be a pleasure if you follow the advice outlined in the previous pages. Here are the key points, plus a few extras, to remember:

1. Plan a short trip.
2. Do not take young children on your first voyage.
3. Always wear old, tie-on canvas shoes or strap-on sandals
4. Bring extra clothing in a watertight container or waterproof bag and tie it to a thwart.
5. Protect perishable food from overheating and store it in a watertight container tied to a thwart.
6. Allow time to swim, picnic, and rest.
7. Respect private property.
8. Respect fishermen. Don't cross their lines. Above all, don't paddle into them when they're standing hip-deep in the river.
9. Use litter bags. The fish object if you dump your trash in

their water. Everyone objects if you leave a dirty picnic site.

    10. Strap on glasses and sunglasses.

    11. Lock valuables in your car or leave them with the livery operator.

    12. Take no more than three people in a canoe.

    13. Protect yourself from the sun and storms.

    14. Enjoy but do not disturb the wildlife or pick the wildflowers.

    15. Don't overload your canoe.

    16. Don't leave canoe or equipment unattended.

    17. Don't stand up in your canoe—until you've learned the proper way to do it.

    18. You might want to take a bottle of wine, or perhaps a touch of something more spirited, but only for sipping around the campfire.

    19. Even when it's hot, wear your life jacket.

    20. Drink alcoholic beverages only in moderation.

A Short Overnight Trip

The canoeist who yearns to put his or her skills into an outdoor wilderness adventure of several days, or longer, would be well advised to make that first foray a short overnight weekend trip. This is equally true for the experienced camper and the woodland novice.

Livery-Arranged Overnight

One of the most pleasurable short-trip options for those who want to paddle by day but do not want the work of setting up a campsite at night is an inn-to-inn trip offered by some liveries. For these trips the liveries provide a guide and canoes, paddles, and all associated necessities, plus lunches on the river and dinner and lodging in motels and inns near the river at night. As with other rental arrangements, costs vary and group discounts and packages are available.

Similarly, you could arrange to spend the night at a campsite arranged by the livery outfitter. Some will transport sleeping bags and other equipment for you.

Do-It-Yourself Overnight

Your best source of information on where to take a shake-down weekend by yourself is someone who knows the route and can advise you about distances, campsites, and other pertinent information. Canoe livery and outfitter operators are reliable folks to

The Megiscane

You have to toss your canoes and gear onto a freight car yourself when the eastbound Canadian Pacific railroad brakes to a halt at Senneterre in the forested wilderness of central Quebec. Three hours later the train stops at a water tank called Monet only long enough for you to drag everything off.

It will be almost two weeks and 130 miles before you paddle the Megiscane River to Lac Fallon. There a pre-arranged truck will haul you, canoes, and empty food bags back to your cars.

Be prepared for a magnificent and lonely trip. You'll see an occasional moose, maybe a bear, and Eagles, but rarely other paddlers, if any at all.

Start scouting the shore for a large enough space to pitch your tents in the thick woods right after lunch. Carry map and compass to poke your canoe through island-spattered lakes. A lightweight Kevlar is more fun to haul across portages several thousand yards old, thick with blueberries, than a classic shoulder-bending wood and canvas behemoth.

talk about your trip with, and, finally, there is an increasing library of guidebooks to river and wilderness regions for paddlers.

Canoes, like car trunks, have a limited capacity. Unlike the trunks, everything in the canoe must also be protected against the weather and an accidental upset. Wrapping everything inside plastic garbage bags is fine for a single-day jaunt. But you'll need far sturdier waterproof packs to protect gear hauled in and out of canoes several times on a weekend trip. If you are used to a 30-pound behemoth of a family tent, you'll find quickly enough that because of weight and bulk it won't make a good companion in your craft. Heavy cooking equipment and large camp stoves also pose difficulties. The chapter on wilderness camping provides information on suitable camping and cooking equipment.

In planning menus remember that everything will be sitting in bright sunlight in the canoe for a couple days. Unless properly protected, fresh foods can spoil. Choose foods not seriously affected by temperatures. For clothing you'll need items similar to those suggested for a day trip, but you should bring an additional set of clothes.

If your first weekend jaunt includes at least one pesky portage, good! The pain and irritation of poor packing and excess weight is a lesson you'll remember next time. If children are involved, you'll learn how well the wee ones take to a couple days sandwiched between the gear in a canoe and both the contributions and problems older children create in the wilds.

With this experience tucked under your PFD, you're ready now to enjoy the unique pleasure that comes only to those who point their bow into the wilderness and start paddling.

Popular Canoeing Rivers

Most recreational canoeists know local rivers and the liveries that serve them, but some have only a vague awareness of the hundreds of other rivers and lakes filled with paddlers served by liveries in the United States and Canada.

For those keen about canoeing in other areas throughout North America, for one day or a week, here is a run-down on what the Professional Paddlesports Association (PPA) lists as the nation's most popular canoeing waterways and nearby towns or cities with liveries. All of the rivers have long stretches for casual canoeists. Many also have whitewater for paddlers with advanced skills. For the names, addresses, and telephone numbers of local liveries serving the rivers you want to paddle, write to the PPA at P.O. Box 248, Butler, KY 41006; or call (606) 472–2205.

State	River	Location of Liveries
Arkansas	Buffalo	Ponca
California	American	Sacramento
	Russian	Windsor
Florida	Everglades	Everglades City
	Escambia area	Milton
Maine	Allagash	Millinochet
	(the first river in the nation protected as a Wild and Scenic river)	
Michigan	Au Sable	Grayling
Missouri	Merrimac,	Steelville
	Courtroix,	(U.S. population
	Huzzah	center)
Nebraska	Niobrara	Valentine
Nevada	Colorado	Las Vegas
	(below Hoover Dam)	
New Hampshire-Maine	Saco	Center Conway, New Hampshire
New York-Pennsylvania	Delaware	Barryville, New York

North Carolina	Nantahala, Chatooga	Bryson City
Ohio	Mohican	Loudonville
Oklahoma	Illinois	Tahlequah
Pennsylvania	Youghiogheny	Ohiopyle
South Carolina	Edisto	Canadys
Tennessee	Ocoee (where the 1996 Olympic paddling water sports events were held)	Nashville
Texas	Guadalupe	New Barunfels
Viginia	Shenandoah	Front Royal

A superb source on the rivers of America and the outfitters and liveries that serve them in all fifty states is *Paddle America,* by Nick and David Shears. The 1997 edition contains 871 listings of canoeing, kayaking, rafting, and sea kayaking outfitters accross the country.

One significant point the Shears make is that when you plan to paddle a new river and must depend upon unknown liveries, "you may want to write or call five or more companies to request brochures and information. Doing so you will find that each outfitter has his or her own distinctive character, level of service, and array of trip offerings."

If *Paddle America* ($15.95) is not in your local outdoor store, you may order it through Starfish Press, 6525 32nd St. NW, Washington, DC 20015.

CHAPTER SIX

CANOEING WITH KIDS

There aren't many times that we are closer to our children than when we take them canoeing with us. In this environment it is the family working together, paddling together, making camp together, and facing the cold or the rain together that brings us into a tight-knit closeness that can be achieved and felt in no other way. No outside influence interjects its opinion on what is right, or wrong, or smart, or stupid. You and your spouse and your kids are alone together—learning, teaching, and sharing together.

One early September, my wife, Gail, and I took our four-year-old twin daughters, Hilary and Rebecca, on a weeklong canoe trip in the great Adirondack wilderness region. We had imagined a fall setting of idyllic beauty, but as we drove north the idyllic vision faded as storm clouds scudded in patches along the horizon. By late afternoon rain began to fall and we headed for a motel instead of our intended campsite. The next morning was damp and chilly. Now the question arose: To go or not to go in the face of inclement weather?

The sunset of another perfect canoe day. Shhh. Can you hear the loons?

We considered the facts: (1) We had everything we needed for a week's trip—proper clothes, the right tents, adequate foods, and basic medical needs plus a few extra items from our pediatrician; and (2) we had prior experience on weekend camping/ canoe trips that had taught us what it was like to canoe with the girls in our craft, how they reacted to a camp setting, and what items they needed to enjoy the trip on their level. We decided to go.

Sure, the weather was lousy the first two days, and we spent more time in camp than on the water. Still, it was a wonderful trip. The weather became glorious, and with the help of our excellent maps, we found a campsite whenever we needed one. Since it was after Labor Day, the great, wild region was virtually free of canoeists, and the isolation provided a splendid setting for a family adventure.

This chapter will help you prepare your family for the invaluable experience of weekend or wilderness canoeing. It includes advice on the clothing, sleeping bags, packs, and tents most suitable for children. Special recommendations on medications, safety equipment, foods, and safe behavior on family trips are provided along with ideas for enjoying and learning about the gifts of nature you will see along the way.

"Gee, Mom, this is fun. I want to paddle some more." Take the kids on an easy river. It will be a family outing of pleasure.

It should be noted that basic canoeing skills are necessary for any backwoods trip with children, even if you are paddling only lake or easy river waters. Don't take the family along on *your* first canoeing experience. Older children who will be paddling should be given some instruction before you set out.

Your first family trip should be a short one, especially if the children are young. As you make your plans, try to involve the whole family. The wee lads and lassies can be prepared for canoeing and camping through illustrated children's books; older children can be consulted as you plan menus, work out distances to paddle, look at maps for potential campsites, choose points of interest to visit, and tend to all the other details of trip organization.

Equipment

As with adults, children probably already own much of the equipment they'll need for canoeing, especially if their family has camped or hiked previously.

Clothing

From hats to shoes, every item of clothing takes on a more significant role in the wilderness. If you underpack, you can't go to the closet and find what you need. If you overload, you can't escape mess and confusion in camp. Choose sensible garments of good quality and take only what the kids will really need on that particular trip. Don't take a complete set of clothing for each day of the trip. They'll wear some items more than once or twice, and you can wash clothing in a bucket outdoors just as well as you can in the automatic washer at home. (Leave all detergents at home; bring only biodegradable laundry soap. Wash and rinse clothes, hair, and dishes in a bucket *away* from the water.)

Even in midsummer, mountain lake and river temperatures are cooler than city temperatures; in fact, they're often downright chilly at night. Plan to bring clothing that can be layered, so that as the weather changes, layers can be removed or added. Here's our packing list for each of our girls for a one-week trip on which we expected chilly nights and warm days:

1. Two sets of regular-weight underwear
2. One set of winter underwear
3. One pair of lightweight long pants
4. One pair of heavier weight long pants
5. Two pairs of shorts
6. One turtleneck
7. One wool sweater
8. Light jacket that can be worn with or without the wool sweater
9. Ankle-length poncho with hood (*Note:* Ponchos pose no danger for young children in a canoe)
10. One lightweight wool shirt with long sleeves
11. One T-shirt
12. One pair of gloves
13. Two pairs of shoes (one pair of play shoes, such as sneakers, and one pair of leather, ankle-high lace-up boots, pretreated with water-repellent silicone)
14. A complete extra set of clothing to be left in the car to use for the trip home

Packs

Certainly it would be easiest to stuff all the children's clothing into the adults' waterproof packs, but that takes some of the fun out of the camping experience. Hilary and Rebecca each have a small daypack for which they can take responsibility. The bags contain a few items of clothing and each girl's "special things." Since the packs are not waterproof, all of their contents are packed in plastic garbage bags first. The rest of their clothing and other gear is packed with ours. Older children usually need bags as large as adult bags. All their gear can be packed in one bag, but they may also want to have a day pack.

Sleeping Bags

You can buy child-sized sleeping bags for young children, or you can buy an adult bag they will grow into—the choice is yours. We decided to buy the half-pint models, filled with top quality, synthetic fibers and large enough for several years' use before the girls would outgrow them.

In shopping for a kid's bag, remember that the design that keeps an adult warm and comfortable is the design kids need, too. A bag with a total loft (thickness when zipped shut and lying flat) of 4 inches will keep an adult or a child comfortable to a temperature in the twenties. An inexpensive bag with sewn-through seams is useless; the cold seeps right through the seams.

You may also choose to put off the investment in a good sleeping bag while the kids are very young. Some parents bring a double-bed comforter or a couple of warm blankets instead. Fold the blankets and fasten them together with large safety pins, making a cozy bag that can be adjusted as the child grows.

Sleeping Pads

The body weight of very small children is not sufficient to flatten the synthetic fibers in a sleeping bag, so they may not need a sleeping pad. Older and heavier children may need some extra padding and insulation. The closed-cell ensolite pads favored by backpackers are excellent for this purpose. Air mattresses, on the other hand, do not provide good insulation; the air circulates with every breath and movement so that body heat is not absorbed and retained.

An upside down canoe as a table. Quickly strung tarps. It's dinner time. Raining? Not on us.

Tents and Tarps

Many large "family tents" are available to sleep a group of six or even eight comfortably. They are tall and roomy, but they are also heavy and cumbersome. I do not recommend them for any kind of family camping, whether you drive up in a car or paddle to a site in a canoe. Neither do I recommend that you buy a good quality, lightweight double-wall tent for the adults and a cheapy "backyard" single-wall tent for the kids. I recommend that you buy *two* good quality, lightweight double-wall tents. Mom and Dad will stay warm, dry, and comfortable—

and so will the kids. Mom and Dad will have mosquito netting over the tent door and a water-resistant floor—and so will the kids.

It is possible, of course, to buy a top-quality, lightweight four- or six-person tent with all these features, but that means you all will be sleeping in one tent. It may be fun the first night, but then it becomes a confounded nuisance. Gear and clothing scattered all over and no privacy for Mom and Dad or anyone else.

When your children are young (three- to ten-year-olds), pitch the tents so that the openings face each other. Before they went to sleep, our girls practiced crawling from their tent to ours so they would be secure in the knowledge that if they awoke in the middle of the night they could find their mother quickly and easily. You'll probably want to keep infants and toddlers in the adult tent; preteens and teens may actually enjoy a campsite of their own.

In addition to the two tents, we carry a rain tarp. Mine is a 9-foot square of long staple cotton, both lighter and easier to carry than a nylon tarp. It makes an ideal shelter from rain or hot sun when no shade trees are handy to offer protection.

Special Needs

Children, especially preschoolers, enjoy the comfort and security of a special toy, stuffed animal, book, or other small item from home. Each of our girls chooses a few favorite treasures and puts them into her own pack. Toy paddles are also a great diversion for small children.

Kid Food

Planning a healthful diet for kids out-of-doors depends only partially on what you "know" your children will eat. Parents often discover that their usually finicky eater develops a ravenous appetite in the woods. The child who will eat only highly sugared and refined cereals at home may develop a taste for oatmeal and Cream of Wheat in the great outdoors.

Milk on a wilderness jaunt is no problem. Powdered milk is available in skim milk packages at your neighborhood store; many outdoor specialties stores also carry powdered whole milk. Use bottled or purified water to mix a pitcher of milk.

Though your kids may love the prepackaged instant oatmeal with its tasty fruit bits, they will probably gladly forgo other prepackaged meals for the opportunity to cook outdoors. If you cook your own foods in camp, let the children help—even the littlest ones.

You might want to enhance a meal with edible wild plants growing near your campsite. An excellent guidebook is *Edible Wild Plants of Eastern North America* by Fernald, Kinsey, and Rollins

(Harper & Row). One warning: If you don't know what you're picking, don't pick. Some plants have edible leaves or fruit but poisonous roots. Some plants are completely poisonous. Nonetheless you can choose from a vast variety of plants that are tasty and easy to find (see p. 174).

Safety First

Outdoor enthusiasts know that too much risk and not enough caution can spoil the fun they intended to have. This section provides ideas for ensuring that the kids stay safe and enjoy every moment of the adventure.

The Medicine Chest

Talk to your family doctor or pediatrician before you take your children into the wilderness, especially if you will be out of touch from any source of help for several days. Find out if the kids are overdue for any booster shots, and ask for recommendations for medications that might be useful in an emergency. Our pediatrician, for instance, advised us to take Epipen auto-injectors because our girls are slightly asthmatic and can react violently to a wasp or bee sting. She also prescribed a broad-range antibiotic to be used only according to her description of when and under what circumstances it should be administered. If any of your children take medication on a regular schedule, make sure you take along enough to last the whole trip, especially if you will be in a remote area.

First Aid

The most common first-aid problems on a canoe trip are the same ones that occur at home: cuts and abrasions, burns, slivers, and insect bites. The first-aid remedies that work at home will work in camp. Bring an extra supply of Band-Aids or other tape bandages.

Children rarely think to use insect repellent. If you see them scratching or complaining about mosquitoes, give them a coating of repellent several times a day. Use any repellent recommended by your druggist that does not contain DEET, which is not suggested for use on children.

The whole family should be carefully examined every night and every morning for ticks, which can carry Lyme disease and wood tick fever. Ticks may be found anywhere on the body, but they are especially likely to attach themselves in the hair, under the arms, and around the crotch. Remove ticks promptly with tweezers or a fingernail. Wash the wound with soap and water after all of the tick is removed.

Nessmuk's "receipt" for insect repellent:

"Three ounces pine tar, two ounces castor oil, one ounce pennyroyal oil. Simmer all together over a slow fire, and bottle for use. . . .

"Rub it in thoroughly and liberally at first, and, after you have established a good glaze, a little replenishing from day to day will be sufficient. And don't fool with soap and towels where insects are plenty. A good safe coat of this varnish grows better the longer it is kept on—and it is cleanly and wholesome."

Ideally all adults should have first-aid training. On a family outing it is essential that at least one adult have more than a vague memory of what to do in the event of a major accident, severe wound, broken bone, or a potential drowning.

The ability to administer artificial respiration is of paramount importance. If no adult in the family is familiar with mouth-to-mouth resuscitation or other artificial respiration techniques, *run*—don't walk—to the nearest competent agency (American Red Cross, YMCA, or local Visiting Nurse Association) that offers a course in first aid.

Children in their early teens can also study first aid; the previously mentioned agencies often offer such training as do scouting groups. Who knows? The kids may save *your* life.

PFDs

A properly fitting, good quality life jacket is more than important—it's absolutely necessary. Even if you are renting from a livery, I strongly urge that you buy each younger child his or her own life jacket to ensure that you are putting the kids in the PFDs most suitable for them. A Type II horse-collar style with a crotch strap to keep it in place in case of an accidental dunking is the best device for the littlest children.

A child's life jacket should be a bright, even fluorescent, color. My choice is yellow because it is highly visible, especially if left ashore where you stopped for lunch.

Water Safety

Safe behavior while canoeing or swimming is preached so regularly it is almost a cliché. Some parents forget, however, that a child will mimic parental behavior more than he or she will listen to their words. If the adults are sitting on their PFDs, that's what the kids want to do.

It is not uncommon to see parents without life jackets on insisting that the children wear theirs. On a recent trip a friend and I assisted in the rescue of a father canoeing with his young son. The man, not wearing a life jacket, was thrown from the canoe as it passed through a stretch of fast currents. The boy, wearing his PFD, held desperately to the gunwales while the man, floundering in the currents, tried to grab the canoe. My partner and I were able to grab the man and the canoe, and in a few moments we had cleared the rough stretch and reached calm water. After we had made sure the boy and his Dad were safe, I told the man none too gently, "You know, if it's important for your son to wear a life jacket, isn't it for you? It would be a helluva mess if you got drowned and the boy was alive." The man agreed. He thanked us again and kept on agreeing with what I had said.

An hour later, as we were paddling through another fast, rough stretch, I saw the same canoe, the same dad, and the same son we had rescued earlier. The boy had on his PFD. Again, the father did not.

Swimming

When the weather is warm, your kids and perhaps you, too, will head to the water for a pleasant swim. Parents should insist that young children or nonswimmers keep their PFDs on when playing in the water. Even a mild river current can carry a person downstream; and a lake may have sharp drop-offs hidden under the water.

Old canoeing shoes should be worn to protect the feet from stones under water. Do not permit diving into an unknown pool until the bottom has been inspected for underwater obstacles that could cause serious head, neck, or back injuries.

Paddling

If you're a family with very young children, the small four-person crafts known as family rafts are increasingly popular on our rivers (and, by the way, are especially suitable for people with physical disabilities). Families with infants are attracted to the rafts because they are as safe as any watercraft can be for very young children. Not long ago I saw a threesome in a family raft; Mom was nursing the baby while Dad gently steered the craft downriver.

By age nine or ten, youngsters will be able to do some genuine paddling, especially on easy rivers and lakes. Although they start out enthusiastically, most youngsters of this age can paddle only for short periods. You thus have a choice: two adults and one child in a canoe, with the paddlers rotating, or one adult and one child per canoe, with the adult prepared to use an increased amount of energy to keep the canoe moving when the bow partner's vigorous strokes at the start of the day turn into little dippers after a few hours. Make sure you know your child's skills and limits before you plan a major outing. Short day trips provide the opportunity to assess their stamina.

Teens often want to take a canoe out on their own as soon as you make camp. Before you give them permission for a fishing trip or exploratory adventure, make certain you are aware of their route and agree on a time when they will return. On a lake with numerous small islands, it is quite easy to get lost. As for free time paddling on the river, always start them *upstream* rather than down. Currents may carry the kids much farther down than they intended to go. If a brisk breeze is blowing across the lake, have them begin their trip paddling into the wind. On the return to camp, the breeze will be a pleasant asset.

Enjoying the Trip

Kids who have never camped or canoed may wonder what they're going to "do" on a long trip. This section provides ideas for fun, educational activities on the water or in camp.

In-Camp Days

All canoeing days are not glorious, and you may opt to stay in camp when the weather is wet and windy. Even on beautiful days you may feel like loafing instead of paddling. For the youngest campers, bring along a few games and small toys so that they can play when the going stops going. For older kids, consider taking along a couple of books especially suited to the outdoors. Books on outdoor sports, plant and wildlife identification guides, and titles on nature crafts and observation usually include lots of information to keep kids busy.

Basic Mountaineering, published by the Sierra Club, discusses rock climbing techniques, and *Mushrooms and Fungi* by Moira Savonius (Crescent Books) has more than one hundred color illustrations to help campers identify and collect wild mushrooms. Teenagers may enjoy a U.S. Department of the Interior publication entitled *How to Mine and Prospect for Placer Gold* (Bureau of Mines Information Circular 8517, available through the U.S. Government Printing Office, Washington, DC 20402). It includes an excellent chapter on how to pan for gold. Send the kids out with some tin plates; a few flecks of gold could pay for your vacation.

The famed Petersen guides to birds are superb, as is the Audubon Society's Pocket Guide paperback *Familiar Mammals of North America.* It includes outstanding photographs of each mammal and information about its usual habitat and footprints.

Hell's Bay

South of Miami, U.S. 95 ends at the Everglades National Park. That's where Hell's Bay Canoe Trail begins weaving its way through the Everglades, a confusing and beautiful maze of mangrove tunnels, creeks, marshes, and ponds on the six-mile route. The S, U, and M turns are well marked, a marker on the left means turn left—immediately—on the right, swing right, now!

In the bays you'll startle herons, wood storks, gulls, and egrets. Keep your camera handy.

We spent the night on a chickee. These are not weird monsters but 10x12 foot wooden platforms built on stilts, well above the snap of hungry 'gators teeth, for overnight Everglade campers. Remember, only self-supporting tents will stay erect on the wooden slats.

For Everglade exploration beyond marked routes, go only with a guide.

Two outdoor classics mentioned elsewhere in these pages are informative for adults as well as older teens. *Woodcraft,* written by George W. Sears in 1888 under his Indian name Nessmuk, was the first outdoor book to focus on lightweight, nondestructive camping and the critical need for mankind to conserve the American wilderness. Perhaps the most plagiarized outdoor book ever written is Horace Kephart's *The Book of Camping and Woodcraft,* first published in 1905. It is full of fine information still useful today. Both books are available at better bookstores.

Conservation

Few activities lend themselves so fully to an understanding of conservation as a canoe trip does. Take advantage of this. If the waterway is suffering from any kind of pollution (it usually is), educate yourself about this and point out to the children the effect of the pollution on plant life, fish life, and bird life. Show your children how the food chain begins with our streams and rivers. Discuss the effect of an unnecessary dam on the nature of the valley you are paddling through. Ask the children to think about what would happen if wooded shores were replaced by housing or industrial developments. Conversely, ask them to imagine how beautiful the river and valley must have been before its shores were developed or its waters polluted.

Those parents with an ardent bias toward conservation and

beauty are the ones who will help redress the damage humanity has inflicted upon nature. Lessons on conservation are learned best in the outdoor classroom where the teacher-parent can show children the beauty and the destruction firsthand.

Capturing the Wilderness

A camera can help you capture memories of your trip that will last a lifetime. After you take pictures of all the humans in your group, let the older children use the camera to photograph birds, animal tracks, and unusual plants. Those species that cannot be identified on the trip can be identified later in the local library when you develop the photographs.

You might also bring along a diary and encourage the older children to write entries daily. Have the little ones tell you their observations and write their impressions in the diary for them.

If you carry a few cupsful of plaster of Paris, the kids can make plaster casts of animal footprints. They can sprinkle the footprint with a half-inch of the powder, then spray with water lightly until the powder is fully damp. Let sit until the form hardens. They can also mix the plaster of Paris and water into a rather thin solution that can be poured carefully onto a print without damaging it. Let the solution harden; then lift the form from the underlying print.

A tape player with a cassette of camp songs is fun for children in the wilderness, but other music, whether Mozart or Metallica, does not belong in the wilds. It will only destroy the most brilliant sound of all—the sound of the night. Listen. Do not intrude upon it.

CHAPTER SEVEN

WILDERNESS TRAVEL

Many canoeists entertain the fantasy of paddling quiet, distant waters through remote forests—where the laughter of a loon echoes across a lake, where a moose steps out of the edge of the woods as you glide by, where the fish bite willingly.

You can turn this dream into reality through several means. You can join an outdoor organization that runs wilderness trips under the leadership of an experienced volunteer. You can take a trip run by a commercial wilderness outfitter with a professional guide. Or you can plan the most interesting trip of all—the one you take on your own with your family or a few friends.

Planning the Trip

If you set out on a trip of your own creation, remember these three basic rules:

1. Preparation!
2. Preparation!
3. Preparation!

You need no more skill than a low intermediate paddler to enjoy adventures in the wilderness. It would be folly, however, to undertake a trip of a week or two without prior experience in canoe-camping on familiar rivers. Regardless of who goes on a wilderness trip, preparation (a few long-weekend trips, for instance) and planning are essential elements of its success.

The Guest List

The first step in planning your trip is choosing the members of your party. The most important consideration in that regard is the canoeing skill level of those you'd like to include. If you all are capable of handling a canoe on quiet waters, ten thousand routes are open to you. If your group consists of skilled canoeists seeking challenging waters, another ten thousand trips await you.

Second, consider the compatibility of each paddler with the others. All members of a group on a trip into distant waters must be agreeable and cooperative. We all know friends who are great to have around when the sun shines and everything goes smoothly but complain at the first drop of rain on a tent at night. For long trips choose personalities that can handle the discomforts as well as the pleasures of the journey; the going may be tougher than you imagined from the comfort of your living room.

Third, examine the motives of each person who would like to go along. The trip will be more pleasant if you all have the same reason for going. If one of you is an ardent photographer who wants to stop for every "spectacular shot," another is a dedicated angler who would rather fish than paddle, and a third is a gung-ho physical fitness buff who wants to leap out of the tent at dawn and paddle all day without letup, you may not have a terrific trip. Diet may also cause other problems. Hearty meat eaters and dedicated vegetarians really don't dine well together.

On a weekend trip such differences may only ruffle a few feathers. On an extended wilderness tour, however, strong differences may create more serious difficulties.

The Group Size

If you will be out of touch with any form of civilization for more than a couple days, I recommend a minimum of three canoes. If something goes wrong, one set of paddlers can remain with those who need assistance while the other can go for outside help. On the other hand, I hesitate to recommend a trip with more than five canoes, simply because the impact of a large group upon the environment is usually negative. Just the acts of putting up five or more tents, walking around, and gathering firewood will have an adverse effect. Numbers aside, you'll have to determine whether the region in which you will be canoeing has campsites; you may have to search for clearings large enough to pitch your tents. In the thickly wooded Precambrian shield country of northern Canada, for instance, clearings are few and far between.

The Length of Your Trip

No group is stronger than its weakest paddlers. Carefully estimate the distance the group is capable of paddling and plan the length of your trip accordingly. The following chart may help you plan a trip in terms of distance. It assumes that you will paddle approximately five hours daily: Keep in mind that this is only a guide. Distances can be affected by the weather, water levels, and paddling with or against the prevailing winds.

	Flat water, no portages	River, 1–3 mph currents, no portages	River-lake, mild currents, 1–2 portages daily	River, 3–10 mph currents, Class II rapids, 1–2 portages daily
Advanced novice to low intermediate	10–12 miles	12–15 miles	7–12 miles	10+ miles
Strong intermediate	12–15	16–18	10–15	15+
Expert	15+	18+	15+	20+

The Route

There's more to wilderness tour planning than simply knowing your group. It is mandatory that you also thoroughly know the route you will be paddling.

One of my wilderness trips involved six people—three men and three women. Their canoeing level was low intermediate; two had limited camping experience.

Our goal was a two-week trip that would allow a full layover day once each week. We wanted to paddle a remote waterway instead of the well-marked canoe trails that can be found in state and national parks and forests. We wanted the primitive solitude the fur traders experienced two hundred years ago.

I called an old friend, Claude Contant, a mining engineer by profession and a native of central Quebec, who loved and knew the region well. Did he have any suggestions?

Claude wrote: "Everything considered, I would suggest the Megiscane River, from Monet to Senneterre. You can see what it's like from the small-scale topo maps (1:50,000 scale). The entire trip is 180 miles, but you can take out at either 150 or 120 miles."

Claude noted some specific places on the river where we would have to portage. One was about 2 miles. The rest were only a few hundred yards each.

The Megiscane sounded ideal. I assembled our group, and we carefully studied the maps and Claude's letter. Only after we were fully familiar with the maps of the area and what the terrain would be like was a final decision made to spend two weeks on the river.

One of the group asked why it was necessary to spend so much time studying maps and talking to Claude about the trip. My reply: "What we don't know can hurt us. What we do know we are prepared for." In other words, the same three rules apply to everyone who would take any wilderness trip: Preparation! Preparation! Preparation!

It was a magnificent canoe trip. Beautiful days. Chilly nights. A few storms. Occasional sightings of moose, bear, and beaver. Eagles circling overhead. A 12-pound pike that fought our one fisherman with endless fury.

We ran into an unexpected problem on an anticipated stretch of Class IV and V water roaring through a gorge. As we neared it, we began searching for the portage take-out, knowing at best it would be a small clearing in the thick brush along the water's edge. Some limited lumbering in the area several years earlier had obscured the original take-out, which probably had been used by canoeists for hundreds of years. We paddled cautiously into the first of a series of minor rapids, got out, scouted the bank, and still could not find the take-out.

I assembled the paddlers and explained that we had two choices: We could tie up our canoes and continue to hunt for the portage, or we could unload the canoes, carry the gear along the rocky shore, and line the canoes through the gorge. Either choice would require at least a full day's work. The consensus: Line the canoes through.

It turned out to be a rough experience. Everything went slower and was more difficult than we'd anticipated. By evening we were halfway through the canyon and desperately searching for space on the rocky shore to pitch our tents and spread out our bedrolls.

The camp that night was on two flat rocks, each just barely large enough for maybe five people. Our cooks were up to their ankles in water half the time while turning out a hot meal on our single-burner Optimus 111B.

It was past noon the next day before we got through the chasm and could reload our canoes for the last leg of our journey on the wide and gentle water of the Megiscane.

The delay in making our way through the gorge posed no problem on our trip. We had three take-out points and would easily make the one at the 120-mile post, so we paddled on. The sun was warm, the breezes light; we were becoming wilderness veterans. On our last morning we paddled 15 miles down Lac Fallon to Abel's Rest Camp, the first sign of civilization in two weeks. The camp at that time was a collection of small cottages largely inhabited by enthusiastic fishermen during the summer. It also boasted a tiny four-table restaurant with a bar that was overcrowded if five people tried to approach it.

We got permission to pitch our tents on a swath of lawn behind the cottages and, after hot showers, dined in the restaurant.

Camp Chores

Every camper knows that along with the fun there's work to be done. How will a group divide the camp chores? Each of you can choose to do the jobs you particularly like before the trip begins, or you can rotate assignments.

A family trip is easiest of all to structure. A group of friends makes the division of labor a bit more complex. My strong suggestion whether you're with friends or family: Work out and write down a schedule of jobs so that everyone knows, no one complains, and no one forgets. If a group has six or more members, use a formal assignment chart in which jobs rotate every day at dawn and last the entire day. There are six jobs; if there are more than six people, some are "off" each day (which should be noted on the chart). The job descriptions are as follows:

- *Cook:* Prepares, cooks, and serves each meal.
- *Bull cook:* North Woods term for KP; washes all dishes, pots and pans, and personal gear.
- *Fire:* Starts the camp cooking fire and keeps it going throughout the meal. *Note: Everyone* helps bring in firewood.
- *Water:* Hauls water for cooking and dishwashing; keeps a full pot of water on hand at night in case of emergencies.
- *Safety:* Keeps a sharp eye out for any unsafe practices in camp; makes certain canoeists wear PFDs when required; is sweep canoe (last canoe in line) when underway.
- *Area cleanup:* Takes care of all garbage; sees that fire is dead out; carries the day's nonburnables in a plastic bag in his or her canoe until it can be properly disposed of.

The following chart is a typical duty roster. Notice that people work in pairs.

When I organize a duty roster, I never team up those who pad-

Day	Sat.	Sun.	Mon.	Tues.	Wed.	Thurs.
Cook Cook	Françoise Harlan	Rel Herb	John Art	Kevin Joel	Françoise Harlan	Rel Herb
Fire Water	Rel Herb	John Art	Kevin Joel	Françoise Harlan	Rel Herb	John Art
Bull Cook Bull Cook	John Art	Kevin Joel	Françoise Harlan	Rel Herb	John Art	Kevin Joel
Area Cleanup Safety	Kevin Joel	Françoise Harlan	Rel Herb	John Art	Kevin Joel	Françoise Harlan

dle together. Why? First, working with a new partner helps create new friendships. Second, paddling partners are given a chance to separate for a while after a day of paddling when all may not have gone well.

You can also use a more informal roster if you prefer a casual approach. Write down the duties and make the assignments based on each person's favorite or best task. Hand rosters out or post one so that you avoid arguments in case a person forgets his or her assignment. The following list works well as an informal roster:

- *Breakfast and lunch cooks:* John and Betty.
- *Dinner cook:* Harry and anyone who wants to help out
- *Wake-up call and morning fire:* Ann (don't forget your alarm clock).
- *Cleanup:* Everyone does their own dishes, but Bill hauls water and heats it for washing and rinsing and washes the pots and pans. We all help him at every meal.
- *Dinner fire:* Wendy. Everyone gets firewood.
- *Lead canoe:* Changes every day—Monday, Ann and Bill; Tuesday, John and Wendy; Wednesday, Betty and Harry; Thursday, Ann and Bill; Friday, John and Wendy; Saturday, Betty and Harry.

Leadership

Is it necessary to have a trip leader? If so, what are his or her responsibilities? If you're traveling with a small group of close friends, you may have little or no need for a "captain." Consensus is the usual rule. But if a trip expands to more than an intimate few, and includes strangers, then leadership becomes a greater necessity.

Planning a wilderness trip with six good friends who have paddled together before is accomplished fairly easily. In a typical planning session, we chat about what a great time we're going to have and answer questions that arise: Who has a first aid kit? How much will the food cost? Do you think we should find a motel to spend the night in on our way to the river? Does anyone know the canoe rental fee? Can we bring individual tents? How long are the portages? Has anyone talked to any of the folks up there about the river? Who's buying the maps?

A few friends can raise questions and find solutions among themselves. When a group of strangers is involved, however, there is a stronger need to coordinate the tasks necessary to prepare for the trip. That means leadership.

Who selects the leader and what are his or her responsibilities? The assumption is that the organizing spirit behind the trip will be the leader. The group should have a meeting, however, to finalize the choice by common agreement.

It amazed early western travelers that native Americans rarely walked across a portage, but tossed their canoes on their backs and ran, whether the portage was short, or miles long.

The leader has two key responsibilities. The first is to see that all advance preparations are made, including planning menus, getting food, purchasing necessary maps, arranging for canoes, checking the first aid kit, and such other items necessary to ensure a safe and enjoyable wilderness experience. The leader can handle all the details or assign them to others. But he/she is the one responsible for every advance requirement.

The second responsibility is during the trip. It is the leader who, both in consultation with others or, if necessary, by himself or herself, has the heavy responsibility of keeping the trip on schedule and the pleasurable responsibility of making certain everything goes well in camp.

Portaging, Lining, and Tracking

Your opportunities to enjoy the sweaty pleasure of toting canoes and equipment across a portage, past an unruly set of rapids or from one body of water to another, improve substantially when you and your friends head off to paddle a wilderness region. On the short one- and two-day trips set up by liveries, portaging is almost never necessary.

In many wilderness recreational areas in the United States and, to a lesser extent, in Canada, portages are easy to locate. Usually they are indicated at the start of a portage by a large yellow sign with a silhouette of a person carrying a canoe. The official recreational maps of the areas generally indicate all portages.

In less traveled and more remote wilderness regions, however, portages are not marked. They may be indicated on the detailed topographical maps you should always carry of your route. Or a notation may be made on the map of an R or a V on a river, indicating rapids that probably will necessitate the sweaty work of portaging the canoes and the gear past the problem spot. Some topographical maps also will show an R plus a number from II to VI, indicating the International Rating of the rapids. The higher the number, the more likely it is to mean a portage.

Alas, many topographical maps of wilderness areas may not have such symbols. In such cases, a knowledge of contour lines will be helpful in determining where a set of rapids or a waterfall is likely. A contour line crossing a river usually is indicative of a drop in the river gradient, meaning, in canoe language, portage.

Signs along the water point to portage trails and warn paddlers of dangerous waters. Tent silhouettes indicate campsites.

Locating the Take-out

It's a wonderful day, sunny and pleasantly warm, and as you paddle the wide, easy river, you begin to hear a faint roar in the distance, the warning rumble that tells you your canoes are slowly approaching a dangerous set of rapids that you will need to portage around.

If a sign has been placed on the route to warn you of the need to portage, it may appear only 100 or so feet from the portage trail, which itself may be found within a few hundred feet, or less, of the place dangerous waters begin. Finding the portage trail on a little-used waterway is often no easy matter. Perhaps you were told that the portage is on the right bank. As you paddle along the right shore line, begin looking for a small area where the natural vegetation is trampled back into a tiny bay large enough for one or maybe two canoes to put ashore. The roar grows more thunderous. You've paddled 200 yards, and still there is no sign of a portage. Did you miss it?

Probably not. Generations of canoeists have always agreed on one point: the less walking the better. As indicated before, the take-out is apt to be much closer to the start of the rapids than you might consider prudent. Keep looking. Sad to say, there are times, such as our experience on the Megiscane, when searching fails. In these cases line down (see p. 138).

In this version of the two-person canoe-carry on a portage, the lead canoeist holds the canoe in both hands, just high enough in the air for trail visibility. Another method is to place the tip of the deck on one shoulder; this can be done by either person or by both.

Obvious Routes

If you are not certain of the portage, remember several considerations. First: A portage almost inevitably will take the shortest route possible from take-out to put-in. Thus, if the rapids occur on a bend, the portage will cut across the curve. Second: If there is one steep bank and one low bank, look for the portage on the easiest slope. Third: If there is an island in the middle of a river with heavy rapids on either side, the portage well may be on the island itself. This is especially true if the down-river end of the island is level with the water, and both banks are rough cliffs gouged out by the river over the millennia.

Scouting

Once you've located the take-out, scout the trail thoroughly—whether it appears to be well used or is so faint as to be scarcely passable. Follow the portage from end to end before you begin to carry the canoes and gear. Few treks are more useless than loading up and starting on a portage trail only to find that it is a seldom-used path to a fisherman's cottage hidden in the woods. Scouting also will reveal dangerous or difficult points on the trail.

Portaging

You and your partner can choose to portage by the one-person carry method or the two-person leapfrog method. In the first instance one person shoulders the canoe and the other hauls the equipment. It is easier, of course, to handle a one-person canoe carry if your craft is an ultra-lightweight Kevlar craft weighing 45 to 55 pounds. The method is not quite so manageable with the average 70- to 80-pound wilderness canoe.

Generally, canoeists favor a two-person carry method. The canoe is hoisted upside down onto the shoulders of both portagers. The canoe can rest on your shoulders, or you can tuck your head inside the canoe, supporting it with your hands on the gunwales. (I prefer to carry the bow on one shoulder.) The person in the stern position can use a one-shoulder carry with his or her head outside the canoe or a two-shoulder carry with the head inside the canoe.

Before lifting the canoe, tie paddles and extra PFDs to the thwarts. If your PFD has over-the-shoulder flotation padding, leave it on. If it does not, use a sweatshirt or other similar gear to pad your shoulders before you hoist the canoe.

First, carry the canoe a few hundred yards; put it down—gently. Next, go back for the gear and bring it up to the canoe. Put the gear down, hoist the canoe, and pack it onward another few hundred yards, and go back for the gear. In this method, all the gear is brought forward in small incre-

"Each paddler grab a gunnel!" Or if the portage is more than 100 yards, its "unload, carry, and reload."

ments that allow your shoulders to rest as you go along.

On trips with several canoeists, it may be possible to haul each canoe across a short portage without unloading, using a six- or eight-person carry, three or four on each side of the canoe. Simply pick each canoe up, gear and all, and carry it across.

Though it should be unnecessary, I caution you to inform, in advance, everyone in your party that on every portage each canoe team is responsible for its own canoe, all its gear, and any community equipment it carries.

Color

What does color have to do with portages? Plenty. As we all know, green and camouflage colors are popular for outdoor gear. Make yours bright red or yellow. You will have enough difficulty unloading and reloading on a portage without losing packs because they blend into the terrain.

Lining

An alternative to portaging is the technique of lining, or maneuvering a loaded or unloaded canoe down a rough stretch by attaching painters to the bow and stern. The two canoeists get out of the canoe and, holding onto its painters, walk downstream along the bank while maneuvering the canoe through the water.

In turbulent waters with violent currents and rocks jutting up everywhere and a shoreline broken with huge boulders and trees, lining is not the simple task some writers would have you believe. In such a situation it is best to unload the canoes, backpack the gear along the bank, and then start lining. Of course, in these waters canoes don't behave reasonably at all. They get stuck on rocks or half swamped from waves, and someone must wade into the water to free them. Obviously, lining canoes in such waters is an act of necessity, not of choice.

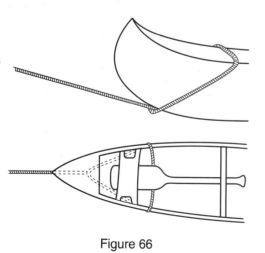

Figure 66

Tracking

Tracking is done exactly like lining, except that the term refers to hauling a canoe upstream. In tracking there is a tendency for the bow to be pulled under the water. This can be controlled with an under-the-keel bridle in the bow (fig. 66). The loop is made using a bowline knot. The same bridle is also used when towing a second canoe behind the first.

Ropes

As mentioned earlier, a loose-weave polypropylene ⅜-inch rope that floats and does not rot from being wet is the best all-around rope for canoeists. The only ropes that should be avoided are those designed for rock climbers. Climbing ropes have a built-in ability to stretch under heavy loads or sudden impact. This is a virtue in a climbing fall, but a liability for the canoeist. If a rope with a high stretch capacity breaks or comes loose under pressure, it can snap back with a stinging force powerful enough to break a person's arm. You can readily visualize that painters used in lining a canoe through rough water are subject to all the strain the rushing water is putting on the canoe.

Orientation Equipment: Maps and Compass

It would be beyond folly to head for a wilderness cross-country canoe trip without a thorough knowledge of map and compass. If you are already familiar with them, this section will illustrate how valuable they are and how I make use of them. If you are a hopeless novice at working with a map and compass, then I would strongly urge that you learn how to make use of them before putting your paddle into the water and heading off into the misty distance. An excellent instruction book is *Be Expert with Map & Compass,* by Bjorn Kjellstrom, which is available through American Canoe Association Book Service (8580 Cinderbed Road, Suite 1900, P.O. Box 1190, Newington, VA 22122). Another is *Maps and Compasses, a User's Handbook,* by Percy Blandford. It is available through the Appalachian Trail Conference, P.O. Box 807, Dept. SD, Harpers Ferry, WV 25425 (304–535–6331).

Three essentials for wilderness travel: map, compass, first aid.

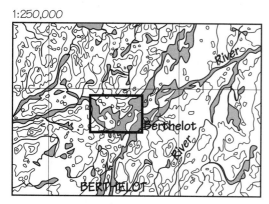

Figure 67

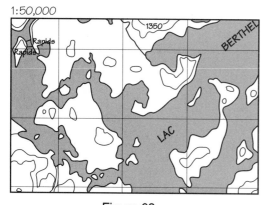

Figure 68

Map Study

For my wilderness travels, the first requirement before buying a single package of food or looking at the road maps is to acquire topographical maps of our water route.

In preparing for a trip on the Megiscane, I ordered a set of small-scale, 1:250,000 series maps, in which 1¼ inches on the map is equal to 5 miles on the ground, and a set of large-scale, 1:50,000 series, in which 1¼ inches on the map is equal to 1 mile on the ground.

It's a good idea to purchase, study, and take along both kinds of maps. Why? First, the small-scale map gives the canoeist the "big picture"—an overview of the entire region that provides a rough indication of the trip's general characteristics. Secondly, the very detailed large-scale map supplies precise information on the shape of small islands and the contours of the bends in the river; often, it contains additional information about rapids and abrupt changes in land elevation. To see the substantive difference in the two scales, notice the details revealed by the maps of the Lac Berthelot region (figs. 67 and 68).

The first detail I check is the average gradient from our put-in to our take-out. In the case of the Megiscane, we began our trip at an elevation of approximately 1,450 feet at Monet and expected to take out at an elevation of approximately 1,000 feet at or below Lac Fallon. This drop of only 450 feet was slightly less than 4 feet per mile.

If the drop were constant, that would mean we would canoe a sluggish river with mild currents. In the Precambrian shield region, however, rivers tend to wander short distances, then empty into lakes, and turn again into rivers. The gradient changes all occur on the river stretches or, in some cases, in a waterfall at the outlet of a lake. What this means, in general, is that the currents will range from mild to strong, with possible stretches of rapids on the river segments.

A lake-river combination might drop only 40 feet in 10 miles, but if the contour lines show that the 40-foot drop occurs on one 2-

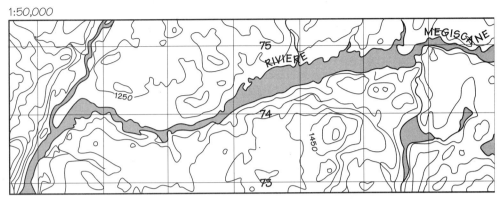

Figure 69

mile stretch, you can conclude that the stretch will include Class II to Class III rapids; the contour lines may also indicate a waterfall. In either case it's likely that this is portage country.

In tracing the course of our Megiscane trip, I found the small canyon Claude had referred to clearly indicated by a close grouping of contour lines. The most abrupt change of elevation on the entire trip was in that canyon. As I looked at the map at home, I knew that the stretch could be a long run of Class III to Class IV rapids, but I also guessed that it was likely to include some short, flat stretches of Class V rapids. (See fig. 69.)

Home Preparation

After I check out the general course of a planned route, I prepare the maps for the trip, making detailed notations on them while I sit at my desk under a pleasant electric light—a much more comfortable position than kneeling on rocky ground under the glare of a camp lantern.

First, I assemble the maps in the sequence in which they will occur on our trip. I clearly label each map according to that sequence (i.e., Section I, Section II, Section III, and so on). If the route meanders across only a tiny section of one map, I cut it out and paste it to the next map.

Second, I trace the entire route with a colored pen in such a way that no essential information is obscured. When the map is spread out before me in a canoe, I can tell at a glance where we should be paddling.

Third, I gather all the bits of information I have collected from others who have canoed the route, outfitters, and guidebooks, and I make notations on the maps as to possible campsites, major hazards, portages, and points of interest. If you have a guidebook of your route, bring it with you. Since I always keep a map spread out in front of me for instant reference, I write notes from my guide-

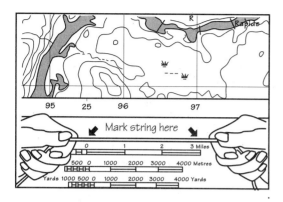

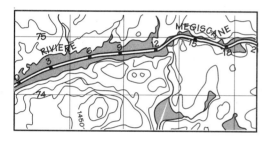

Figure 70

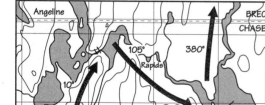

Figure 71

books right on the map so that I don't have to dig into a pack for the book. You might try that method as well.

Fourth, measuring against the mileage scale at the bottom of the map, I mark a piece of string into 3-mile segments. Placing the string carefully along the route, I make a slight mark every 3 miles *on the map,* again being especially careful not to obliterate any map information. (See fig. 70.) This marking system is invaluable when you are underway. The mileage markers help you see at a glance the progress you have made on a particular day or in any given time period; they also give you an instant update on the distance to your next take-out. As I make the mileage markers, I also roughly estimate the distance I think we can travel each day; I note that to one side of the route with a special mark such as a star, an arrow, or a triangle.

Finally, when I spot an area on the map that might be confusing to paddle through, I use numbers (degrees) and arrows to indicate the direction we should take. You'll still have to check your compass and landmarks when underway, but you won't have to stop for any serious map reading as you figure out the direction in which you should paddle (fig. 71).

Too Much Work?

Aach, you might say, looking over my shoulder at the maps on the table. Come on. It's simple to know where you are and where you're going when you have the maps. Aren't you overproducing this scenario?

Hey, man, say I, it's one thing to look down on a map on my dining room table and examine all the details carefully. It's another to struggle with a map in a canoe on a windy, murky day with rain threatening. See those three islands? One's big; two are tiny. In a canoe they all look the same size as you stare ahead trying to figure out which is which.

Staying on Course

Take a glance at figure 72, a detail of the 1:50,000 map we used to paddle a difficult section of the Megiscane. We were paddling north *from* A, heading toward H through the scattering of islands on Lac Canusio. Our route would carry us past C, through the eastern channel emerging at E, then past F, swinging over to the western shore as we passed the islands at G. The weather was poor, and a brisk breeze turned into a strong wind as we headed up the channel from C to E, buffeting us badly as we left the channel marked F.

Look at our dilemma. Imagine that you are studying this map and its islands not from the quiet security of a chair but in a canoe scarcely higher than a fish's eyeball, with strong winds blowing across your canoe from the left.

1:50,000

Figure 72

Though the map clearly indicates otherwise, your line of sight makes it impossible to distinguish the islands from the shoreline a half-mile ahead or to find a clear indication of the entry to channel H. Note the two X marks on the map. If you know, without question, that you are west of the western X, you should have no difficulty paddling into the Megiscane channel. But, if you become confused by the *eastern* X channel, you could easily paddle up the St. Cyr River.

Like our group at the time, you have to determine your position before proceeding. Don't compound your confusion by a trial-and-error expedition—you risk getting turned around or swinging far off course. The best solution is simple: Look at your compass.

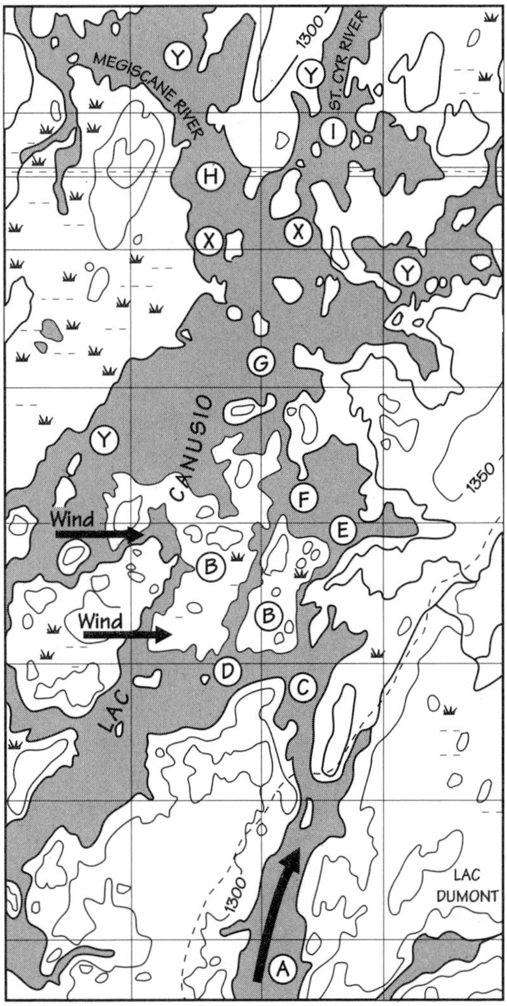

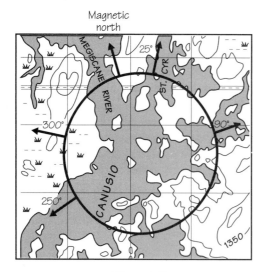

Figure 73

In our actual case we drifted off course and had headed up the St. Cyr River channel (I) before I noticed the wrong direction on the compass fastened to my thwart. The compass showed that our bearing was approximately 25 degrees. (See fig. 73.) We should have had a bearing of approximately 300 degrees. We swung back down the St. Cyr channel, paddled the St. Cyr–Megiscane Point, and headed up the Megiscane River. Thank you, map. Thank you compass.

Incidentally, as I mentioned earlier, I had marked many junctures of our route with directional arrows and compass bearings in degrees while studying the map at home. The marks made it easy to confirm our error and correct our course without delay.

Lost

Sooner or later every cross-country canoeist paddles a waterway on which every island looks the same and bays are indistinguishable from channels. For a moment the canoeist is lost. Panic won't help, so he or she stops and takes a deep breath or two. It wasn't long ago that the canoeist was well oriented, so he paddles back to the last known point and starts again. This procedure is a good method of reestablishing location and redetermining the route to the destination.

But what happens if the canoeist can't retrace the route to a known point? Paddlers in this predicament must know how to use a compass and techniques such as triangulation.

On a Canadian wilderness trip, my group and I were 10 miles from our final take-out, in a spot where the river emptied into a vast lake region, dotted with islands and inlets. Some local fishermen near the island we lunched on gave us a tip they said would save us miles of paddling. Following their course when we got back into our canoes, however, led us to an impassable swamp. They had incorrectly identified our island. We turned around and paddled a couple miles back to what we thought was the island where we had eaten lunch. Then we had to establish through triangulation that it actually was the same island. We went ashore.

An hour later we soon found the island and went ashore. Accompanied by two canoeists familiar with map and compass, I

climbed to the highest point, a relatively low ridge that was, at
least, above the water line, giving
us a better view of the surrounding terrain.

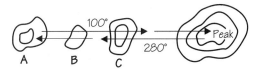

Figure 74

Step one: A couple of miles
across the lake was a distinctive
peak, sloping gently on one side
and with a steep face on the other.
We soon found the peak on our
contour map. Then I took a compass bearing on the peak. It was
exactly 100 degrees. If I were on
the peak, looking toward our
group on the island, we would
have been at a direction of 280
degrees.

Step two: I oriented our map—
that is, I laid it flat on the ground
with the magnetic north arrow on
the map exactly in line with the
magnetic north arrow on the compass. Step three: I drew a line running 280 degrees from the peak

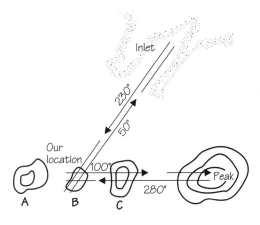

Figure 75

(fig. 74). That line passed through three islands. So now the question was, Which, if any, of the three islands were we really on? Step
four: Across the water, not a half mile away, was a distinctive inlet.
I took a compass reading from us to the inlet. Fifty degrees. The
reading from the inlet to us would then be 230 degrees. Step five:
I drew a line of 230 degrees from the inlet. The two lines inter-
sected on one island (see fig. 75). Ours. We knew precisely where
we were. We passed a small bottle of medicinal brandy around, and
everyone had a celebratory sip, saving enough for a final toast
when we got to our final take-out.

Compasses

Every wilderness traveler should have two very good compasses. The style you choose is a matter of personal preference. The two
basic compass styles are the floating dial and the needle. In both
cases they always point magnetic north. The needle points north.
The dial points north, with the direction, N, marked on the dial
(figs. 76, 77).

Both of my compasses are floating dial. One is the Finnish
Suunto KB14, a superb compass for getting an accurate fix on a
given point. It will give a reading within less than ½ degree of
accuracy when hand-held. The other is an army-style lensatic com-

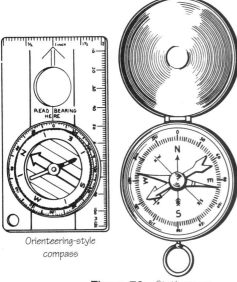

Orienteering-style
compass

Figure 76   Stationary or
fixed-dial compass

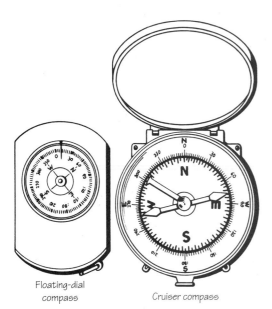

Floating-dial
compass

Cruiser compass

Figure 77

pass, an expensive model. The more popular compasses at present are needle in a rotating dial on a base plate with adjustable declination. Those with a sighting mirror are the most accurate.

The Suunto, hanging around my neck from a cord, is tucked into a shirt or vest pocket, available for instant sighting whenever necessary. The army compass is affixed to the thwart in front of me so that at a glance I know our crude direction in degrees. Alongside the army compass is the current map, tucked inside a plastic envelope and securely fastened to the thwart. Two sets of maps are mandatory when you are paddling unfamiliar terrain. Each set should be protected in a waterproof envelope and should be kept in separate canoes.

Personal Wilderness Equipment

Most of the rules for personal wilderness equipment are the same for canoeing as for backpacking. Dress warmly, but pack light. Consider comfort, quality, and durability when you're comparing prices of new equipment—you often get what you pay for. By all means bring what you need, but leave extras and unnecessary gadgets at home.

Canoeists can pack more pounds of gear than those who backpack through the mountains, but they can't pack *everything,* as it seems car campers do. Your canoe can hold a good amount of gear, but you'll be responsible for it in camp and on portages, so *don't overburden yourself.* On a portage the overequipped struggle valiantly with their excessive gear but have little capacity for carrying community gear. Sharing a tent with a partner who over-

The most famous lightweight canoe ever to cruise American waters was Nessmuk's Sairy Gimp, built to prove that "ten pounds of well-made cedar ought to carry one hundred pounds. . . . Her dimensions are: Length, 10½ feet; beam, 26 inches; rise at center, 9 inches; at sterns, 15 inches; oval red elm ribs, 1 inch apart; an inch home tumble; sterns, plumb and sharp; oak keel and keelson; clinker built of white cedar."

A small man weighing in at around 115 pounds, Nessmuk spent one summer touring several hundred miles of Adirondack waterways in her. He later bragged that he paddled equipped for a week, with canoe and luggage combined weighing a total of 25 pounds.

packs is its own special torture.

First-timers often overload unnecessarily. Examine your gear carefully before you leave home. Will you really use it all? Do you really *need* it all? At home you may wear a shirt or a sweater one day, then wash it or send it off to be cleaned. On a wilderness trip you can't be too finicky about wearing clothing more than once. Your clothes are apt to have a smoky odor from the campfire, but as long as you keep clean they're unlikely to be offensive from other causes. Keep in mind that you can wash clothing on your trip; use your painter as a clothesline.

When you return from your first overnight trip, check your pack. Could any gear you didn't use be left at home next time?

Clothing

Pants and shorts. Take two pairs of pants. One pair should be a comfortable fabric of your choice, suitable for the season and climate. The other pair should be 100 percent wool. Why wool? It's warmer than cotton or synthetics and has the same ability to hold moisture as a wet suit; if it gets wet, it provides a layer of warmth next to the body. The all-wool pants should be a tight weave such as worsted. Soft weaves will pick up the sticky seeds and weeds that line the portages and abound in campsites. A heavy 20-ounce fabric is excellent if you expect cool or cold weather.

Jeans are popular for outdoor wear, but make sure they are not tight. They will not be comfortable when you're paddling all day. If you're most comfortable in jeans, be sure to wear a loose-fitting style (remember, though, that when jeans get wet, they stay wet). Shorts are optional for summer weather, but keep in mind that you'll probably be fairly cool on moving water, anyway, and the sun may burn the tops of your thighs.

Shirts. I bring one lightweight wool and one heavier wool for chilly weather. The latter doubles as a jacket. Whatever shirts you bring, remember that long sleeves help protect the arms from sunburn, mosquitoes, and other biting and stinging insects.

Long johns. Long underwear is often overlooked by summer canoeists, but if the weather is wet and cold, you'll appreciate it no end. It also makes fine pajamas on unexpectedly cold nights. My first recommendation is the light, polypropylene ski underwear. My second choice is a wool-cotton blend thermal underwear, such as Duofold. Avoid the bulky thermal underwear made of 100 percent cotton—it's useless, in my opinion.

Gloves. For cool-weather paddling consider preshrunk 100 percent oiled wool mitts, wool gloves, or the synthetic gloves that are molded to fit a paddler's hand. The molded synthetics are *not* comfortable for camp wear. If you prefer them for paddling, you will need a second pair of wool or leather gloves for use in camp.

Socks: Every canoeist should have at least two pair. For north-country travel they should be heavy, all-wool socks such as Ragg wool or polypropylene ski socks. Make certain your shoes fit over all-wool socks before you start out.

Shoes

My preference is to bring a pair of comfortable canvas shoes to wear while paddling and a pair of lightweight boots to wear around the camp or on a long portage. The canvas shoes shed water easily; in cold weather wear them with wool socks. Wet-suit booties are also an excellent option for paddling. Once ashore, remove your wet shoes and put on your second pair. Lightweight hiking boots are widely available in sporting goods stores. I prefer an all-leather style, which I treat with a waterproofing silicone solution available at shoe stores.

If your leather shoes get wet, dry them slowly in the open air—don't prop them near the campfire. Heat shrinks leather and makes it brittle. Likewise, avoid propping your wet canvas shoes too close to the fire—the canvas may scorch or burn, and the rubber soles may melt.

In all cases, avoid loose-fitting shoes for canoeing. They can slide off your feet quite unexpectedly in a swift current. They also may stay behind in the mud as you clamber up the riverbank or hike a portage trail.

A pair of light, plastic overshoes to slip on over your canvas shoes will also keep your feet reasonably comfortable in wet weather.

Outerwear

Hats and Caps. A wide-brimmed hat is useful for shedding the rain and cutting the bright glare of the sun. Hats blow off easily in a high wind, so wear one that has a chin drawstring or can be pulled tightly on the head.

A light, close-fitting wool or cotton skullcap will help you stay warm at night around camp and in your sleeping bag when the temperature plunges. (A pair of clean, dry wool socks will also help you stay warm in your sleeping bag.)

Rain Gear. Nothing is more practical for keeping dry and comfortable on a rainy day than a rain suit. Like all outdoor gear, these come in a variety of materials and styles. Gore-Tex is highly popular for outdoor wear because it allows body moisture to escape while keeping rain out, but it also has a serious drawback. When it is soiled from grease or oil, the rain will penetrate. I recommend suits made of nylon or Dacron coated with PVC (polyvinylchloride). These come in both light and heavy-duty fabrics and are fully waterproof even if soiled.

As I have said before, avoid ponchos. In case of an upset, a poncho can entangle the feet, as can long plastic rain coats.

Getting up and down in a canoe, kneeling one moment and sitting the next, will pull and tug on rain pants. Sturdy suspenders will help you keep them up.

Be cautious about buying ultra-lightweight rain suits. They are not designed for sitting on all day, and the seat seams may leak. In fact, unless the seams are electronically sealed, they *all* leak. Coat seams with a seam sealer before your trip.

Lightweight dry suits are excellent rain gear only if they are made from breathable fabric, with neck, wrist, and ankle gussets that can be opened.

Windbreakers. A light, long-sleeved windbreaker is a pleasure to paddle in on a cool day or to wear around camp in the evening. If it is not water-resistant, treat it with a water-repellent spray. (You'll still need a waterproof jacket for rainy days.)

Vests. A top quality down vest is worth the cost. It can be scrunched into a tiny bundle when you don't need it, and, ounce for ounce, it is warmer than any other material. If you can't afford a down vest, buy one filled with synthetic fibers such as Quallofil, PolarGuard, or Hollofil II. A heavy wool sweater is also an option.

Camping Gear

Sleeping Bags. The wilderness canoeist should look for a three-season bag with a loft of about 4 inches, anticipating night temperatures in the low 30s. The bag must be made without the sewn-through seams often found in inexpensive bags; cold will penetrate along sewn-through seams. The fill should be the finest material you can afford; if it's within the range of your pocketbook, I recommend down.

I know that some canoeists will shriek at the thought of a paddler using a down bag instead of one with synthetic fill. The argument against down focuses on its characteristics when wet: It collapses like a paper bag, provides no warmth for sleeping, and is slow and difficult to dry. Synthetics, on the other hand, can be wrung out when wet and will instantly regain their loft, though they remain somewhat soggy. In addition, they are easier to dry.

Weighing both sides of the argument, I prefer down. In all the years I've been canoeing and backpacking, no more than a small corner of my down bag has become even damp. The possibility remains that I might get my sleeping bag wet sometime in the next twenty-five years, but against those odds I'll still opt for the fill that gives me the greatest warmth for the least weight and rolls up smaller in my pack than the best quality synthetic.

If you decide on down, you must take special care in choosing a waterproof stuff sack for your bag; use a heavy-duty plastic garbage bag or a PVC pack bag. Keep the sleeping bag in its stuff sack packed with other gear in a larger waterproof pack. When you shop for the sleeping bag itself, remember that not all down is equal. Down from southern ducks and geese is not as fluffy or firm as down from northern birds. In addition, some bags contain down mixed with an excessive amount of feathers. A simple test called the expansion factor determines the quality of the down. A factor of 550 means that an ounce of down will fill at least 550 cubic inches; a factor of 500 means that an ounce will fill 500 cubic inches. Prime down has a fill capacity of at least 550. Never buy a "down" bag that does not specify the fill factor. If you cannot afford prime down, you might consider a top quality synthetic.

After you decide on the fill you want, you'll need to choose a style. Sleeping bags are commonly available in three standard shapes. The mummy bag is shoulder-wide at the top but narrows at the bottom; it often includes a contoured hood with a drawcord and usually unzips only about two-thirds down the side. The rectangular bag is the same width from top to bottom and usually has a full-length zipper that opens along the side and bottom to allow the bag to open flat like a comforter. Two rectangular bags can be zipped together to form a large double bag. Semirectangular bags are slightly narrower at the foot and, like mummy bags, usually unzip partially down one side.

Mummy bags often contain four-season insulation and are great space savers for backpackers. The rectangular bags are the roomiest and most versatile bags. The full zipper also allows you to unzip the bottom on a warm night and stick your feet out to keep comfortable. You can't do that with most mummy bags.

Some sleeping bags have hoods that cover the head on cold nights. Though fine in principle, this feature won't work if you twist and turn. If you're concerned about your head getting cold, wear a light wool or cotton nightcap when it's chilly outside.

Some bags are designed with a lighter layer of insulation on one side than on the other, the idea being that you can sleep with the heavy layer on top on cold nights and the thinner layer on top on warm nights. Again, this works if you never twist or turn; if you're an active sleeper, you can shuffle the top and bottom within minutes.

In any case, try before you buy. Get into a bag on the showroom floor and determine for yourself—not on the advice of the salesperson—the style that suits you.

Sleeping Pads. When the ground is cold you will be chilly in all but a mammoth sleeping bag simply because your body weight compresses the fill under you. The solution is a sleeping pad for both comfort and warmth.

The thin, closed-cell ensolite pads are the choice of many backpackers because they are lightweight and provide insulation. They also are damned uncomfortable. A rock or twig underneath you will poke up like a bony finger. Far more comfortable is a 1-inch pad of open cell foam. This is a bulky solution, however, since it does not roll up in a small package.

Freestanding double-wall dome tents are excellent for camping. Left tent has been covered with a fly; right tent does not yet have its fly attached.

The best product yet developed for the ground sleeper is the Therm-A-Rest pad, a waterproof nylon shell filled with an open-cell foam core that self-inflates when the pad is unrolled and compresses when rerolled. Equipped with high-flow valves for superfast inflation, they are available in several widths and lengths.

Avoid air mattresses if you can. They take lots of time and energy to inflate; the air circulates as you move, so you never have a warm spot beneath you; and they develop leaks somewhat easily and never at a convenient time.

Tents. A light, easily erected tent that can withstand wind and rain is an obvious choice. The most practical style with these characteristics is a double-wall tent with mosquito netting over the openings and with a water-resistant floor. Tents like this are widely available in a variety of shapes and sizes—modified A-frame or geodesic dome, small enough for one person or large enough for six.

Weight and packed size are important factors for canoeists to consider. Large, so-called "family tents" are not suitable for carrying in a canoe and across a portage. The most practical sizes are those designed for two or three people; the four-person size is pushing the outer limits of manageability.

In choosing a tent consider how comfortable you will be if you have to sit out a daylong rainstorm in one. This should not be the only important factor, but it might rule out a tiny backpacker model barely tall enough to sit up in.

No matter what size or style you choose, make certain that all the seams are properly sealed. In the rain even an expensive tent will leak through sewn-through seams. To test for proper sealing, erect your new tent in the backyard and spray it well from the hose. If it leaks (most tents will), apply seam sealer to every seam before you take your portable home into the wilderness.

Unlike sleeping bags, which usually are packed with the rest of your gear, tents are usually carried separately. Pack yours in a water-resistant tent bag or nylon stuff bag before tossing it into your canoe.

Ground Cloths. Most tent floors are made of a highly water-resistant, but not waterproof, material. This means they will get damp in a storm or on wet ground. Solve this problem by spreading a ground cloth (a tarp or a sheet of plastic) under your tent before you erect it. Lay it out carefully. In the event of rain, water pouring downhill can flow over the ground cloth and dampen the tent floor. To avoid this, roll the outside edges of the ground cloth so that no water can flow into it, and tuck it well under the tent edge to prevent water from pooling on it. You can also place the ground cloth inside the tent, but the tent floor will be damp when it is time to break camp.

Small Essentials

Toilet Kit. Your toilet kit should include a minimum number of those items that will make you feel clean and comfortable. A small container of shampoo, a conditioner, a bar of soap, insect repellent, sunscreen lotion, deodorant, toothpaste, toothbrush, and shaving and grooming articles are among the most-needed items. Bring perfume or aftershave if you'd like, but keep in mind that insects like them, too. A small metal mirror can be useful.

A few small plastic bags are useful for storing a bar of wet soap or a wet washcloth, shaving brush, or toothbrush. Big towels are wonderful luxuries for day trips. A small towel and a washcloth are all you need for one or two weeks in the wilderness.

Of course, you should also include any medications prescribed by your doctor as well as any over-the-counter products recommended for you. If you are subject to colds or hay fever, bring a few tablets of an appropriate antihistamine (ask your doctor to prescribe a product that does not cause drowsiness). Drop in a few small bandages and, if you feel it necessary, some antacid tablets and a small supply of aspirin or other pain reliever. I recommend Advil because it relieves joint aches and muscle pains as well as headaches or other discomforts.

The Meramac

The most delightful part of paddling the Meramac river, in Missouri's Onandaga State Park, near Leasburg, is the scenery. It is a mixture of bluffs, caves, wide gravel banks, and woodlands. The gentle and easy water is ideal for novices and beginners, and refreshing for a summer dip.

The Blue Springs livery at Sullivan can drop you and your canoe far enough up river for either a one- or two-day trip, each about five hours paddling time.

Camping along the river is no problem. Pick out any large, white sandbar, pitch your tent. Best bet: Carry a small camp stove for cooking, and a jug of fresh water for drinking.

The most pleasurable time of the canoe year is when the countryside bursts into bloom in the spring. Summer can be a problem with heat and humidity.

Women should bring a supply of personal hygiene items because a change of diet and environment may cause a change in the menstrual cycle.

Flashlight and Candles. Whether you choose a mini-light or a standard flashlight, start with *fresh* batteries, plus an extra set of batteries and a spare bulb. Mini-lights are popular but of limited value in a night emergency. My choice is a so-called "miner's lamp," which fastens to the head by a flexible band. Mine is a three-battery affair in which the batteries are carried in the pocket and a slender cord attaches to the lamp. Headlamps that use AA batteries contained in the headband are neither efficient nor comfortable. As for batteries, an alkaline D battery will burn approximately ten hours; AA alkaline batteries will burn about four hours.

A candle lantern is a highly useful camp item. Only about 10 inches long when extended, the lantern holds a candle that burns for up to eight hours. Since the candle is inside a Plexiglas shield, it will not drip wax and poses minimum fire hazard when used carefully inside a tent. If you use a candle lantern, you also need matches or a cigarette lighter.

Knife. You can separate the novice from the veteran by his or her knife. The veteran's is small and always sharp. Large hunting knives are ungainly, awkward to use, and poor substitutes for a good hatchet. Choose a sheath or case knife with a blade no longer than 3 inches. A knife of good quality is made of 440-C stainless steel and has a minimum hardness of C57-59 on the Rockwell scale. (A competent sporting goods salesperson can explain the meaning and importance of the Rockwell scale.)

Canteen. A 1-quart canteen or plastic bottle is handy in your canoe or in your tent at night. Fill it with properly treated water.

Alarm Clock. A small travel alarm clock is helpful for waking you up before noon. The hand-wound models are more practical than battery-operated ones. Batteries fail or can short out if they become damp.

The Ditty Bag. Though the origin of the expression is unknown, ditty bags were originally used by sailors to hold small, useful articles of gear such as needle, thread, and tape. You, too, should pack a bag with items you think may come in handy on a wilderness trip. Mine is a small, water-resistant bag with a drawstring closure. I just checked its contents: three fishhooks, medium size, and 10 yards of line; some long-forgotten 10-cent stamps in a glassine envelope; a couple of dollars in change, both Canadian and U.S.; an 8X Zeiss monocular; a Suunto ME-D compass; an empty 8-ounce plastic bottle that starts each trip filled with medicinal brandy or rum for a night cap in camp; a working butane lighter; an extra buckskin shoelace; a spare flashlight bulb and three D-cell alkaline batteries; some matches inside a 35mm film container; a notepad and pencil; a miniature sewing kit and several buttons; a paperback volume of Robert Service's totally necessary Yukon poems for reading around the campfire at night; an ancient mouth harp I cannot play (nor have I yet found a paddling companion who could).

Recreational Gear

Fishing Equipment. Canoeing fishermen must hold their gear to an absolute minimum. As canoeists they already have lots to carry; a rod, reel, tackle, and perhaps a net are about all they should bring. Check in advance about the cost of a fishing license where you will be paddling. No angler is too remote to avoid the observant eye of fish and game wardens who patrol their territories either in helicopters or in planes equipped to land on water.

Cameras and Lenses. The same rule applies to photographers as anglers: Hold your gear to a minimum. A single body, with a variable focus lens, a couple of filters, film, and a fresh camera battery or two should take care of your basic needs. In the wilds I use a Nikon FE-2 body, one 35–70mm lens, and a 2X extender. I have a UV filter chiefly to protect the lens and a polarizing filter to reduce the glare of sunlight reflected off the water. If using black-and-white film, such as Kodak Tri-X 400, I also carry a yellow filter for excellent separation of shades of green and a red filter for dramatic sky effects. My usual color film for slides is Fujichrome 50D or 100D or Kodachrome 64.

I put my equipment in Ziploc plastic bags, place it into a water-resistant nylon stuff sack, and carry it in my day pack. If you want something more substantial, all camera stores carry waterproof carrying cases for cameras and lenses. When you look at them, keep in mind that they have to be stored while you are paddling and carried during a portage.

Binoculars and Monoculars. Binoculars are an asset but not a necessity for the canoeist. They are helpful for locating outlets invisible to the naked eye as well as for sighting birds and looking at distant points of beauty. I recommend binoculars with a 7- or an 8-power magnification and no less than a 20mm objective lens. In binocular language that's an 8x20. Remember, the larger the diameter of the objective lens, the more light the binoculars will admit, thus improving their use in dim or late-day conditions. I also carry an 8X Zeiss monocular not much larger than my thumb. It's small, lightweight, and powerful.

Musical Instruments. On one trip a few years ago, Bill, a waiter from Philadelphia who hoped to become a professional folk singer, brought along his guitar. Almost every evening after dinner Bill left the light of the campfire and sat down in the darkness, where he strummed the guitar softly and sang, faintly but clearly. Bill and his guitar brought magic to the night. You or others in your party with portable instruments should bring them with you if you can. Your music will add to the beauty of the wilderness.

Packs and Frames

Waterproof Bags. I can't recommend one "best" waterproof pack that will keep your gear dry in the heaviest storm and protect it unconditionally should it tumble into a swift stream, but I know of several products that offer superb protection and can withstand a great deal of banging around.

As mentioned earlier, Northwest River Supplies in Moscow, Idaho, manufactures a top quality, PVC-coated Dacron bag that has shoulder straps for carrying it into camp or on a portage and a small handle for easy maneuvering in a canoe or tent. Another popular Northwest River model is a tough nylon bag with a separate inner lining of especially heavy plastic. Some styles have a single shoulder strap and carrying handle; others are made with two shoulder straps.

You also can make an excellent waterproof bag using two laundry bags and a plastic garbage bag. First, insert the plastic bag inside one laundry bag. Next, insert the second laundry bag inside the plastic bag. This "sandwich" bag, consisting of an outer fabric layer, a plastic inner barrier, and a fabric liner, makes a serviceable waterproof bag at low cost.

Regular backpacks with internal or external frames also can be converted into waterproof packs if you pack all your gear into plastic garbage bags before you put it into the backpack. Divide your gear into small groups of items (such as socks and underwear), each in its own plastic bag.

Pack Frames. A handy gadget for carrying a homemade pack that does not have its own carrying straps, a sturdy pack frame will save you a great deal of sweat and trouble if you must haul your equipment across a portage.

Day Packs. This is a knapsack-sized pack that carries enough gear for a daylong excursion: a lunch, a change of clothes, and a few first-aid items or other small articles—the limit of its capacity. A good day pack usually features carrying straps and one or more zippered pockets.

I carry a day pack instead of a small thwart bag. My pack is not waterproof, but I use it for carrying all the small items I may need at any time, most of which are stuffed into a water-resistant ditty bag that goes inside the pack. Anything that must be kept secure from damp or storm is stuffed inside a plastic bag. In the canoe I lash the pack to a thwart by its own straps.

Last but Not Least

As a Boy Scout experiencing the thrill of climbing the 10,000-foot peaks of the rugged Bannock mountains around my hometown of Pocatello, Idaho, I always packed one special item for overnight trips—an old pocketknife with one badly nicked blade. At night, when the thin wind whistled through the giant pines, I always slipped it inside my blanket. Today I have another pet that goes with me on outdoor trips—a slightly battered Sierra cup that has been my companion for twenty-five years.

Not until I read Horace Kephart's 1905 outdoor classic *The Book of Camping and Woodcraft,* did I realize that carrying a special trifle, not necessarily useful, is common among outdoor enthusiasts. Kephart wrote: "The more absurd this trinket is, the more he loves it." It is an amulet, a "medicine" that keeps the "spooks and bogies," called the "Koosy Oonek" by Native Americans, far from tent and camp. You, too, may have a special amulet. Whatever it is—an old magnifying glass, a keepsake cigarette lighter, your one and only woodland cap—carry it along. You'll feel prepared for the wilderness with your secret "medicine" to protect you from the pranks of the Koosy Oonek.

The Ultimate Test

The test for determining how secure your equipment will be and how comfortable your clothes will be during foul-weather canoeing is a simple one. Try it at home, following these directions:

1. Dress as you would if you were expecting rain on your canoe trip.
2. Pack your gear and your tent in the bags you intend to use on your trip.

3. Put on your rain gear.
4. Put on your hat.
5. Shoulder your pack.
6. Step into the shower. Turn on the *cold* water and slosh around in it for fifteen minutes.
7. Step out of the shower. Fill the tub half full of cold water. Drop your pack into the tub and kick it around a few
    times.
8. Take off your rain gear and open your pack.
9. How dry and comfortable are you? How dry is your gear?
10. Make necessary adjustments, mend patches, and seal seams while you're still at home.

Community Wilderness Gear

Personal gear is only a part of what you need on a wilderness trip. You must also equip a kitchen, carry general camping items and emergency equipment, and prepare a first-aid kit. Each person could bring his or her own set of all the supplies necessary, but this would mean a lot of duplication. Do six people need six hatchets? Do two couples need two full sets of kitchen gear? Is it necessary to carry eight first-aid kits if eight people are in your group? Of course not. Members of the party can divide the list of community equipment, each taking responsibility for bringing and carrying one or more items.

Kitchen Gear

Two considerations are important in organizing a kitchen: the menu and the size of your group. First create a menu, planning every dish for every meal of the trip. This means a fair amount of work, but it is necessary. Plan meals that require the fewest possible pots working simultaneously; for example, avoid four-pot meals if you have one two-burner stove and are trying to limit your gear. Similarly, don't plan a meal in which you must use the same pot for two different courses, or you'll be washing dishes between bites.

Pots and Pans. Your largest pot should have a capacity of one pint per person. It can be used for soup, one-pot meals, and washing dishes. You'll have no trouble finding other uses for it.

Your basic cooking should be done in nesting pots, not pots and pans brought from home. Home equipment with long handles is awkward to pack, and pots with short handles are difficult to use. In addition, the home items will quickly become blackened if you cook over a campfire.

Camp cookware kits of sturdy spun aluminum or stainless steel with copper-jacketed bottoms are excellent. A good set will have lids that can be placed upside down on pots filled with warm water and used to keep food warm. Some manufacturers claim that such lids can be used as small frying pans, but they are not really satisfactory for this use. We carry a separate 10-inch aluminum frying pan. You also can buy excellent cast iron or teflon-coated frying pans or small aluminum griddles specially made for camp use.

Avoid the almost-toylike lightweight aluminum kits. The thin metal loses heat instantly when removed from the fire and is easily dented and damaged.

Cooking Accessories. I take most or all of the following: a medium-sized wire whisk, one or two metal spatulas, a long-handled dipper, a can opener, a bottle opener, a large serving spoon, a 1-liter plastic bottle with a wide mouth and watertight lid (used for mixing powdered milk or such other purposes as you may devise), an 8-ounce measuring cup, a set of measuring spoons, a flat, round, oriental-style long-handled sieve (useful for straining unwanted fly-in guests from a pot of soup, plus the usual purposes), a pair of metal tongs, a long-handled serving fork, a vegetable peeler, two sturdy aluminum pot grippers (available at better sporting goods stores), a pair of oven mitts, and a kitchen knife. Ours is a fisherman's filleting knife in a plastic sheath that has a small, built-in sharpener; it's an excellent product.

On a short trip with three or four friends, I include a 2½-gallon plastic water bag. For a larger group I take two such water containers. (Keep in mind that if you use your cooking pots to bring water to the campsite, they can't be used for cooking as long as they are filled with water.) You might also want to bring a large plastic bowl in which to mix foods.

Tableware and Utensils. For each person bring one stainless steel cup, one large bowl, either sturdy plastic or enamel, and a stainless steel knife, fork, and spoon. To avoid arguments over who belongs to which cup and bowl, use red nail polish to mark each piece with each person's initials. This is especially important if you are using the same style of equipment for everyone.

Portable Stove. Never travel without one lightweight mountaineering stove; if your group is large, bring two. They are a blessing in the pouring rain when you have no dry wood or in areas where wood fires are prohibited. They are also handy when you'd like to put ashore on a chilly day and swiftly heat up water for coffee or tea.

Outdoor stoves burn gasoline, kerosene, butane, propane, or alcohol; each type has its merits. Alcohol burns clean but is expensive and produces less heat for weight than any other fuel. Propane and butane stoves are extremely convenient, and both fuels burn without fuss or muss. Butane, however, is difficult to light at temperatures below 32 degrees F. Also, there is no easy way to know when a butane or propane cartridge will run out of fuel. (Empty fuel cartridges should be carried out with you.) Kerosene is used most often by those who paddle in foreign regions where gasoline is not available.

Gasoline is an excellent fuel. The newer stoves that use gasoline are designed to burn either white or leaded gas; some also will burn kerosene. Among the miniature gasoline stoves highly suitable for two or three people are the self-cleaning SVEA 123R, the Optimus 99, and the Phoebus 725. Larger models like the MSR, the Phoebus 625, and the Optimus 111 can be used to cook for as few as two or as much as a one-pot meal for ten.

Coleman produces two stoves that burn either gasoline or kerosene, the Peak 1 Feather and the Peak 1. MSR and GAZ both make lightweight stoves that burn butane or isobutane.

While weight must always be considered for a wilderness canoe trip, be cautious about buying the extra-lightweight, fist-sized mountaineering stoves. They may be quite satisfactory for one or two people for minimum cooking but are not sturdy enough to stand up to the abuse and use they might suffer on a canoe trip for four or six people. As I said earlier, a large group may prefer two mountaineering stoves to a camp stove with two burners. Even medium-sized pots on the two-burner at the same time are crowded. Two stoves allow two people to cook at once without stumbling over each other. The double camp stove and two mountaineering stoves weigh about the same and take up the same amount of space.

Fuel. If your stoves burn gasoline, there really is no safety problem in carrying a can of white gasoline or filling fuel bottles with gasoline. Include a small funnel to spare yourself the indignity of spilled fuel when you resupply your stoves.

Grill. A sturdy campfire grill is one of the most important items you can carry if you will be cooking over wood fires. You can buy them or, as we do, use a shelf from an abandoned refrigerator. Rectangular grills are more useful than the round or square models. For a large group, carry two of them.

Dishwashing Gear. Bring only biodegradable bar soap, along with a couple of metal or plastic scouring pads, some small sponges, and a packet of disposable but reusable dish towels such as Handi-Wipes. Air drying is favored for camp dishes and pots. If you need to use the towels, they can be washed and hung up to dry for re-use.

Water Purification Pump. A few years ago, hyped by the promotional literature and advertising claims, we added a water purification pump to our wilderness kitchen. Since then, I've had serious second thoughts about how really effective a pump can be, and I probably will *not* take one on our next wilderness travel.

Here is the reasoning behind this decision:

An article in the American Canoe Association journal touting the advantages of purifying water by use of a pump filter or, as a

The Olympic Ocoee

No, not even if you have your own canoe and are a whitewater wild-cat can you paddle the 1996 Olympic course on the Ocoee River in Tennessee. The world-class stretch is afoam with water only when it is released from a TVA power dam for an event as important as the Centennial Olympics. Otherwise, the water from the dam is detoured through a flume that empties well below the skillfully designed Olympic course.

Will water someday be released regularly into the dusty Olympic stretch? Local and TVA authorities are sort of, maybe, thinking about the prospect.

However, where the flume water roars back into Ocoee you can begin a five-mile run of whitewater rafting or challenging canoeing for experts. A few miles below another TVA dam, a beautiful five-mile stretch of easy Ocoee water tempts the casual paddlers.

second choice, boiling it for at least ten minutes prompted a reply by William W. Forgey, M.D., from Mellville, Indiana. Dr. Forgey has published scientific articles on the use of chemicals for water purification.

The doctor pointed out that all filter systems are limited in their capacity to absorb harmful organisms. They cannot eliminate polio, rotovirus, or other viral pathogens, but they can be of help. The most significant weakness, for example, among the filters is that they reach a point where they no longer are effective. The First Need filter for instance, says it is "good for up to 100 gallons filtration capability," but that "up to" depends on the quality of the water. And, in a normal situation, who, if any of us, knows when a filter has reached its limit?

Dr. Forgey also said that chemicals, such as chlorine or iodine, to purify water are highly effective. He warned, however, that they must be used according to directions. He added that pregnant women and people with thyroid conditions should not use chemically treated water any longer than one or two weeks.

Dr. Forgey concluded his comments about water treatment with filters and chemicals with this observation:

"Of all the techniques we have for making water safe to drink, only bringing water to a temperature of 50°C (122°F) is foolproof. All of the other modalities work as long as they are used properly and we understand their limitations."

It may come as the same surprise to you as it did to me to learn that heating water only until it is very warm, but not as hot as the water that comes from our house taps, is "foolproof."

Camp Gear

Toilet Paper. Plan on at least half a roll per person per week. Don't use your share for blowing your nose or any purpose other than toileting.

Poncho. Take a sturdy, serviceable poncho for the community pack. As discussed earlier, use it as a "tablecloth" to spread on the damp ground or as a cover for a woodpile. Strung overhead, a poncho provides a quick shelter for a small group caught in a rainstorm. You're likely to find other uses for it as well.

Folding Shovel. A small folding shovel or heavy-duty trowel will be useful in many ways, such as digging a latrine pit, clearing debris from a fire site, or covering a dying campfire with dirt.

Axe and Saw? I make that a question because you may or may not really want to add one to your gear. Neither item is especially necessary in woodland regions. On the other hand, we carry a small hatchet for such tasks as hammering tent pegs, occasionally cutting kindling, cutting a long center pole for the tarp if we need to put it up because of inclement weather, or cutting and trimming an emergency tent pole if one breaks.

Repair Kit. We carry a small pair of pliers; two small screwdrivers—one Phillips-head, the other regular; a few tacks, nails, and wood screws; a sewing awl; a bobbin of light wire; and the universal savior of more situations in the woods than any other item in your kit: duct tape. This silver-colored tape has so many uses it's hard to imagine being without it. You can cover a leak in a canoe, mend a broken paddle, repair a tear in a tent, or even patch the hole in a burned shoe. Take a large roll.

We also carry a tent repair kit that includes a tube of seam sealer, a couple of tent pegs, and some heavy cord. Finally, we bring a small sewing kit with needles and safety pins and a few sheets of aluminum foil folded into a small pack. On one trip someone broke the glass on our single-mantle Coleman lantern; we made a reflecting shield out of aluminum foil, and it worked just fine.

Tarp. On short trips that will not involve portages, we carry a 10- by 10-foot plastic tarp, complete with poles. On longer wilderness trips we take a 9- by 9-foot lightweight cotton tarp, without poles, and string it from trees. We use a tarp to shelter the kitchen on rainy days.

Lanterns. Two kinds of lanterns are widely available—those that burn propane or butane and those that use gasoline. Recommendation: Choose a lantern that uses the same type of fuel you need for your stove. Bring an extra generator, a repair wrench, and a supply of mantles.

Emergency Wilderness Equipment

The need to carry emergency equipment increases significantly on remote wilderness trips. There was a time, not too far in the past, when the most critical "item" in our emergency pack was telling the outfitter who was to pick us up at our takeout that if we did not arrive within 24 hours of our preplanned arrival time he was to notify the appropriate authorities. They then could initiate a search and rescue operation, usually with a single-engine aircraft that would follow the map route we had given the outfitter.

With our electronically changing times, we now carry two sophisticated "items." One is a hand-held VHF marine radio, and the other a small Electronic Positioning Radio Beacon, or EPRB. With the VHF, one can broadcast on channel six and speak to whoever picks up the signal, describing your problems and location. The EPRB transmits a distress signal that is relayed by satellite. Anyone hearing the signal knows that whoever is transmitting needs help and can locate the source of the signal within a few hundred to a a few thousand yards.

In addition to a small AM/FM radio for weather broadcasts, throw rope, snap links, and emergency rescue knife, we always tote along on any canoe travel, when heading into the wilderness, the following emergency equipment:

- An extra compass
- Extra matches in a waterproof container
- Three "Skyblazer" self-contained launchers—flares that reach an altitude of 200 feet. The "Skyblazer" flares are Coast Guard–approved.
- A couple of whistles
- Coast Guard–approved red signal flags, which can be spread on the ground, hoisted in the air, or waved from the end of a long pole
- Two tubes of Coast Guard–approved red dye. Spilled on the water, the oil spreads into an ever-widening circle to alert aircraft.
- A metal rescue mirror to flash a signal to passing aircraft or even a distant boat
- A complete extra set of maps securely wrapped in a waterproof plastic envelope
- A half-dozen various fishhooks and a package of fishing line
- A hand-sized set of ratchet pruning shears (I use the Florian model), which can cut through ropes and vines in a fraction of the time it takes to cut through them with a "diver's" or "river" knife. In an emergency, time is of the essence.

Packing the Community Gear

How do you carry all the community items? Everyone could, of course, stick a few pieces here or there in their personal packs. You may find it more convenient, however, to use the "Gordon Pack System" (see fig. 78). Here's how it works: All the kitchen equipment, including personal bowls, cups, and flatware, is kept together in a single pack. It must be sturdy, but it need not be waterproof. It should have straps for carrying across a portage. This bag is marked (in big, readable letters printed on duct tape and stuck to the side) KITCHEN UTILITY.

Figure 78

Next, all the general camp items such as repair kit, shovel, tarp, poncho, hatchet, portable saw, fire tube, and camp stove are put into another bag clearly marked CAMP UTILITY.

Food preparation and packing are discussed in Chapter 8 in which I review several methods for putting your food together. All the spices, salt, pepper, coffee, tea, hot chocolate, and other items that you'll use for nearly every meal should be packed in their own bag, clearly marked FOOD UTILITY.

All of the emergency items are to be kept together in a sturdy *red* bag marked EMERGENCY.

Making Camp

Low-impact Camping

As a Boy Scout in a long-ago era, the highlights of our school vacation were backpacking in the mountains. Once each summer good ol' Troop 7 planned a special weekend trip to learn the skills of "camp making."

Tramping several miles into the nearby mountains, our scoutmaster would find an open area in the woods, with a stream running nearby. Once we had chopped away ground cover and dug deep pits around our tents to keep out any wayward water from a storm, we would study camp craft—as practiced in those days.

Aspens were chopped down, trimmed, and used to make a cook-

The ability of a bat to pinpoint an object through "echolocation" is so acute it can detect something as thin as a human hair. That's why a bat flying around your campsite can locate and eat up to 600 mosquitos and gnats an hour—and it won't touch a hair on your head.

ing tripod for each of the three patrols, which cooked meals over their own hunter's fires. These were made from live trees chopped into 6-foot logs at least a foot in diameter. Other trees and green branches were cut into suitable lengths and trimmed to make a 5-foot "signal tower" that could support the weight of one Scout.

A bridge was made from two sturdy pines cut, trimmed, and laid across the water, then covered with short branches.

We learned to make an emergency shelter by chopping down endless pine-tree branches and stacking them against a standing tree in such a way that they formed a rude "branch tent."

Of course, we proudly cleaned up after we left. All the unburned wood was neatly stacked by the three fire sites, which were doused with water to make certain the fires were truly out. The fire sites, with their hunter's fire logs and tripods, were untouched. The bridge and tower were left as testimony of our skills. Tin cans and garbage were buried.

We hiked home proud of our new-found camp skills.

But that was years ago, when *conservation* was a word few had heard and none of us worried about. The mountains and rivers and forests had been here for untold eons, and neither hunter, camper, fisherman, canoeist, nor Scout was a threat.

In present times, everyone who travels our shrinking wilderness is, in a sense, a threat. This in no way implies that wilderness is sacred land and can be saved only if closed to human use. But it does mean that we can destroy what we love by thoughtlessness, by carelessness, or by not recognizing that conservation is a responsibility of everyone who walks the earth, or paddles its rivers, or flies through the skies.

For those who love and use the wilds, yesterday's profligate and misunderstood maltreatment of the out-of-doors has been replaced with what we now know as *low-impact camping*.

Go. Enjoy. But, within the tradition of the original Americans, leave a minimal impact upon the untamed lands and clean waters so when our grandchildren hike the trails we have hiked, canoe the rivers and lakes we have canoed, and camp where we have pitched our tents, they still will be able to relish its tranquility, its remoteness from the stress of cities, and take the same joy in the magnificence of the wilds as you and I do today.

Choosing a Site

On trips through our state and national parks and forests, canoeists should have no trouble determining where to camp. On popular canoe routes, campsites are marked and often maintained. Some have Adirondack shelters; some have privies with doors that lock.

In remote regions you may have more difficulty finding sites. In heavily wooded areas where trees grow to the waterline, making camp often is a matter of when, not where—that is, whenever you can find a suitable place. In such regions we begin scouting the shoreline early in the afternoon. Given the choice between stopping somewhat earlier than planned because we've found an excellent site or continuing a few more miles and then looking depends on how frequently we've been seeing good sites. I favor the "grab it early" system. On more than one occasion those few extra miles led us to make camp in a miserable spot because we were running out of daylight and muscle power.

The first criteria in locating any camp area is to inflict as miniscule damage as possible to the terrain. If there is an existing tent site use it rather than tearing up brush or destroying grassy areas to make a virgin place for your weary butt. Always locate a fire in an existing fire ring if there is one, even if it obviously hasn't been used for years. Avoid damaging trees, brush, or saplings as much as possible. So what if a root nudges one side of the tent? Chopping it out certainly won't help the tree.

Nails carried on a wilderness trip are for emergencies. Hammering them into trees to hold a lantern, gear, or clothing is no emergency.

Unless you are learned enough in wilderness lore to recognize edible roots, berries, leaves, and mushrooms, don't pick anything that grows if you do not intend to add it to your menu. If you want to take something home for identification, take its picture.

In seldom-visited timbered wilderness, there is an exception to the oft-cited phrase: Leave no trace. Should you stumble upon a good camp area when exploring for a clearing in heavy woods, follow the old-timer's tradition of hanging a small red ribbon from a tree that can be spotted by passing paddlers. If such a dangling bright strip leads you to one, you will be grateful.

Here's a fine way to set up camp. The inverted canoe, used as a table top, is safely away from the fire. The fire is built between two walls of rocks to support a grill and is kept small for good cooking without waste of fuel; the wood supply, in the lower right corner, is within easy reach.

If canoeing in the spring or early summer in regions where clouds of mosquitos relish a refreshing sip of your blood, place your camp, if at all possible, in an area *partially* open to the prevailing breezes.

Even a light wind will help sweep away the mosquitoes dying to have you join them for dinner. Avoid sites completely in the open, however, because you will have no protection against storms or high winds.

We ran into just such a situation on a trip on the upper Ottawa River. The first night we camped on a low bluff covered with light brush. Most of us pitched tents on scattered bare spots. Only one of us chose to pitch a tent in the scant protection a few nearby trees offered.

A storm crashed into us shortly after midnight. Thunder roared and lightning bolts hurtled down, brightening the night in a ghastly blue that revealed the damage the winds and beating rains were causing. Dome tents were spun half around and shoved from where they had been pitched. Two double-wall A-frames were nearly felled from the pounding winds. The one tent among the trees was wet but standing.

That storm taught every camper a lesson. At our next campsite tents were pitched within the protection offered by trees, the A-frames were properly secured, and the dome tents were pegged to the ground.

Work Areas

Even as paddlers climb out of their canoes and search for sites for their individual tents, give thought to where the community facilities will be. Choose a kitchen area, a fire area, and an equipment-storage area. Reserve an appropriate spot for erecting a tarp and for firewood.

Keep these areas to one side of the tent area. If the community areas are centrally located, you will have a steady stream of people walking through the work areas on their way to visit another tent or to go to their own tents.

Tents

In picking a tent site, look for the flattest ground available. On even a slight slope, weary paddlers may find they are slowly sliding downhill in the middle of the night. If you can't avoid a slope, sleep with your head uphill.

Do not "ditch" tents—that is, dig a small ditch around the uphill side to keep rain away from the tent floor. That may have been smart camping a century ago, but modern tents have highly water-resistant floors to keep the rain out. The no-ditching rule is a matter of conservation. Future storms can turn those small, abandoned ditches into deep erosion ditches. If you're concerned about the water resistance of your tent floor, use a ground cloth or plastic sheeting under your tent.

It is bad policy to hang clothes or other items on your tent. Using the tent as a clothes dryer adds unnecessary weight and pulls at the seams, thus leading to seams that leak. Use your painter as a clothesline instead.

If you value your tent, be careful inside it. Take off your shoes before walking in it and clean out any debris before you pack it up.

The Cooking Fire

Although we carry portable gasoline stoves for occasional or emergency use, we basically cook with wood fires. There is a continuing argument by some outdoor enthusiasts who staunchly maintain that fires should never be built in the wilderness. Their argument does make sense, in certain circumstances, such as high-impact areas subject to continual use by campers, hikers, or canoeists; or in areas where tree life is so minimal that it is threatened by even a single fire.

On the other hand, there is no intelligent need, from a conservation point of view, to eliminate the use of wood fires if traveling a well-wooded, little-visited region.

Consider by way of example: Wood is a renewable resource. The dead branches and twigs used for a fire today will be replaced in the spring by new growth. Trees will continue to mature. The local ecosystem will not suffer when moderate fires are lighted for cooking or the pleasure of a small campfire at night.

Now, consider problems actually caused by total dependence on stoves for cooking. First, their fuel is nonrenewable. Once burned, it's forever burned. Second, neither the resources consumed in making or in transporting a metal stove are renewable.

Even the most dedicated fire builders, however, must recognize that the concern over the indiscriminate use of wood is valid. Conservation is a critical element in maintaining our ever shrinking wilderness. What this means is simple: Keep night fires small. Roaring cooking fires or camp bonfires are anathema to all who love, and use, the lands beyond the boundaries of civilization.

Build two walls of rocks and put the grill on top of them. If you can't find rocks, drag in a couple of logs and put the grill atop them. Wet down the support logs frequently so that they don't turn into firewood.

Some birch bark and a few lightweight twigs will start a fire, even in the rain, in a matter of minutes.

Types of Fires

There are as many ways to build a fire as there are campers to light them, but only these four are basic to how a fire should be built: the hunter's fire, the trench fore, the trapper's fire, and the Indian fire.

Here's how they are built:

Hunter's Fire. Traditionally, a hunter's fire was built from the butt ends of two freshly cut trees, about 1 foot thick and 6 feet long. They were placed about 6 inches apart at the end facing into the breeze and 15 inches apart at the other end. The fire was lit between them at a width that would support the pots and pans.

The modern hunter's fire is built either of two parallel walls of heavy rocks, about 12 to 18 inches high, or a couple of dead logs, only far enough apart to support the camp grill, and aligned with the prevailing breeze. A large rock or slab of wood is placed against the windward opening if the breeze becomes too strong.

When breaking camp, the smoke-blackened stones should be tossed into the underbrush if they were not used in an existing fire ring, and the fire site should be covered with ground debris.

Trench Fire. A trench fire is, in effect, a hunter's fire below ground level. Dig a trench 1 foot to 18 inches deep, only wide enough to support the grill, and with one end sloping so that wood can be fed into the fire. Pile the dirt to one side.

When breaking camp, shovel the dirt back onto the pit and cover it with natural ground detritus.

Trapper's Fire. A trapper's fire is a combination portable fireplace and cooking fire that was popular in days long past with hunters and fishermen who would be in a remote wilderness camp for several days. It consists of a 6-foot-high back-wall, made of stones or of green logs, at least a foot thick, slanting slightly backward. The fire in front of the back-wall would be for cooking by day, and it was kept burning at night. The heat would be reflected into an open lean-to built on the opposite side of the back-wall.

Indian Fire. Building a fire out of long branches placed butt-to-butt in a pattern of spokes radiating from the hub of a wheel is known as an Indian fire. As the wood is burned, the branches are shoved into the burning center.

Efficient Fires

For cooking, the most efficient fires are the trench and hunter's fires. In both the heat is concentrated between the walls and reflected upward to the cooking pots.

An open fire with a self-supporting campfire grill with four legs, a standard among a majority of campers, is the least efficient use of fuel. The direct heat is blown away by every wandering breeze. It may take two to three times as much fuel to cook a meal over an open fire as it does with a trench or hunter's fire.

Take full advantage of the fire. As soon as it is lit, put a pot of water on. Sooner or later, the camp will need the hot water.

On one trip we lost our grill. We still built parallel rock walls for the fire and found flat pieces of slate every night to make a stove top. Once the top rocks were heated, they held the heat and distributed it evenly.

A large cooking fire is foolish. It should be large enough only for cooking, not wasting fuel. Keep in mind that when cooking over a fire, the fire shifts, flares, and dies away. Move your cooking pot as the fire shifts.

For grilling, bring a fire to a high pitch of flame, then let it burn down to a bed of hot coals. Build a second, smaller fire at the edge of the main bed of coals, shoveling its new coals into the main fire as the fire burns down.

Bringing in firewood is everyone's job. The only wood you should collect for a fire is downed wood and dead limbs. Cutting live trees is destructive and may also be illegal in some areas. Chopping or sawing the dead wood is usually unnecessary. Large dead limbs can be snapped into smaller pieces by bracing them against a close pair of trees and pushing the limb until it breaks.

Look for smaller slivers of dead wood and the tips of dead branches for kindling to start a fire. If you see birch trees, peel off sheets of their outer bark and use them as a starter fuel. Even when wet, the bark will burn because it is saturated with birch oils. Pine pitch is also an excellent starter. So, too, are plastic knives, forks, and spoons.

Before lighting the fire, make sure you have a large kindling pile plus a good supply of larger pieces on hand to keep the fire going.

There are two standard methods for helping the first hint of flame to keep burning until the fire is well started—crouching down and blowing on it, or fanning it with a hat or frying pan. But the standard methods are, bluntly, lousy.

Something better? Yes, an old Indian technique, which involved the use of a hollow reed. You can use the same technique, but replace the reed with a 3-foot length of runner or plastic tubing at least ⅜ inch in diameter. Put one end in the mouth, hold the other close to the flame, and after a few brisk blows, voilà! It's burning.

Before turning in at night, put aside a stack of firewood and cover it with a poncho or slip it inside a tent so you'll have dry kindling to get the fire going again in the morning.

The Work Table

An inverted canoe makes an excellent work table. Treat it with respect. No cutting, no hacking, no chopping directly on its surface. It is, after all, a canoe. To turn a canoe into a table, invert the canoe and shove some large rocks or a couple of logs under the bow and stern gunwales to make it stable. The space under a canoe is excellent for the storage of camp gear, food bags, and other equipment you want to keep dry and protected.

A canoe is inverted for use as a table. The flatter the hull, the better the table. Note how rocks or logs are wedged under the bow and stern decks to stabilize the canoe.

Food Preparation

General Camp Order No. 1: "Under no circumstances and at no time will any person, male or female, who is a participant in any canoe trip bother or interfere with the cook(s), in any way whatsoever, while they are engaged in the preparation of food."

It is an irritant when you are cooking a dish in your own kitchen and someone noses around to taste or offer advice. In camp it can be a disaster.

To prevent the cook(s) from wielding a sharp knife upon the hapless hide of a person who invades the cooking area during prep time, provide a diversionary snack such as gorp or crackers and cheese placed far from the cook. A dish of crudités is exceedingly effective on a short camping trip where refrigeration of vegetables is not a problem.

Animals and Food

In the wilderness animals can range from pesty to dangerous. The porcupine, on the annoying edge of the spectrum, gnaws at anything that contains salt. It will chew on a well-used paddle handle permeated with salt from perspiration, as well as find gourmet delight in anything from shoes to pack straps. Pack rats will drag small items from an untended tent. Raccoons are a delight to watch if they come sauntering into your camp looking for food. They also are clever at getting into loose bags that contain your edibles.

At the hazardous end are bears. The most dangerous are the grizzlies, whose Latin name is, appropriately, *Ursus horribilis*. Their habitat is largely confined to the northern Rockies, Alaska, and remote Canadian wilderness. Grizzlies are rarely known to invade a camp in search of food, but they will. The most common camp problems elsewhere are caused by the much less aggressive black and brown bears.

In bear country keep your camp site clean. If fishing, clean your fish well away from the camp. Never, ever, bring any food into your tent—not even a delicious candy bar.

It is imperative to state the obvious: If a bear comes strolling into your camp, sniffing for a meal, it wants food wherever it is. If you catch sight of a bear, make noise, flash a light, whistle, holler, or throw sticks or stones from a distance. This type of noisy activity almost—almost—inevitably frightens it off. If it doesn't, then it is the better part of valor to make a hasty retreat.

Protecting food from small animals is largely a matter of keeping it stored in food bags. To safeguard food from bears at night, some wilderness paddlers recommend hanging the food on a line stretched between two trees. If you choose this method, the food sacks must be more than 10 feet off the ground and well away from branches. A big bear can rear up and easily knock down a low-hanging sack. Agile, smaller bears can scramble up branches and, intelligently, rip at the line to knock the packs down.

A method we have used for more than a quarter century is the old "scare 'em with noise" system. We stack all the food in a single pile, cover it with a poncho, and stack all the pots and pans on top of the pile. The theory is that if a bear comes nosing around, it'll knock the pots and pans down, frighten itself, and run off. Keep in mind, however, that a bear may not care one wit about theory. Once I was awakened by a terrible clatter and saw a small brown bear lumbering off, dragging a day's food bag with him. When we recovered the bag later, the only food missing was some chocolate-covered candy!

Cleaning Up

All washing of dishes—and people—should be done away from the body of water you are canoeing. Buckets of water should be hauled ashore for kitchen and personal washing and rinsing. The two-pot method is excellent for cleaning up the kitchen. One pot of hot water is used for washing; a second is used for rinsing. To ensure sanitary rinsing, use water that has been heated first.

Dishes and kitchenware need not be towel-dried unless you're

Wipe the Dishes? Not a problem for smart canoeists. Let 'em air dry.

in a hurry to get underway. Air-drying works fine, especially if you're camped for the night.

Garbage and Toilets

In frequently traveled areas flammable garbage, including left-over edibles, should be burned. Refuse that cannot burn (aluminum foil, tin or aluminum cans, dead batteries, empty butane or propane cartridges, and so on) should be taken with you. In seldom-visited remote regions, it is not necessary to burn leftover edibles, but you should scatter them far from the campsite.

Bathroom functions should be performed at least 200 feet away from any water and well away from camp. The camp shovel or spade and a roll of toilet paper in a plastic bag should be highly visible in the camp. Use them both. It takes only an extra moment to toss a spade of dirt over one's private contribution to the wilderness manure pit.

Care of Equipment

If you have time in the morning, air out your sleeping bag on a branch or painter clothesline before rolling it up and stuffing it into its pack. Otherwise, air it out in the afternoon when you make camp. Be careful, though—don't let it hang out after sundown when the dew falls.

Sweep the sand and grit out of your tent every morning before putting it away. If you spot any dampness along a seam, apply seam sealer. If you see any evidence that water has dripped onto the inner lining of the top of the tent, check the outer fly for leaking seams.

Wash your clothes using the same procedure you use to wash your dishes. Use two pans, one for washing, one for rinsing; away from the stream or lake; biodegradable soap only.

The Koosy Oonek has a nasty little habit of turning your flashlight on when it is carefully tucked away. To foil this little imp you can take the batteries out or, as I do, slap a piece of adhesive tape over the switch.

Prepared campers always have a sharp knife. If you forgot to bring a small sharpening stone, borrow one.

Even if you've paddled for days in bright sunlight under cerulean skies, make certain all of your gear *always* is securely packed in waterproof bags or packs. Better dry than sorry.

The Campfire

The campfire provides perhaps the most beautiful and satisfying moments on a canoe trip. Use the small evening campfire time to talk over the events of the day and to share the emotional experiences of the trip. Bring out your musical instruments to add music to the beauty of the night, and enjoy the display of moonlight and starlight you will never see in the city.

Telling stories around a campfire is an experience shared by humans since the dawn of communication. If you have no stories of your own to tell, bring a favorite book with short stories that fit the time and place. Among the greatest of wilderness poets is Robert Service. His verses about the Klondike, gold panning, and saloons, where the ragtime kid beats out old songs on a broken piano, still come alive, especially on a wilderness journey.

Safety Check

Before you go to sleep, take a tour of the camp. Are all tents secure? Is all equipment put away? Is the food stored? Is the woodpile covered? Has the fire died down to embers that will cause no problems if the wind increases? Are the canoes all ashore, tipped upside down to keep out rain? Are PFDs and paddles safely tucked away? Once you're satisfied that all is well, head for your tent and get some rest for tomorrow's adventure.

Survival Techniques

It was a cloudy afternoon with a brisk breeze. Eight of us paddled along the shores of a lake in the lonely wilderness of northwestern Quebec. We were pushing to reach a sandy shore near the lake's outlet where we could set up camp before the vaguely threatening sky turned to rain.

A canoe is brought ashore, inverted, and safely tucked away for the night.

From a previous trip several years earlier, I knew the outlet was at least a 50-foot drop of wildly cascading water, and that the portage was a narrow wisp of a trail probably not used by more than a dozen paddlers a year.

We rounded a slight bend, and ah, there it was, our personal, beautiful wide stretch of beach. The flotilla swung instantly toward the shore. Canoes were beached. Canoeists quickly jumped ashore, dropping hats, paddles, or personal floatation devices (PFDs) to mark the chosen spot for their tents. As we bustled about setting up camp, we spotted two canoes, the first people we had seen in more than a week.

We waved. They paddled over.

"Lots of room to camp here," I called out.

They were not looking for a camp site. One of the men was a fishing guide familiar with the region. The other three were fishermen. The guide knew of a spot across the lake where they would make their camp that night.

"First we go fishing below falls," the guide said, in a thick, friendly Canadian French accent. "Then we have some great fish for dinner. Maybe leave one big fish for you, okay?" He laughed.

"We'll eat it," someone said.

They paddled on, rounding a point at the end of the beach.

Once our tents were up, community gear stored under a tarp tied between trees, and a fire area cleared, we sort of relaxed. No rush. Every paddler knew his or her duty for the day. Dinner wouldn't be started for another hour or so. The cooperating clouds began to break up.

Several of us decided to check out the portage and visit the roaring falls. We eased canoes into the water and paddled around the point. There, on another spit of sand, was the clearing marking the start of the carry. The two canoes from the fishing party were pulled up on the shore.

The wind was sending light waves splashing up on shore as we beached our canoes, dragging them high above the water. Even as we did, two of us simultaneously saw one of their canoes, both loaded with gear, rocked by rolling, small waves, edging off the sand and into the water.

Racing madly, we splashed onto the water trying to reach the canoe. Too late. It drifted further from shore then, propelled both by the current and the wind, floated directly into the outlet and disappeared.

Checking to see that their second canoe was safe, we started down the portage, weaving through bushes and slipping on the steep, narrow path. The guide and one fisherman were rushing up the path. They stopped for a brief moment.

"We lose canoe. Now portage other canoe down and find things," the guide shouted before they raced on to get the second canoe.

Eventually, they found the errant canoe, badly battered but with enough duct tape it could be made fit to be paddled gently. Their gear and food were another problem. Two paddles were broken. One paddle was not recovered. Bags were ripped apart. Food, clothing, tents, and sleeping bags were scattered on the waters.

Some were lost. Salvage was plucked from wherever it showed up by two men in the second canoe paddling below the falls.

Before they were able to paddle to their own camp we had loaned them two of our paddles, and given them some extra food from emergency supplies we carried. They accepted, reluctantly but thankful.

There is a significant point to this true experience. What would have been the outcome if this had occurred to a couple paddling the wild country's lakes and rivers and there had been no well-equipped group of canoeists to lend a helping hand and paddle?

Accidents do happen in the back country. Once you paddle into the wilderness, it is not only important to go well prepared with equipment, but also with the knowledge of basic survival skills if that accident should happen to you.

Emergency Rescue Equipment

In addition to the Emergency Wilderness Rescue Equipment (see page 162) carried by the group, individuals also are responsible for three personal items on them at all times. They can be your personal life-saving equipment if lost on a remote trip.

1. Waterproof matches in a waterproof package.
2. A whistle.
3. A sharp sheath or folding knife.

Consider the key elements in simply staying alive if your canoe, with all its gear, disappears over the lip of a waterfall, or is lost in a heavy storm while crossing a lake, and little, or none, is recovered, but you manage to reach shore.

Key element no. 1. Stay calm.

Key element no. 2. Stay calm.

Whatever the problem you, and most likely your paddling partner, are alive. No gear. No food. No canoe. Maybe a pocket knife and waterproof matches. Now your survival will depend on your ability to stay alive until rescuers, who will come searching for you because you didn't show up at your take-out on the day you said you would, find you.

The critical first problem for survival in the wilderness that one usually faces is finding water. Since, as a canoeist, it's right beside you, let's move on the the next step: Shelter. Food comes third. You can survive a week or two without eating a damn thing, but you could die of exposure in twenty-four hours if the weather turns cold and rainy.

Is a cave handy? Scout around. Small is better than big. If you can't find a cave, consider making a "tree tent" for your first night out. This is done by breaking off branches, the thicker with leaves or pine needles the better, and placing them tips down a couple

Pend Oreille

When you pitch your tent for the night after a day cruising the Z-canyon waters of the Boundary Dam Lake, camp well above the water level. At night, the dam waters rise because of a drop in the need for electricity.

Only 17 miles long, the dam waters, about 100 miles north of Spokane, Washington, are ideal for a weekend outing. You can paddle through a rock arch, stare in awe at the Pee Wee Falls, or edge into a beaver cave that glows green. The rugged hills are heavy with coniferous trees.

What paddlers may most enjoy is that the waters attract few power boats.

feet from the base of a tree, and leaning the butts up against the tree. These slanting branches make a sort of crude half-tepee for one or two to crawl under. Pile up leaves or pine needles a foot or 2 deep inside. This shelter will help you keep warm at night or in cold weather.

If it appears after a day or two that you'll need better shelter, make a hollow tepee at least 3 or 4 feet high out of large dead branches or logs braced against each other. Clear the interior of small branches and cover the outside with reed, plants, rushes, or small, live branches to make a "roof."

If you can light a fire, build a semi-circular stone wall from 3- to 4-feet high in front of your tepee. The stones will act as a reflector for a fire on a cold night, throwing heat into the crude shelter.

The location of your wigwam is crucial. It would provide the most shelter if built deep into the woods, or a defilade, to protect it from the wind. However, it must be on a beach or clearing easily visible from a passing boat, plane, or helicopter. Don't hide from help.

The universal wilderness signal of distress is three. Three blasts on a whistle. Three shots from a gun. Three fires on the beach.

Pile up three stacks of firewood on a beach, make them 6 or 8 feet high and located 10 feet apart, so they can be lighted instantly if you hear the noise of boats or aircraft. For fast fire starters, make a large mound of birch bark, or a handful of pine pitch, covered with tiny twigs, in the center of each wood pile. The bar or pitch will burn whether wet or dry. If you can find neither pitch nor birches, then fashion a large pile of tiny, dry twigs, topped with slightly larger pieces of wood, inside each huge stack of wood.

There also may be some value of lighting the fires and keeping them going for a couple of days. Much wilderness is regularly patrolled by rangers for signs of fire or other problems. Occasionally, game wardens fly about in helicopters to check on wildlife and hunting and fishing parties. They could spot the smoke from your fires by day. A passing plane might see the fires at night. A single fire might be ignored, but three in a line should attract help.

If you are on a beach, tramp out "help" in huge letters on the sand.

Beating Starvation
Natural Foods

Meanwhile, naturally, you've been eating any kind of available berries with which you are familiar to satisfy the growing, gnawing hunger pangs while you've concentrated on vital shelter.

Piñon Pine

Now consider some of the edibles available in wilderness regions popular with canoeists in the United States and Canada that could keep you alive for weeks, if necessary. The list below is only a brief summary of some of the more common wild foods from trees and plants that a lost or starving canoeist might not even be aware of that are at his fingertips, and can be eaten raw or cooked. There are a number of excellent guides to edible plants. Any of them would be a source of advanced knowledge that could save your own life, or provide interesting new foods that you didn't buy to sample on a wilderness junket.

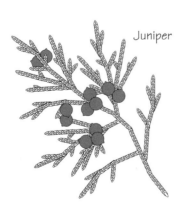
Juniper

Juniper

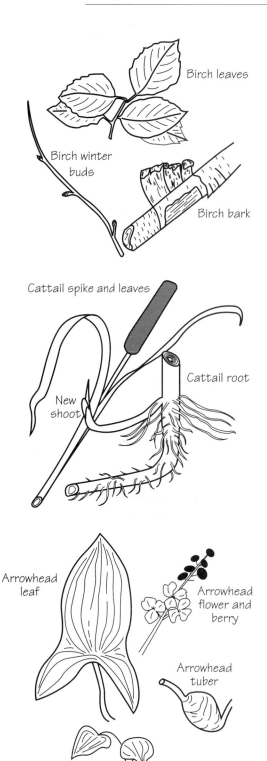

Birch leaves

Birch winter buds

Birch bark

Cattail spike and leaves

Cattail root

New shoot

Arrowhead leaf

Arrowhead flower and berry

Arrowhead tuber

Location of tubers

For example, the thin cambium layer, or inner bark, of pine tree (*Pinus*) is rich in Vitamin C. Both raw and cooked, it was long a part of the diet of Native Americans and often gathered by pioneers to dry and grind up with regular flour.

Young pine needles also are pleasant tasting and nutritious, to a point. Eat sparingly, they could lead to diarrhea. Tea made from them can be used to treat constipation.

The large seeds of Pinons, a low-growing conifer largely found in the western United States and Mexico, are considered a delicacy. The cones can be charred in a fire, which roasts and loosens the seeds, which may be eaten shelled or ground up, shell and all.

The fleshy stems and branches of cactuses, peeled of their scales or spines, are edible.

The blue berries from Junipers (*Juniperus*), also a member of the pine family, are nutritious but bitter. They will lose some of the bitter taste if you pound and boil them. Junipers are common in the desert regions of the west.

In the more northerly climates, Birch trees (*Betula*) can be a lost paddler's department store. The cambium layer is edible, raw or cooked. The outer bark can be peeled off in short strips for starting fires. Large sheets can be formed into almost anything you need, from cups to plates to pots to roofing for your private wigwam.

Cattails (*Typha*) are a miniature supermarket. The tiny shoots in the spring are edible. Even when they start to mature and become somewhat tough, they can be boiled and eaten. Other edible parts include the white inner section of the first foot or so of the mature plant, and the

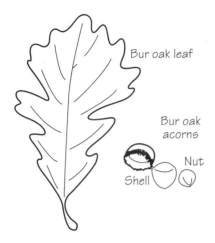

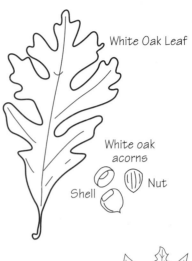

roots. The roots can be eaten raw, boiled, baked, or roasted.

Arrowhead, also known as Arrowleaf (*Sagittaria*), is common and widespread in North America. It is found on the borders of ponds, streams, and swamps. It has deep green arrowhead-shaped leaves that may protrude from the water, or lie flat. In the fall and spring, small tubers on the roots growing in the mud are edible. The tubers have a stinging sensation when eaten raw. They should be baked or boiled, like potatoes.

The tasty watercress (*Nasturtium officinale*), growing in thick mats in clear water and springs and looking exactly like the watercress sold by the supermarket, is a superb flavoring when added to turtle soup.

As the ancients saw it, "Giant oaks from tiny acorns grow." The acorns from any species of oak (*Quercus*) are palatable when pounded into flour between two stones, then leached thoroughly to remove the tannic acid.

Mushrooms are an excellent food—if you know which to pick and which to avoid.

The leaves of Dandelions

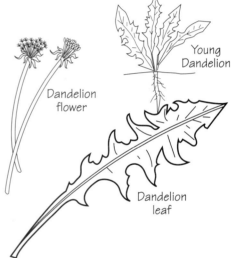

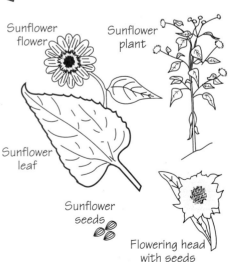

(*Taraxacum*) are a source of nutrients. The younger leaves are the most succulent.

The journals of Lewis and Clark reported on Indians in western Montana drying sunflower (*Helianthus*) seeds, then pounding them into a fine powder. "Sometimes the add a portion of water and drink it thus diluted," they reported in 1805.

Wild strawberries are even tastier than those in the grocery store, but much smaller.

The uncurled fiddleheads of young Bracken ferns (*Pteridium*) are a popular vegetable sold by many green grocers in the spring for salads. They are also nutritious when you find them growing out of doors. The fern is rather coarse and covered with a hairy felt at the base.

Insects, if one can bring one's self to eat them, broiled, fried, or simmered in a soup, are an excellent source of wilderness nutrition. Recommended insects (for food value not gourmet dining) include grasshoppers, locusts, crickets, cicadas, and katydids. As a general rule all insects should be cooked because many harbor internal parasites that can be harmful.

Grubs and caterpillars can add protein to your soup. Avoid those with hair or fuzz. Some are slightly poisonous. If you stick to the hairless ones, you should be okay. Snakes and salamanders are excellent food. Behead, skin, and gut snakes before dining.

Don't overlook the nutritional value of snails and fresh water mussels, as well as crayfish, stone flies, and other nymphs beneath rocks in streams. These may be found any time from early spring to late fall.

Ants of all species, from tiny red and black to the large carpenter ants, were widely used by Native Americans living in arid areas. Indians would roast them, grind them into powder, and add them to a stew cooking over the fire.

Virtually any wildlife you are able to catch—from pack rats to pachyderms, turtles to tree frogs—is a source of survival. To dine on turtles, tear off the shell, clean the sides, and slice up the edible meat. If you have a pot, make turtle soup. It's delicious.

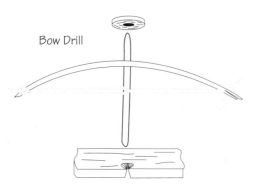

Bow Drill

Wilderness Stoves

The painfully obvious first step in cooking is to build a fire. Those with matches should have no problem. For those whose matches are somewhere in the foaming rapids, there are a variety of techniques for lighting a fire without using matches, none of which have much value unless learned and practiced before they are needed.

If you have a magnifying glass, use it to focus the sun's heat on a pile of dry moss. It may, or may not, set it on fire. However, at the first hint of smoke, blow lightly and carefully to create a flame and immediately place the burning moss under the tiny pile of twigs or shreds of dry kindling, or scraps of birch bark you have already gathered. If one has a watch, remove the glass face, fill it with a few drops of water, and use it as a magnifying glass.

Making a fire starter using the Indian bow and now string technique to twirl a piece of dry wood against a dry slab might work if you have a tough cord to use as a bow string. If you don't have one in your pocket, try a shoe string, lace or leather.

Few who suffer the indignity of finding themselves lost or stranded in the wilderness are fortunate enough to have a couple pots and pans handy for cooking. However, the lack of such common items should in no way deter the determined—who can build a fire—from having cooked foods.

By way of an example, three long, sturdy sticks can be formed into a tripod, the tops bound by any wild vine. Cleaned meat or dressed birds can be suspended from the tripod over a fire by other vines. Fish can be cleaned, cut in half, with each half fastened flesh side out to a slab of wood, and cooked by the reflected heat of the fire.

An excellent primitive stove can be made by building a hunter fire. Erect two parallel low walls of stones about 12 to 16 inches high. Place flat pieces of slate across the top. Build a fire under the slates and use them as frying pans. Lacking rocks, dig a long, narrow trench in which to build a fire. Use flat pieces of slate across the top for your frying pans.

Try steaming food clam-bake style. Scratch out a fairly deep hole by hand or by sticks. Line the hole with rocks and build a fire in the hole. When the rocks are hot, cover them with a heavy layer of fresh moss or grasses. Place the food on the greens. Cover it with another deep layer of greens. Top with a layer of rocks or dirt and let the foods steam for several hours or overnight.

A large piece of birch bark can be soaked in water, then formed into a pot, using twigs or cord to weave the edges together. Built with skill, such a pot will hold water. Drop sizzling hot rocks into the water to bring it to a boil. Or the bark can be simply shaped into the form of a pot and placed in a hole. For cooking, fill with water, then drop in the sizzling rocks.

The wilderness wanderer need not be an expert in all the skills necessary to live off the land for a few months. But he or she must have enough knowledge to survive for at least several weeks, with or without fire, until hearing the welcome shouts from a search party.

CHAPTER EIGHT

OUTDOOR CUISINE

As Hiawatha once said: Canoeists travel on their stomachs. Of course, there is more to filling one's stomach than thinking in terms of quantities of food. Some consider nutrition the only important factor in a meal. Others frown on cooking as a waste of time; they are content to open a few cans or pour some hot water into a freeze-dried meal in a plastic packet.

Many canoeists, however, consider their meals as pleasurable as paddling distant waters. To them, planning menus and cooking over a campfire are worth the extra effort. How better to crown a day's paddling than by sharing an excellent meal with good friends?

Freeze-Dried Meals

Freeze-dried meals are prepared by adding hot water to precooked servings of freeze-dried foods. The packages are lightweight, easy to pack and carry, and can be served within minutes of putting ashore. Unfortunately, they are often bland and lack the vibrance of freshly cooked meals. In many cases they are oversalted to mask the lack of flavor (though the judicious addition of spices or wine often improves their dullness). Since the weight factor is more appealing to backpackers than canoeists, you might consider leaving the freeze-dried meals for emergencies and plan a more sophisticated menu for your greater enjoyment.

Meals for Weekend Touring

On short trips of one to three days, you can enjoy almost any dish in camp that you enjoy at home. Fresh meats and poultry, as well as vegetables with a short shelf life, are fine for such trips. Preserving such foods is elemental. Freeze the meats and any other foods (margarine or butter, bread, rice, and pasta) that will not be adversely affected by freezing. Foods that cannot tolerate freezing should be thoroughly chilled in your refrigerator. When you are ready for the trip, take the foods from your freezer and refrigerator and pack them immediately into an ice chest, along with a couple of frozen containers of "ice" solution. For additional insulation, line the ice chest with slightly crumpled newspaper. In camp, store the chest in the shade.

Meals for Wilderness Trips

When a trip extends over longer periods, we limit our fresh foods to a last meal at our put-in. All other dishes use canned, freeze-dried, dehydrated, smoked and (occasionally) salted or pickled meats and vegetables, plus pastas, rice, potatoes, and precooked or regular legumes such as beans and lentils. In addition, we carry a range of spices to complement each meal on the menu.

Read the Label

If you are planning to use precooked foods, from the freeze-dried varieties available in the supermarket, read the labels before you buy. You'll want to know what the meal contains and, even more important, how the manufacturer figures the quantity per person. Make sure that if the label reads FOUR SERVINGS, the quantity per person is enough to nourish a hungry, tired adult paddler.

Menu Planning

Working out a trip menu can be a chore, but it should not be a bore. Plan an interesting variety of dishes, both familiar and innovative. Your favorite cookbook will yield a shopping cart of ideas for camp dishes.

You like chili made from ground beef and beans? Substitute canned corned beef for the fresh ground beef. Your family enjoys paella? Substitute canned shrimp and canned chicken for the fresh products. For that wonderful soup made from a rich chicken stock, replace the stock with chicken bouillon cubes. Turn a package of dehydrated soup you bought at the supermarket into a Chinese soup with a dash of soy sauce, some ground, fresh ginger root, and dehydrated shiitake mushrooms.

You get the picture.

Breakfast Ideas

Our camp breakfasts are a combination of carbohydrates, which provide quick energy when the well-stuffed paddlers climb into their canoes, and proteins and fats, which continue to stock the energy furnace many hours later.

It was not the biggest rally ever held in Washington. But it was among the most unusual. More than 100 paddlers portaged their canoes and kayaks to the steps of the capitol in the summer of 1996 to protest legislation that would permit an increase of motorboat use in the Boundary Waters Canoe Area. Action on the measure was postponed after the demonstration.

Hot instant cereals such as oatmeal or Cream of Wheat are exceedingly popular with most campers and are prepared simply by adding hot water. You can also prepare them with the tasty liquid from a fruit compote (made by simmering minced dried fruits for ten to fifteen minutes in water). Serve the cereal topped with the fruit compote.

Cold cereals are also popular. Select nutritious brands, avoiding those that are highly sugared. Cold cereal also can be served with a fruit compote. You can use fresh milk on short trips or dehydrated powdered milk on long journeys.

If you are beyond the reach of fresh eggs, powdered or freeze-dried eggs are available at most outdoor specialties stores. Egg mixes that contain extra ingredients, such as bits of meat or veggies, are much more expensive than plain freeze-dried eggs. I suggest that you look for freeze-dried eggs with a butter mix, then add spices to give them more flavor. Hint: Freeze-dried eggs are much more like fresh eggs than dehydrated ones.

Potato pancakes, or latkes, are an excellent carbohydrate source and are more substantial than pancakes made from refined wheat flour. Serve potato pancakes with applesauce.

Canned ham, salami, and sausages (which can go without refrigeration for some time) are fine sources of meat protein. These meats can be fried in a skillet or broiled over a fire.

Camp Lunches

Medium-hard and hard cheeses, salami, gorp, canned fish such as tuna, salmon, or sardines, peanut butter and jelly, crackers, firm breads, dried fruits, hard candies, sun-dried tomatoes, and powdered drink mixes are good lunch foods for short or long trips.

Gorp, supposedly an acronym for Good Old Raisins and Peanuts, can be a homemade combination of any of the following foods, in addition to the raisins and peanuts: other nuts, toasted soybeans, sunflower seeds, M&Ms, Cheerios, dried fruits such as dates, apricots, banana and apple chips, and sugared pineapple, coconut shavings, sesame twigs, or any other high-protein, quick-energy food. Gorp is usually carried as a loose mixture served by

Root River

Three forks flow together to form the Root in southeast Minnesota, near Lanesboro. For more than 100 miles the river is a great paddling trip that novices can handle. The river begins in an area of limestone bluffs and hardwood forests. The countryside slowly changes into pastureland.

A number of liveries make it possible to arrange trips that run from one to five days. Camping is permitted at designated sites on State Forest lands. Many canoeists find it unusually pleasant to put ashore at several of the small towns along the river, and spend their nights at different bed and breakfast motels.

The beauty and charm of the Root river are protected by the Minnesota Department of Natural Resources' Canoe and Boating route program.

the handful from a large plastic bag or container. It can also be minced in a food grinder or food processor and molded into sausagelike portions, packaged in small plastic bags and nibbled on like a granola bar.

Dinners Alfresco

Our camp dinners always begin with soup. *Always*. During an active outdoor day, summer or winter, the body loses a substantial amount of fluid. If you do not drink enough liquid to counteract the loss, the result may be anything from a mild, unexplained headache to nausea, constipation, or leg cramps. Soup is a wonderfully tasty way of helping the body restore its fluid balance. Unless you are on a low-salt diet recommended by your physician, use salt in cooking. The salt is essential for helping the body retain fluid.

In addition to soup, camp dinners should include a good proportion of carbohydrates, along with meat, fish, or poultry.

Desserts? But of course. Scan the supermarket shelves for dishes easy to prepare in camp. Try to avoid those that involve a lot of cooking and long cooling unless, of course, you're going to bake something as pleasant as a cake on your reflector oven.

Finally, why not a nice wine? The wines sold in the collapsible plastic containers are especially good to have on a wilderness trip for two reasons. One: They don't break. Two: They collapse as the wine is consumed, thus preventing air from getting in so that the wine retains its tasty quality for many days.

It is essential to go fully supplied with food when paddling long distances, even where the rivers and lakes are reputedly filled with hungry fish. As every fisherman knows, sometimes the hungry fish aren't hungry. When the fish are biting and someone reels in a wriggling walleye, bass, or trout, we often use it for dinner, sometimes dicing the flesh and making a chowder. We also broil whole fish or cut large ones into fillets as a side dish for dinner or breakfast. We follow one absolute rule: Fish that are not going to be eaten are photographed, unhooked with care, and returned to their native waters.

Quantities

A critical part of menu planning is figuring quantities of foods accurately so that every person eats heartily and there is neither waste nor a scarcity of food. I base my estimate of the amount of food needed on a outing, whether the group is small or large, on the invaluable chart on recommended quantities in the Sierra Club Totebook *Food for Knapsackers and Other Trail Travellers,* by Hasse Bunnelle.

As a basic rule, the quantities listed are for a trip of one to several days for an average group of adult men and women. For trips lasting a week or longer, we increaase quantities by 10 percent. For an all-male group, increase basic quantities by about 15 percent. And for young males in their teens and early twenties, satisfy their voracious appetites with an additional 5 percent.

Don't worry about calorie counts or excess amounts of protein or fat. An active canoeist can burn 3,000 to 4,000 calories on a day of steady paddling, and the slow-burning fats act as a source of energy long after carbohydrates and proteins are burned off. Whether a strenuous, lengthy canoe trip can cause problems for paddlers who are strict vegetarians is a question I am not qualified to answer. Vegetarians should consult a physician to make sure their needs are met.

In the Sierra Club Totebook, *Cooking for Camp and Trail,* co-authors Brunnelle and Sarvis note:

"Carefully planned diets contain sufficient quantities of vitamins and minerals for most people, but because cooking destroys vitamin C, supplements of that are advisable on any trip more than a few days long. If there is any question about the nutritional content of your canned or dried foods, add vitamin and mineral supplements."

Sierra Club Estimates

Breakfast

Food	Ounces per person per day	Calories	Comments
Dried fruits	1.5	110	Excellent when eaten dry, mixed with cereal or simmered.
Cereals: compact cold cereals such as various granolas, Familia, Grape Nuts, etc	1.5	150–180	Avoid presugared cereals, or cereals with high sugar content. Sugars add bulk without adding nutritional value.
Instant hot cereals: Quaker Oats, Wheatena, Cream of Wheat, etc.	1.5	150	Some are prepared by simply adding hot water, others must be boiled for a minute or two. Cereals with such extras as raisins, fruits or flavorings are especially popular. If the cereal does not contain any, add them yourself.

(*Note:* Cereals commercially packaged into individual servings usually contain portions too small for husky camp appetites. Figure on one and one-half packages per person.)

Food	Ounces per person per day	Calories	Comments
Bacon, Spam	1.4	250–300	For long trips buy the canned varieties. Use the grease for cooking.
Boneless ham or shoulder	1.4	160	Take precooked only.
Eggs	two per person	170	Whether fresh, freeze-dried, or dehydrated, eggs are a breakfast staple.
Potatoes, dehydrated and prepackaged	1.0	150–200	Available in supermarkets; exceptionally popular.
Pancake mixes	2.0	200	Popular, but drags out a breakfast. Reserve for days when you'll be in camp.

Lunch

Food	Ounces per person per day	Calories	Comments
Crackers, such as RyKrisp	1.5	175	Keep well and are excellent with peanut butter and jelly.
Firm "German" or Westphalian pumpernickel	1.5	100	Also keeps well, but is more likely to be crushed than firm crackers.
Various dry salamis and bolognas	1.5	120–150	Many varieties keep well without refrigeration.
Cheeses	1.5	170	Look for hard cheeses (such as Monterey Jack, Swiss, or provolone) or those canned cheeses that do not need refrigeration. On shorter trips try the canned French cheeses such as Brie and Camembert. Avoid cheeses with unusual and strong flavors.
Tuna fish, salmon, sardines	1.5	125	Canned tuna can be served as is or mixed with mayonnaise or sandwich spread.
Deviled meats	1.5	Varies	Sample at home; some types are quite spicy.
Gorp	1.0	220	Use salted nuts or salted soybeans when mixing gorp, especially in hot weather.
Nuts, various	1.0	1.75	
Peanut butter	1.0	200	A luncheon favorite.
Jelly	0.3	80	To add a touch of something special to the peanut butter.
Candy	0.5	75	Avoid candy that melts.
Dried fruits	1.3	100	Raisins and apples are the most popular.
Powdered drink mixes, including instant ice coffee and tea.	Varies		The label will give you the approximate amount per cupful.

Dinner

Food	Ounces per person per day	Calories	Comments
Soup, dehydrated	Varies		Check on label. Packaged soups specify the servings in either 6- or 8-ounce amounts. Figure on 12 liquid ounces per person.
Sauces and gravy mixes	Varies		Check on label. Usually a package makes an 8-ounce cupful. Popular with almost every starch dish from mashed potatoes to couscous.
Meat, fresh—steak, boneless	5.0	250	A fine main course the first night in camp.
Fowl, fresh—chicken, turkey	16.0	140	Chickens broil in about 40 minutes; turkey takes much longer. Also best the first night at your put-in.
Canned corned beef			
Canned roast beef	3.0	200	
Canned ham, boneless	3.0	230	For large groups, buy the meat in No. 10 cans. Quantities and servings are usually clearly specified and accurate.
Canned chicken, turkey	3.0	220	
Canned tuna	3.0	250	
Freeze-dried beef, chops, patties	1.0	130	
Pasta, noodles	3.0	300	
Precooked rice	2.0	200	
Dehydrated mashed potatoes		160	
Dehydrated potato dishes, such as au gratin or scalloped		210	Servings specified on the label are about 50% less than hungry adults will eat in camp.
Couscous, kasha	1.6	160	Serve with a light gravy mix.
Desserts: Jell-O, instant pudding, instant cheesecake, etc.			Number of servings listed on the package.

Staples

Item	Ounces per person per day	Calories	Comments
Coffee, instant	0.15	0	
Tea, instant	0.15	0	
Tea bags	2 bags	0	
Hot chocolate mix	1.0	150	
Nonfat dry milk		100	Buy in prepackaged 1-quart envelopes; figure on 1½ quarts per day per four people.
Flour or biscuit mix			The box will indicate the number of biscuits its contents will make; judge accordingly. Mixes also can be used for thickening instead of ordinary flour.
Sugar	1.0	100	An artificial sweetener will substantially reduce the amount of sugar bulk you must carry.
Dehydrated soup greens	0.1		For enriching many dishes.
Dehydrated onion flakes	0.1		For enriching many dishes.
Dried mushrooms	0.15		Buy dried Chinese mushrooms.
Margarine	1.0	230	Read the label; some require no refrigeration and will keep for several weeks.

Staples (continued)

Item	Ounces per person per day	Calories	Comments
Condiments (*)			Based upon your own preference and specific recipes.
Salt			
Pepper			
Basil			
Thyme			
Oregano			
Chili powder			
Curry powder			
Fresh ginger root			
Tarragon			
Cloves			
Red pepper			
Sesame seed			
Chervil			
Parsley			
Bouillon cubes			
Garlic or garlic powder			
Rosemary			
Cumin			
Marjoram			
Cinnamon			
Maple flavoring			Useful if you make your own syrup out of sugar.

(*) plus any others your recipes call for

Shopping and Packing

Shopping and packing are relatively painless—even fun—if you figure quantities carefully, shop with a detailed list, and bring in other members of your group to help out. Use the following steps in preparing your list: (1) Plan a complete menu for every day and write down recipes for every dish; (2) make a chart listing each food, the number of meals it will be used in, and the quantity of each food necessary for each meal; (3) add the quantities used in each meal to arrive at a trip total and make a master shopping list.

For example, a chart for four persons for a four-day trip (three breakfasts, four lunches, three dinners) might look like this:

Foods	No. of meals	Servings per person	Total	Notes
Oatmeal, instant	3	1½ packages	18 packages	Mixed varieties
Freeze-dried eggs	2	2 eggs	2 packages	Equivalent of 8 eggs per package
Dehydrated soups	3	12 ounces		Check package label
Bacon	2	2 slices	16 slices	Check amount in package
Spaghetti	1	¼ pound	1 pound	
Fresh steak	1	5 ounces	1¼ pounds	Buy boneless

Continue, until all the dishes for all the meals are itemized on the shopping list.

When the list is completed, head for the supermarket or place mail orders. (Mail-order shopping must be done well in advance of your departure date.)

Next, assemble members of the group for a repackaging party. Open outer packing materials and discard them; repack individual packets (such as instant oatmeal) and dried foods (pasta, potatoes, and so on) in plastic bags *with directions*. Transfer all liquids into plastic bottles. Put spices in small plastic bags or transparent Fuji 35mm film containers. Label all packages in indelible ink.

Finally, pack for the trip using the Gordon Bag System. I put each day's food—breakfast, lunch, and dinner, along with menus and recipes—into separate nylon stuff sacks with inner plastic-bag liners. Then I mark the outside of each bag like this: Monday, Day 1; Tuesday, Day 2; Wednesday, Day 3, and so on. Coffee, tea, spices, hot chocolate, salt, pepper, sweetener, and other items used at every meal can be placed in the separate pack marked FOOD UTIL-ITY. This system keeps you from digging elbow-deep into food packs to find the necessary ingredients for each meal. Two or more days of food bags can be consolidated in a Duluth pack or other large carrying pack.

CHAPTER NINE

FIELD MEDICINE

You must be prepared for medical emergencies whenever you travel far from medical help. This is as true for the wilderness canoeist as it is for the mountain climber or the fisherman at a remote lake.

I remember a weekend canoe trip on the Delaware River when a canoe flipped in a set of Class II rapids. The stern paddler was thrown out, crashed into a rock, and suffered a broken arm. Luckily, circumstances were in his favor. First, he had on his PFD. Second, we were able to paddle over to give him assistance as he floated half-dazed through the foaming water. And third, within an hour he was in a local hospital for treatment of shock and a broken arm.

How would he have fared if he had been on a trip with you and some friends a day or more away from professional medical help? Emergency treatment in a wilderness setting requires more know-how than is needed in an emergency close to civilization. Elementary first aid is concerned with alleviating anguish or preventing further injury during the time necessary to obtain competent treatment for the victim. If that time is a matter of days rather than hours, you may have to administer some basic medical treatment before professional care arrives.

Primary care in a remote setting means you should know basic first aid and CPR (cardiopulmonary resuscitation), as well as the administration of antibiotics and proper procedure for moving (or not moving) an injured person. In other words, you should feel confident that you can do what is necessary, even though you may be called upon to administer treatment that under normal circumstances you'd leave to a paramedic or physician.

The First-Aid Text

The first item to put into your kit is a first-aid text. Among the books I would recommend are these: *Wilderness Medicine* by Dr. William Forgey (available from American Canoe Association Bookservice, P.O. Box 1190, Newington, VA 22122-1190); *Mountaineering Medicine* by Dr. Fred Darvill (available from

Skagit Mountain Rescue Unit, Inc., Box 2, Mount Vernon, WA 98273); or *Emergency Survival Handbook* by the American Outdoor Safety League (available through the Appalachian Trail Conference, P.O. Box 807, Dept. SD, Harpers Ferry, WV 25425, Tel: 304–535–6331). In this chapter I will discuss, in general terms, two of the most likely serious problems that can occur on a canoe trip. One is hypothermia, the other is drowning. Please remember, however, that this information is no substitute for a thorough knowledge of how to treat both situations. That must come from a certified first-aid course by such an agency as the American Red Cross, augmented by the information in a qualified first-aid textbook.

The First-Aid Kit

You can buy a first-aid kit stocked and ready for use, but it may not contain the same items you would choose. In that case, make your own kit. Pack the equipment into a waterproof box clearly labeled and marked with red crosses (use red tape or red nail polish). Keep the box accessible at all times but out of the reach of children.

My kit includes the following:
- adhesive tape (two rolls—one narrow, one broad);
- various Band-Aids or similar bandage strips; bring plenty, especially if children are with you;
- adhesive butterfly dressings for holding together the edges of a wound that might need to be stitched by a physician;
- sterile 2- by 2-inch gauze pads;
- a roll of 3-inch Ace bandage;
- moleskin;
- Cutter snake-bite kit (never used one yet, but who knows?);
- extra tube of SPF 25 sunscreen;
- hypo-hyperthermia thermometer (registers temperatures from the mid-70s to the 100s);
- roll of 2-inch sterile gauze bandage;
- single-edge razor blades;
- tweezers (try to find the style with a built-in magnifying glass);
- sterile Vaseline;
- toothache medication;
- aspirin (in addition to its known effectiveness in relieving pain, fifteen grains at night will act as a mild sedative to ease sleeplessness);
- Advil (highly effective in reducing pressure on swollen joints);
- sore-throat lozenges;
- over-the-counter cold medication;
- large sewing needle (useful in digging out splinters);

- several swab sticks;
- fingernail clippers;
- safety pins;
- latex gloves to avoid HIV infection (always wear them if there is any sign of blood);
- several Kotex pads (useful as pressure bandages as well as feminine hygiene product);
- Pepto-Bismol; seems to prevent stomach upset caused by the *Giardia* cyst found in river waters; usual preventative dosage: one large tablespoonful every morning; useful for easing stomach upset and diarrhea;
- small plastic bottle of rubbing (isopropyl) alcohol for sterilizing instruments and wiping off skin before removing splinters;
- Benadryl ointment and tablets (reduces reaction to insect bites and skin poisoning);
- Kaopectate, for controlling diarrhea;
- over-the-counter laxative medication;
- several chemical hand warmers, such as the pouches used by skiers and hunters;
- Tylenol for relief of minor pain; useful for children and for adults allergic to aspirin.

Prescription Medications

The wilderness first-aid kit must contain certain prescription medications normally used by a doctor for treatment. It must be stressed that in acquiring these medications through your physician, you also obtain instructions for their use.

- an antihistamine for the treatment of violent reaction to poisonous plants, insects, or foods;
- a broad-range antibiotic such as tetracycline or ampicillin for treating major infections;
- a strong sleep-inducing medication;
- a medication for use as a sedative or to control hysteria;
- an anti-exhaustion drug when it is critical to postpone rest because of an emergency situation;
- medication to control massive diarrhea;
- ointment to treat eye infections;
- eye drops to reduce severe pain in the eyes as a result of continuous exposure to brilliant sun.

Responsibility for First Aid

You may or may not want to assign responsibility for administering medical treatment to one particular person on your trip. If you decide to elect a "doctor," this person should keep an eye open for

Neches River

Once the unique Big Thicket country, northeast of Houston, covered more than three million acres of Texas countryside. Today, less than 300,000 acres, in scattered units, remain. Canoeists can spend a week or more paddling the Neches where it drifts through Big Thicket National Preserve lands. Here one can absorb the quiet beauty of easy waterways flowing through mixed cypress stands and bayous alive with bird life.

There are no developed campsites. Camping is permitted on sandbars within the preserve lands. However, group size is limited to eight, and in some areas overnight camping is not permitted during the October-January hunting season.

Paddling permits, available from the Big Thicket National Preserve at Beaumont, are required.

any problems that might develop. Paddlers who are nervous about a trip into the backcountry may develop diarrhea or suffer from constipation on the first few days. This is the time to keep minor problems from developing into major problems. Encourage everyone to get past any squeamishness they might have about outdoor toilets (those found behind a large tree) and remind them that stoicism in the face of physical problems is no substitute for medical treatment.

Drowning and Hypothermia

In a water accident there is no time for caution and deliberate medical treatment as long as the danger of drowning exists. Fewer than five minutes without oxygen can cause the brain to slip beyond the point of no return.

Should a canoeist inhale water and lose consciousness after submersion, the most effective method of resuscitation is mouth-to-mouth. This should be started *immediately,* even while the victim is still in the water. If you do not know this method, use the back pressure method to force air into the victim's lungs. The most significant facts to remember are these: Act quickly and *don't quit.* Drowning victims have been revived up to two hours after treatment has begun.

While some authorities recommend CPR instead of only mouth-to-mouth resuscitation, there is a danger in this, as noted by Buck Tilton, director of the Wilderness Medicine Institute in an article in the American Canoe Association magazine, *Paddler,* the only watersport magazine affiliated with the American Canoeing Association:

"In near drownings beware of the shunting of blood from the periphery of the body, an aspect of hypothermia that mimics death. It may make pulses too weak to find. Starting chest compressions on a cold but beating heart often causes it to stop. So take a much longer time than usual, a minute or more, to check for a pulse before beginning CPR on a cold immersion victim. Breathing for him won't hurt, even if he is doing it for himself already. Artificial respiration, therefore, should be begun right away if you think the patient is not breathing."

Not until you have started mouth-to-mouth resuscitation should any thought be given to treating other problems, including hypothermia, which may be necessary even as mouth-to-mouth respiration is maintained without interruption until the patient begins to breathe.

Hypothermia is an ever-present danger in cool, cold, or rainy weather. As a rule of thumb, when the combined air and water temperature falls below 100 degrees F, experienced canoeists who are not dressed in wet or dry suits do not go paddling, and well-managed liveries will not rent them canoes because of the danger of hypothermia in an upset.

The most common cause of hypothermia while paddling is a canoe capsizing. Cold water swiftly robs the body of heat. The victim almost immediately begins to lose physical control and coordination. Rescue efforts, if necessary, must be taken quickly.

Hypothermia also can develop while paddling in wet, chilly weather. The victim often is a thin person who is chilled, wet, and suddenly becomes physically exhausted.

The result, in both cases, is a dangerous drop in core body temperatures, manifested by a rapid increase in pulse and respiration, as well as loss of physical control. Exhausted paddlers may actually collapse in their canoe, or a rescued canoeist may collapse on reaching shore or be unable to stand without help. In the first stage of hypothermia, a person will go into violent chills and shivering. By the end of this stage, the body feels cold to the touch, pulse and respiration slow, and shivering decreases or disappears.

The next stage is confusion and defective thinking as the core temperature drops to about 88 degrees F. Without treatment there is a loss of consciousness, an irregular heart beat develops, and if the core temperature drops to around 81 degrees F, death occurs.

There is only one treatment at any stage: warming the victim's torso as quickly as possible. "Under no circumstances," says Dr. Darvill, "should the extremities be treated until the torso is warmed. To do so will simply further lower the body's temperature."

The choice treatment, if available, is to rewarm the victim in water between 104 and 112 degrees F. Otherwise, swiftly remove wet clothes and hold the victim in the arms of two paddlers, especially warming the back and stomach. Cover the head. Stones can be warmed and placed around the victim's torso. Packaged chemical hand or foot warmers used by skiers—a valuable item for every well-organized wilderness first-aid kit—can be placed under the armpits and to the small of the back. Heat must be maintained until the shivering ceases. If the victim is conscious, offer warm liquids but avoid alcohol or any drinks with caffeine, such as coffee or Coke.

Since metabolic abnormalities are common after significant hypothermia, hospitalization should be effected as soon as possible.

On wilderness trips prevention is safer than treatment when the weather turns wet, windy, and chilly. Experienced paddlers carry extra snacks and eat frequently while on the water. If the weather deteriorates, they will head for shore, set up a protected campsite, build a fire, dry those clammy, wet clothes, and just hunker down for a day or two until it's safe to slide the canoes back into the water and get going.

Wild Animals and Pests

Many visitors to the wilderness worry that they may be attacked by wild animals in the woods. News reports of alleged animal attacks on humans strike fear into the minds of many potential wilderness travelers. A single word describes the great bulk of such stores: bunk.

Humans have feared wolves for centuries, but modern research has established what canny hunters have known for generations: Wolves do not leap out of nowhere to attack humans. In fact, they usually slink furtively away from any contact with us. Bears as well—especially Grizzly and Alaskan bears—are feared for their supposed aggression toward humans. But again, don't you believe it.

Yes, humans have been killed by animals, but investigations into these incidents have revealed that foolish human error usually triggers the attack. Bears, for instance, are attracted by the odors of your food. Keeping food in your tent or taking it with you into a sleeping bag are foolish decisions in bear country. Veteran fishermen in remote areas are well aware of the importance of cleaning their fish and disposing of the offal away from camp so that the odors do not attract animals to the campsite. Cleaning fish in your canoe and hauling the canoe ashore next to your tent is another foolish act. Taking wise precautions will protect you from a potentially dangerous encounter with a wild animal.

Safety Rules

It *is* possible to be attacked by a wild animal, but the likelihood is very slim if you follow these few simple rules:

- *Rule 1:* Remember that you are an unwanted guest in the animal's territorial home. An animal taken by surprise on a trail or near its den may fear that you are about to harm it, and it may attack. When walking through a portage trail, make noise, talk loudly, whistle, or bang on a pot to alert animals to your presence. Nearly all animals will go away from the racket.
- *Rule 2:* Keep the campsite free of garbage and food scraps; where fire regulations permit, burn your garbage in your camp fire or scatter organic waste a distance from camp. Wrap and carry out any other garbage. Raccoons, rabbits, pack rats, and other small animals especially like leftovers, but they're not likely to attack you for them.
- *Rule 3:* If you see a baby animal, do *not* approach it or come between it and its mother. Admiration from a distance is acceptable, but if you separate a mother from her young, she is very likely to be provoked to swift violence.
- *Rule 4:* In an area popular with campers, animals may approach cautiously, searching for food. Under no circumstances should you attempt to attract these animals with food in your hand. The animal may snap for the food and tear away a few of your fingers at the same time.
- *Rule 5:* Do not approach any large animal—a bear, a moose, or even a deer—so that you can get a close-up with your Instamatic. These creatures are not impressed by your desire to capture their beauty and are likely to feel threatened by your approach. Use a telephoto lens and stay well away.

Unless you are paddling in southern U.S. waters that are known to be an alligator habitat, do not worry about wild animal attacks when you are in your canoe on the water. Land animals are simply not in the habit of leaping into the water to pursue you.

Insects

You cannot avoid an occasional bite or sting from the insects in the wilderness, but you can do much to minimize the problem. Keep in mind that most insect problems are seasonal. In the north woods, camping in spring or even in early summer can be brutally uncomfortable because of insects. They tend to disappear or "burn off," as the old woodsmen will tell you, later in summer. You'll be most comfortable in August or early September.

To reduce insect problems, start by considering your clothing. Thin fabrics offer virtually no resistance to a hungry mosquito; wear heavier-weight fabrics and loose-fitting clothing for an extra measure of protection. Next, use insect repellent. A large selection of products are available in lotion, spray, or stick form. Sprays are expensive, but they are also effective. When using them, spray your clothing as well as your skin. Avoid contact with the eyes. If one repellent does not work on you, try another. Because of the mysteries of body chemistry, some repellents are highly effective on one person, but less so on another. Read the label carefully when using a new product. DEET, one of the more effective chemicals in repellents, may possibly contain a carcinogen (on the other hand, it may not). *Note:* Because of the danger from either Lyme disease or spotted fever, the current medical advice is get the bug out promptly. A few products are made with natural oils and extracts repellent to bugs. The choice is yours.

In tick season spray or rub tick repellent on the inside of your socks, pants and sleeve cuffs, and the inside of your collar. Disease-carrying ticks in many areas of the country pose the greatest danger to humans in spring and summer months. Primarily in the western United States is the risk of Rocky Mountain spotted fever; in an ever-widening area of the eastern states is the danger of Lyme disease from infected deer ticks. Both diseases can be life-threatening if not treated.

Search your body carefully every night, especially under the arms, in back of the knees, around the crotch, and in your hair. If you find a tick with its head burrowed in, remove it immediately and cover the bite with an antibiotic ointment.

If you are suffering from insect bites, a superb source of relief is hot water, as hot as you can stand, applied to the itch with a washcloth for at least five minutes. This will suppress the itch for up to eight hours.

Wasp and bee stings can be relieved by a topical anesthetic such as Bactine or a paste made from baking soda and water or meat tenderizer and water. A wasp does not leave a stinger buried in your burning flesh, but a bee does. Examine stings closely; if a bee stinger remains, squeeze it out or take it out with tweezers.

To prevent stings, remember that wasps and bees are attracted to sweet odors, especially those from sugars in candy bars, jelly, etc. They are also attracted to some perfumes and after-shave lotions.

Poison Plants

If you do not recognize the poison ivy plant, it is virtually inevitable that some time or other you will become a victim of its itchy poison. If you have avoided it thus far, keep in mind that

The Yampa

The last free-flowing river in Colorado is the Yampa, near the town of Dinosaur. One of the most popular trips on it is a five-day adventure, with 46 miles on the Yampa and 25 on the Green. Scenery is, in one word, breathtaking. Canoeists paddle between towering sandstone walls and soaring pinnacles, known as "hoodoos."

The trip is so sought after that campsites are assigned by the Yampa River Office at Dinosaur.

Water levels are best from April through June. WIth the exception of the Class IV Warm Springs rapid, the waters are chiefly fast or Class II, and can be handled by an advanced novice.

reaction to poison ivy may vary over the years; a person immune to the effects of poison ivy may suddenly develop a sensitivity to it, so beware. On the good side, however, a person heretofore susceptible may suddenly become immune.

Be wary of two other plants that cause the miseries—poison sumac and stinging nettle. The reaction to nettle is a sharp tingling pain similar to a jellyfish sting and usually quite brief. Treatment generally is not required, though a soothing skin lotion will comfort you. Poison sumac causes a similar, but even stronger, reaction as that of poison ivy, and the itching and burning may last for days.

Among the dozen or so treatments for poison ivy and poison sumac are over-the-counter drugs such as calamine lotion or a paste of water and yellow soap such as Fels naptha. If you know you have come in contact with poison ivy or sumac, the best protection is to vigorously wash the contact area with hot water and strong soap as soon as possible after contact. If the reaction develops anyway, you may be able to relieve the itching with the same hot water treatment that relieves the itch of mosquito bites—soak the infected area with water as hot as you can stand for at least five minutes. The fluid from the blisters that develop will *not* spread the reaction.

CHAPTER TEN

PROTECTING OUR RIVERS

Almost from the day the first Europeans landed on American soil a conflict has waged between those persons who would protect and preserve, as well as use, the woodlands and rivers and those who were dedicated to one principle only: putting the land to "good use." The "good use" advocates were, for generations, in the vanguard of the drive to develop, develop, develop. Rivers were dammed for every conceivable industrial use, from the absurd to the necessary, without regard for the river and the valley that was being used. Forests were felled by the millions of acres, and no one was able to stop those persons who believed that the only good tree was a tree cut up for lumber.

A few voices of protest were raised. William Penn, the founder of Pennsylvania, once proposed that every alternate 100 square miles of the sylvan state be protected against development, creating a checkerboard conservation plan. It died almost as soon as it was conceived. By the mid-nineteenth century, however, the voices of protest became louder. Among them was George W. Sears, the outdoor writer who wrote under the Indian name Nessmuk on the need for what we now call conservation.

In his 1888 book *Woodcraft,* Nessmuk tells the story of a camping trip he took in 1860 with four young men who were new to the wilderness. These men had no particular concern for the need to protect the land and preserve its beauty until he helped them to understand that it would eventually disappear without the vigorous support of those concerned with the nation's out-of-doors.

Thirty years later he revisited their campsite at Poplar Spring in New Jersey. He wrote:

> *Alas for the beautiful valley that once afforded the finest camping grounds I have ever known.*
> *Never any more*
> *Can it be*
> *Unto me (or anybody else)*
> *As before.*

A huge tannery, six miles above Poplar Spring poisons and blackens the stream with chemicals, bark, and ooze. The land has been brought into market and every acre eagerly bought up by actual settlers. The once fine covers and thickets are converted into fields thickly dotted with blackened stumps. And, to crown the desolation, heavy laden trains of The Pine Creek and Jersey Shore R.R. go thundering almost hourly over the very spot where stood our camp by Poplar Spring.

Of course, this is progress; but, whether backward or forward, had better be decided sixty years hence. . . .

The Wild and Scenic Rivers Act

A century after Nessmuk camped at Poplar Spring, dynamic efforts were initiated to protect what was left of our rivers and to clean up our soiled environment. The national Clean Water Act and the Wild and Scenic Rivers legislation are among federal laws that seek not only to stop the continuing degradation of the nation's rivers but also to clean up those so polluted that they threaten plant and fish life and pose a hazard to human health.

Both acts have been strengthened and extended since they were first passed. Unrestricted dumping of sewage and chemical and industrial wastes into our rivers has been federally regulated for more than a quarter century. During that period the Wild and Scenic Rivers Act created special districts to preserve rivers. As the last decade of the twentieth century began, 9,000 miles of rivers were protected under the Wild and Scenic regulations. Five thousand miles were declared "forever wild," prohibiting any type of industrial, commercial, or developmental projects to affect their magnificent beauty and wild setting. In addition, 1,600 miles were classified as "scenic" and another 2,500 miles as "recreational." These classifications protect them in perpetuity from any type of development that would impinge upon their current nature. It does not mean converting them back to wilderness waterways.

Wild and Scenic Rivers under the supervision of the National Park Service are patrolled from the waters by NPS rangers, a welcome sight in their green uniforms and green canoes. Scenic and Recreational rivers under the aegis of other federal, state, or local agencies also provide supervisory personnel to give guidance or assistance to paddlers.

The Wild and Scenic River System offers miles of beautiful canoeing routes for day-trippers and weekend paddlers. The 5,000 miles designated as "wild" actually include long stretches of easy water. The 4,000 miles designated "scenic" or "recreational" offer dozens of easy and lovely routes for casual paddling. For specific

"The lands of the state now owned or hereafter acquired constituting the forest preserve as now fixed by law, shall be forever kept as wild forest lands. They shall not be leased, sold or exchanged, or be taken by any corporation, public or private, nor shall the timber thereon be sold, removed or destroyed."

—Article XIV, Section I, New York State Constitution, which in 1894 established the famed Adirondack State Park of some 2.5 million acres. Laced with rivers and dotted with hundreds of lakes, it is, and should forever remain, a paddler's paradise.

information contact American Rivers, Inc., in Washington, D.C. They can give you the name of the agency that administers the rivers in your area. Your inquiries really are welcome. Along with river information they can send you the names and addresses of the liveries and outfitters that service the specific river you may want to paddle.

American Rivers, Inc.

One of the ardent advocates of protecting our waterways is American Rivers, Inc. In 1988 AR reported that some "60,000 to 80,000 existing dams impound 600,000 miles, or 17 percent, of the nation's rivers and streams, compared to less than three tenths of one percent designed to be maintained in their natural state through the Wild and Scenic Rivers System." The long-term goal of AR is to protect at least 10 percent of the nation's rivers from future development. AR warned that the impoundment of waterways was continually encouraged by pressures such as the growing population and the search for cheap energy. The 1988 report noted that "new dams have been proposed for 6,000 sites in the last ten years alone."

The need for new energy sources is a source of pressure that increases daily. Though dams have drowned tens of thousands of square miles of fertile land and irreplaceable wilderness, completely altering the ecology of the region surrounding each dam, such destruction is viewed by some as necessary for our energy needs. To them, each dam is a "clean and non-destructive" source of power. The demands of the increasing population also threaten the nation's waterways. In 1990 America's population reached a quarter billion. It is estimated that the population will expand by another 30 million by the year 2000.

Kevin Coyle, the president of American Rivers, told *Canoe &*

Kayak magazine in an interview that he considered rivers the very heart of the nation's ecosystems. As he explained: "All life is water-dependent. When you are conserving a river, you are conserving a source of life."

Coyle said that the nation has basically only three ways to protect nature. One is to set aside a natural area for recreation or scenic value. Another is to set aside a region to protect wildlife. But, he said, "we have not yet really learned how to protect entire ecosystems" that cross city, county, and state lines and affect great regions. This would be the third way to protect nature.

"River conservation," Coyle said, "is probably the closest we've come in terms of national policy to actually protecting ecosystems."

The goal of river conservation today is to ensure that both wild and scenic rivers will be free of major structures such as dams and simply left in their natural state. Coyle told *Canoe & Kayak* magazine that he also was concerned about protecting land that bordered protected rivers, keeping it as free from future development as possible.

Coyle agreed that the most useful act today to protect our rivers is the Wild and Scenic Rivers Act, but he said he foresees a time when state action will save more miles of more rivers than will be brought within federal protection.

What You Can Do

There are several things individuals can do to protect and preserve our nation's rivers. Volunteer to work on trash cleanup days, to work with agencies to check on water quality, or to support important state and federal legislation. Or join or contribute to one of the following organizations that are deeply involved in the struggle to protect our rivers as well as our total environment.

American Canoe Association, 8580 Cinderbed Road, Suite 1900, P.O. Box 1190, Newington, VA 22122

American Rivers, Inc., 801 Pennsylvania Avenue, SE, Suite 303, Washington, DC 20003

America Outdoors, 360 South Monroe, Suite 300, Denver, CO 80209; (303) 377–4811

American Water Resourced Association, 950 Herndon Parkway, Suite 300, Herndon, VA 22070; E-mail: awrahq@aol.com

Appalachian Mountain Club, 5 Joy Street, Boston, MA 03108

Defenders of Wildlife, 2000 N Street, NW, Washington, DC 20036

The Yellowstone

When you take out after paddling 17 miles on a one-day trip on the Yellowstone River, between Gardiner and Carbella, Montana, return your canoe to the livery and spend the next week touring spectacular Yellowstone National Park, which is just next door.

This scenic stretch of the Yellowstone is best suited for experienced canoeists. There are clusters of Class IIs, and the four miles through Yankee Jim canyon are filled with Class IIIs.

The towering Absarika-Beartooth and Gallatin mountains are a stirring background for the paddlers who are fortunate enough to spend a day on this historic river.

Environmental Defense Fund, P.O. Box 96969, Washington, DC 30090-6969

Professional Paddlesports Association, P.O. Box 249, U.S. 27 and Hornbeck Road, Butler, KY 41006-9674

National Audubon Society, 950 Third Avenue, New York, NY 10022

National Wildlife Federation, 1412 16th Street, NW, Washington, DC 20036

Sierra Club, 1050 Mills Tower, San Francisco, CA 94104

The Wilderness Society, 1901 Pennsylvania Avenue, NW, Washington, DC 20006

EPILOGUE

In 1854 the government of the United States was negotiating with the Indian chief, Seattle, for the acquisition of more tribal lands. Chief Seattle knew, without doubt, that the negotiations were a mere formality, a polite way of telling him and his people that their ancient lands would be taken—with or without tribal consent. He looked at the formidable array of government officials.

Later, he was quoted as having told the negotiators:

If we sell you our land you must remember and
teach your children
that the rivers are our brothers
and yours
and you must henceforth give the rivers
the kindness
you would give any brother.

GLOSSARY

ABEAM. To the right, or at right angles to the center of a craft.

ABOARD. On, or in, the canoe.

A.C.A. American Canoe Association.

ACCESS or ACCESS POINT. The place on the shore of a lake or river where you put in or take out.

ACTIVE BLADE. When using a double, or kayak, blade, that blade which is in the water at any given time.

AFLOAT. Floating. Not stuck on a rock or sandbar.

AFT. Toward the rear, or stern, of the canoe.

AGROUND. Stuck—usually on a shoal or rock—when you didn't intend to be.

AHEAD. Forward—as in the nautical phrase "Full speed ahead."

AIR LOCK. The pressure of air that holds water inside an overturned canoe if you attempt to lift it straight up.

ALONGSIDE. "Hey, bring your canoe up <u>alongside</u> this rock."

ANCHOR, SEA. Your largest kettle tied to the end of a 20-foot rope and tossed over the stern when you are being driven by a heavy tail wind in a running sea.

ANKLE DEEP. The water level when you get out of the canoe to haul it across a sand bar.

ASTERN. Toward the rear, behind, or in back of your canoe.

AU COURANT. Fully aware of the current.

AZIMUTH. The angle of horizontal deviation from north. When using a compass, the direction in degrees. East, for example, is an azimuth of 90 degrees.

BACK FERRY. Paddling the canoe backward at an angle to the current when crossing a stream laterally.

BACKCOUNTRY. Distant wilderness invaded by those with a sense of adventure.

BACKPADDLE. Paddling backward to slow or reverse the forward motion of a canoe.

BAIL. To empty water from a craft by scooping it out with anything from a sponge to a tin can.

BAILER. Anything used to bail out a canoe. One of the most effective is an old plastic bottle with the bottom cut off.

BANG PLATE. <u>See</u> Stem Band.

BEAM. Width of a canoe when measured at its widest point.

BEAM ENDS. A canoe tipped on its side is said to be "on her beam ends."

BEAR OFF. To push off from an obstruction or an object.

BEARING. A direction with respect to either a compass point, such as north, or to the craft.

BEAVER TAIL PADDLE. A paddle with a narrow blade.

BEFORE. What lies ahead; in front of.

BELOW. Downriver.

BENT SHAFT PADDLE. Paddles with the blade at an angle to the shaft for greater efficiency in canoeing flat water.

BERRY BREAK. What happens when you pass bushes loaded with delicious berries on a long, hot, difficult portage.

BILGE. When a hull is cut in a cross section, the bilge is the point of maximum curvature between the bottom and the side of the canoe below the waterline.

BILGE KEEL. Two additional keels, one on each side of the main keel, that protect canvas-covered canoes.

BLADDER. An air bag inside a kayak which adds to the buoyancy of the craft in the event of a capsize.

BLADE. The wide, flat end of the paddle.

BOIL. Where current foams upward when it is deflected by obstructions under the water.

BOTTOM. The part of the canoe that is under the water.

BOW. The front or extreme forward end of the canoe.

BOW-IN. With the bow forward.

BOW-PADDLER, BOWMAN, BOW PERSON. The person who paddles in the bow.

BOW PLATE. Another term for the stem band.

BOW SEAT. The seat located at the front end of a canoe.

BRACE. A stroke used somewhat like an outrigger to stabilize a canoe. The brace may be a high or low brace. The usual reference is to "throw" or "hang" a brace.

BRIDLE. A line looped around the front end of the canoe to which another is attached under the canoe and used for towing the craft.

BROACH. Broadside to any obstacle-wind, waves, current, or rocks; usually the prelude to an upstream capsize. Don't broach!

BULKHEAD. A partition under the forward and aft decks inside which flotation blocks are attached.

BULL COOK. An ancient and honorable north woods term for the person whose job it is washing pots and pans and cleaning up the kitchen.

BUSH. In Canada, the deep wilderness.

C-1. A one-man covered canoe in which the paddler may kneel or sit. At one time C-1's were made with the bow and stern higher than the middle, but this is no longer standard practice. While a C-1 looks much like a kayak, it has a larger volume and rides higher.

C-2. A two-man covered canoe.

CANADIAN CANOE. In Europe the open canoe is referred to as a Canadian or North American Indian canoe.

CANOE POLE. See Pick Pole.

CAPSIZE. What happens when you are gobbled up in whitewater, or flipped by a combination of wind and waves, or—well, it shouldn't happen.

CARRY. See Portage.

CARVEL-BUILT. A wooden canoe built so the longitudinal sides are laid edge to edge, smoothed, and the gaps sealed with waterproofing material.

CAT HOLE. What you dig at least 200 feet from camp and water when there are no outhouses. Bury the toilet paper, too.

CFS. The flow of water measured in cubic feet per second. A cubic foot contains about 8 gallons of water.

CHANNEL. A stretch of passable water through shallows or among obstructions.

CHART. A map especially prepared for navigation.

CHINE. Where the curving sides of the hull gradually merge into the bottom.

CHUTE. A fast current where part of a stream is compressed and flows between two obstructions.

CLOSED BOAT, COVERED CANOE. Any kayak or C-1 or C-2 where the deck is not detachable but built as an integral part of the craft.

COAMING. A rim around a kayak or C-1 or C-2 cockpit to which a spray skirt is attached.

CONSENSUS. When the leader can't decide how to handle a problem.

CREST. The summit of a standing wave.

CURLER. A steep wave, usually at the base of a drop or chute, that curls back onto its upstream side.

DEAD RECKONING. A way of figuring your position based upon the influence of such things as currents and wind upon your projected course and anticipated speed.

DECK. The triangular piece of material, usually metal or wood, to which the gunwales are attached at the bow and stern. A deck may also be the entire top covering built as an integral part of a kayak, C-1, or C-2.

DEFILADE. A depression in the ground; where you foolishly pitched your tent and it rains.

DEPTH. The depth of a canoe measured from gunwale to bottom amidships.

DOUBLE-BLADE PADDLE. A paddle with a blade at each end, used basically in kayaks but occasionally favored by some canoeists.

DOWNRIVER RACE. A race, usually including whitewater, over a long distance on a river.

DRAFT. The depth of water necessary for a craft to float; the distance between the waterline and the bottom of the keel.

DRAG. The resistance to forward motion. Drag may be decrease by use of special waxes.

DRAW or DRAW STROKE. A stroke in which the blade is placed well out from the canoe and pulled directly toward the side of the canoe; designed to move the craft sideways.

DRY SUIT. A light-weight, totally waterproof suit; usually worn in cold weather over heavy clothing.

DUFFEK STROKE. See High Brace.

DUFFLE. See Gear.

EDDY. A current at variance with the main current, and where the main current either stops or reverses its flow upstream; caused by rocks, obstructions, or the bends in a river or stream. Once avoided as dangerous, eddies now are routinely used in maneuvers and for rest stops.

EDDY HOPPING. Using eddies to maneuver upstream or downstream.

EDDY LINE. The boundary between a downstream and an upstream current.

EDDY TURN. A dynamic maneuver used to enter or leave an eddy.

FACE. The side of a blade pushing against the water.

FALLS. A sudden drop in which the water falls free for at least part of the way.

FATHOM. A nautical measure of depth: 6 feet.

FAULT. What can go wrong, will go wrong. In tandem canoeing, it's always your partner's FAULT.

FEATHER. To turn the paddle so that the blade is parallel to the current or wind and the resistance is reduced.

FERRY. To move a canoe laterally across a current.

FIBERGLASS. Glass threads formed into matting or fabric and used with special resins to form a covering of high strength-to-weight ratio for a canoe or kayak.

FILL POWER. The cubic inches one ounce of down will fill. Top quality fill power ranges from 550 to 700-plus cubic inches.

FLATWATER. Calm river water without rapids; lake water.

FLOORBOARDS. Slats placed in the bilge of a wooden canoe to protect the ribs.

FLOTATION. Styrofoam or air bags placed in a canoe or kayak to help keep the craft afloat in the event of a capsize.

FOLDBOAT. Ingeniously designed kayaks or canoes made of a rubberized fabric with a collapsible wooden frame; can be packed into carry bags for transportation.

FORWARD FERRY. Paddling with the canoe at a downstream angle to the current and crossing laterally.

FREEBOARD. The part of the canoe which rides above the waterline.

FREIGHTER. Canoe with large carrying capacity; often used in wilderness regions as a work craft.

GAUGING STATION. A permanent device measuring the level of water at a given point.

GEAR. Everything you carry in your canoe, from food to foolish items; something you always wish you had more of in camp and less of on a portage.

GIRTH. The circumference of the hull at its widest section.

GRAB LOOP. A loop of rope on the bow or stern of a kayak which is useful for grabbing on to in an upset.

GRADIENT. The degree of inclination of a riverbed, usually described as the number of feet the river drops per mile.

GRIP. The top of a paddle. The two most popular shapes are the pear grip and the T grip. The former is used for general canoeing; the latter is favored by whitewater canoeists.

GUNWALE. The section along the top of the canoe from stern to bow where the sides meet; a strip along the top of the canoe's sides. Pronounced "gunnel."

HEAVY WATER. A huge flow of water through rapids marked by extreme velocity difference in currents and violent turbulence.

HELMET. Plastic head protection worn by skiers, cyclists, roller bladers and whitewater canoeists.

HIGH BRACE. A powerful, dynamic kayak or canoe stroke for entering or leaving an eddy. Also, called the "Duffek stroke" because it was developed by Milovan Duffek of Czechoslovakia.

HULL. The lower half of a kayak or closed canoe, or the main structure of an open canoe.

HUNG UP. When a craft is caught on a rock.

HYDRAULIC. An area of major current changes which in turn create problems normally associated with rocks. Also, the formation of a backflow at the base of a ledge where the current reverses itself.

HYPOTHERMIA. The dangerous lowering of body temperature under wet, cold conditions. Can lead to death due to "exposure."

ICF. International Canoe Federation.

INTERNATIONAL RATING. How violent the rapids really are; range from Class I, marred by light ripples, to Class VI, first, say your prayers.

INWALE. The inside of the gunwale.

K-1. A one-man kayak.

K-2. A two-man kayak.

KAYAK. A decked craft in which the paddlers sit with legs extended and propel the craft with a double blade paddle.

KEEL. A projection below the hull, running from stern to bow, which adds strength to the hull, protects it from damage, and helps the craft maintain straight movement, though the last is a result of the use of a keel, not the reason the keels are built into metal and wooden craft. Keels usually are found only on aluminum and wooden canoes.

KEVLAR. A synthetic material five times stronger than steel; used in making aircraft tires and canoes of exceptional lightness and strength.

KNEE BRACE. Supports attached to the canoe into which the canoeist may slide his knees to gain greater control.

KRISP KNEES. When you forget to put sun screen on your knees and thighs while wearing shorts paddling on a broiling day.

LAPSTRAKE. Construction of a wooden canoe so that each longitudinal board overlaps the one below, like a clapboard house; also, clinker built.

LASH. To make gear secure, usually with a rope.

LAUNCH. To slide a craft into the water.

LEAN. A deliberate tipping of the canoe as a maneuver in ferrying or to regain stability.

LEDGE. Rock shelf which extends at right angles to the current and acts as a natural dam over which the water flows.

LEE, LEEWARD. Away from the wind; downwind. Opposite of windward.

LEFT BANK. The left side of the river when facing downstream.

LIFE JACKET, LIFE VEST. A flotation device to provide buoyancy in the water. Wear one when canoeing! See also PFD.

LINE. See Painter.

LINING. The use of ropes, one fore and one aft, to maneuver an empty canoe downstream.

LIVERY. Where you rent canoes and equipment.

LOB TREE. A tall tree with some or all of the top branches removed to make it a distinct landmark.

LONG-DISTANCE RACING. A term usually used for downriver races of at least 10 miles for senior canoeists and 5 miles for junior canoeists.

MOLD. A form used to make a canoe. A female mold is said to produce a male canoe; a male mold to produce a female structure.

MOUTH. Where a river empties into another body of water.

OFF SIDE. The side opposite to the side where the canoeist is paddling.

OPEN CANOE. The standard North American canoe.

OUTFIT. To equip a canoe for a particular purpose.

OUTFITTER. Commercial companies which supply all necessary equipment for wilderness travel.

OUTSIDE BANK. The outside of a bend.

OUTWALE. The outside gunwale.

OVERBOARD. "Man overboard."

PADDLE. The instrument used to propel a canoe through the water; it is not an "oar."

PAINTER. A rope attached either to the bow or stern, usually from 15 to 25 feet long.

PFD. Personal Flotation Device. The term now used by the U.S. Coast Guard to designate life jackets. Do not use any PFD that is not approved by the U.S. Coast Guard for a person of your weight.

PICK POLE. A pole used to propel a canoe. Also called a "canoe pole."

PIKE. The iron point on a canoe pole.

PILLOW. A gentle bulge on the surface of the water caused by an underwater obstruction. All such pillows have hard centers.

PITCH. A sudden drop in, or steeper section of, a set of rapids.

PIVOT. To turn sharply, or to pivot the craft around a point.

PLAYING. Enjoying running a particular set of rapids several times.

POLE. See Pick Pole.

POOL. A stretch of river with little current.

PORT. The left side of the canoe when facing the bow.

PORTAGE. How you get your gear and canoe across a stretch of land between two bodies of water. A solid reason why canoe-campers, like backpackers, attempt to reduce their gear to the lightest load possible.

POWER FACE. The face of the blade which pushes against the water.

PRY STROKE. A paddle stroke used to move the craft sideways, away from the paddle.

PURCHASE. The application of power on a paddle to get leverage.

PUT-IN. Where a canoe is placed in the water; a launching site; the start of a trip.

QUARTERING. Running at an angle to the wind or waves; a technique for riding over waves at a slight angle to avoid burying the bow in a standing wave.

RAPIDS. Waves, whitewater, haystacks, and similar contortions of water in a fast and turbulent stretch of river.

READING THE WATER. Determining water conditions by the appearance of water formations; used in determining the appropriate route through rapids.

RECOVERY STROKE. Not really a stroke, but getting ready for the next stroke.

RESCUE PACK. A special pack in which is kept all rescue equipment.

REVERSAL. Where the current curls back on itself; usually treacherous. May be caused by large obstructions, either on the surface or underwater. Reversals also may be known as souse holes, hydraulics, curlers, or back rollers.

RIBS. Curved strips from gunwale to gunwale which form the shape of a wooden canoe hull; may also be used to add strength to the hull.

RIFFLES. Light rapids where water flows across a shallow section of river.

RIGHT BANK. The right side of the river when facing downstream.

ROCK GARDEN. A navigable waterway filled with rocks; requires constant maneuvering by the canoeist.

ROCKAGATOR. A sullen rock hiding in the rapids which the bow paddler failed to detect until after it reached up and smacked the canoe, sometimes hard enough to cause a capsize or hangup.

ROCKOPOTAMUS. A huge, sleepy rock over which water flows in a gentle pillow so unobtrusively that no one recognizes it until the canoe slides to a stop atop it.

ROCKER. The upward sweep of the keel toward the bow and stern. The more pronounced the rocker, the easier the canoe is to pivot.

RUNNING. To sail with the wind; in canoeing, to hoist a jury sail and let the wind sweep the craft along.

SCOUTING. To inspect an unknown stretch of water on foot before attempting it.

SCULLING STROKE. A figure-eight stroke with the paddle in the water at all times; used for fine adjustments, or when necessary to keep the paddle in a ready position when running a tricky set of rapids.

SECONDS. What you didn't get when your hungry partners got there first.

SHAFT. The handle of the canoe paddle between the grip and the blade.

SHEER. The fore and aft curving sides of a hull.

SHOAL. Shallows caused by a sand bar or sand bank, especially those which may be exposed at low water. Swift current shoals are also known as riffles.

SHOE KEEL. A wide, flat keel used on river canoes.

SHUTTLE. The art of maneuvering cars and canoes from put-in to take-out points.

SKIN. The covering of a craft; may be fiberglass, canvas, or a sheath placed over a fiberglass or wooden canoe to protect the craft from chafing.

SLALOM. A race in which crafts are maneuvered through a series of gates.

SMOKER. A single violent set of rapids.

SPOON. The curved shape of some types of kayak paddle blades.

SPRAY COVER. A fabric deck used to enclose open canoes when running whitewater. Also called a "spray deck."

SPRAY SKIRT. A garment worn by the canoeist which attaches to the spray cover to keep water out of the craft.

SQUALL. A quick, driving gust of wind or rain.

SQUARE STERN. A canoe with the stern cut off to provide a "transom" for attaching a motor.

STANDING WAVE. Perpetual waves which remain in one place; may be caused by decelerating current when fast water meets slower-moving water, or by obstructions.

STARBOARD. The right side of the canoe when facing the bow.

STEM. The curved outer section of the frame which forms the extreme forward and stern sections of the canoe.

STEM BAND. Also known as a "bang plate." A strip attached to the stem to protect it from damage.

STERN. The rear of the canoe.

STERN PADDLER. The person who paddles from the rear of a two-man canoe or C-2.

STRAINER. Brush or trees which have fallen into a river, usually on the outside of a bend. Current may sweep through, but the obstruction will stop a craft. Can be deadly.

STROKES. The various movements used by the paddler to control the direction and speed of the craft.

SWAMP. When a canoe is accidentally filled with water.

TAKE-OUT. Where you end your trip; the take-out point.

TECHNICAL PASSAGE. A route through a rock garden in which considerable maneuvering is required for safe transit.

THROAT. Where the paddle shaft flares into the blade.

THROW LINE. An emergency rope used to throw out to a canoe in trouble.

THWART. The cross braces which stretch from gunwale to gunwale to strengthen an open canoe.

TICKS. Peer for them every night wherever your hair grows.

TIP. The end of the paddle blade opposite the shaft.

TOAST. The nip of brandy everyone in your party salutes you with after they haul your flipped canoe out of the water.

TONGUE. The V of smooth water which indicates a safe passage between two obstructions.

TOP SIDES. The part of the hull above the water.

TRIM. The angle at which a canoe rides in the water. A canoe may be trimmed so it rides even, down at the stern, or down at the bow.

TRIP LEADER. The person in charge.

TROUGH. The bottom between two waves.

TUMBLEHOME. The curving inward of the upper section of the canoe. This produces a canoe narrower at the gunwales than at the bulging sides. An aid in keeping open canoes dry.

TUMPLINE. A strap which slips around either the chest or forehead to help support a heavy pack.

UNDERWAY. Moving, at last.

VOYAGEURS. The canoe trappers and traders of another era.

WAKE. The temporary trail in the water behind the canoe; also called the "wash." Beginning canoeists should peek occasionally at their wake to see if it is a straight line, which indicates good directional control.

WATERLINE. The line of water on the side of the canoe when it is afloat. The waterline will vary with the load.

WATERSHED. The entire region drained by a single river.

WEIR. A low dam used to divert water; frequently built by commercial eel-trap operators to catch eels and confuse canoeists.

WET SUIT. A garment made of neoprene foam which insulates canoeists, kayakers, and scuba divers against the chill of cold water. Essential for cold-water canoeing to avoid hypothermia.

WHITEWATER. A long stretch of foaming waves and rapids. Also called "wild water."

WHITEWATER PADDLE. A paddle with a large blade with square tips, and a T-shaped grip.

WINDWARD. The direction from which the wind is blowing; into the wind. Opposite of leeward.

WRAPPED UP or WRAPPED AROUND. Said of a canoe or kayak which has slammed sideways into an obstruction with sufficient force to physically bend it in a horseshoe shape around the rock.

YAW. When a canoe swerves from its course.

YOKE. Cushioned shoulder blocks that clamp onto the gunwales or midthwart of a canoe to make portaging by one person easier.

APPENDIX 2

SHOPPER'S GUIDE

Unlike the camper and backpacker or the hunter and fisherman, the canoeist sometimes has to scrounge far afield to find sporting goods or outdoor gear stores that also cater to the specific needs of canoeists.

Many liveries and outfitters have retail stores with products of use to canoeists, but only a few have major outlets with a variety of products such as a broad selection of paddles, a stock of various canoes, or a large selection of PFDs. Some of these stores offer a small selection of outdoor clothing for paddlers, a few dehydrated or freeze-dried foods, some outdoor sports and canoeing books, and videocassettes on canoeing, but for a wide range of products you will need to go to major suppliers.

Major Suppliers

The following list includes some of the larger outdoor specialties suppliers in the country. Most have retail outlets and catalog sales.

Campmor is an excellent outdoor supply store located at 810 Route 17 North, P.O. Box 997-F, Paramus, NJ 07653-0997. For a catalog call (201) 445–5000.

Eastern Mountain Sports. Formerly a leading outlet for top quality outdoor merchandise, the store has focused more and more on stylish sportswear and less on the basic needs of the outward bound. It does not have catalog sales. Retail outlets both East and West. Call (603) 924–9511 for information.

Eddie Bauer is as well known for its vast range of stylish outdoor clothing as for its top quality outdoor gear. For a catalog write to Eddie Bauer, 1737 Airport Way South, Box 3700, Seattle, WA 98124, or telephone (800) 426–8020.

Four Corners River Sports. Carries everything from boats to accessories. Located at 360 South Camino del Rio, Durango, CO. (800) 426–7637. Free catalog available.

Jersey Paddler is one of the better equipped canoe and canoe supply outlets in the east. They have no catalog, but their store at 1748 Route 88, Brick, NJ 08724 is a wonderful shop to visit. Telephone (908) 458–5777.

L.L. Bean. This famous "down-east" outlet in Maine is unique among outfitters. No-nonsense, down-to-earth approach. Wide variety of outdoor goods. The retail store, open twenty-four hours a day, is an insomniac's dream place. Acres of clothing and outdoor goods. For a catalog write to L.L. Bean, Freeport, ME 04032, or telephone (800) 221–4221.

Nantahala Outdoor Center. If it's for the paddler, they've got it. Located at 13077 Highway 19 West, Bryson City, NC 28713. For a catalog telephone (800) 367–3521.

Northwest River Supplies carries everything from outstanding waterproof canoe bags to nonslip canoeing sandals. For a catalog write to Northwest River Supplies, P.O. Box 9186, Moscow, ID 83843-9186, or telephone (800) 635–5202.

Piragus Northwoods focuses primarily upon canoes and supplies for canoeing enthusiasts. Fascinating catalog. Write to Boundary Waters Catalog, 105 North Central Avenue, Ely, MN 55731, or telephone (800) 223–6565.

Ramsey Outdoor Stores. There are three outlets in New Jersey, offering merchandise from dry suits to canoes. The largest is at 226 Route 17 North, Paramus, NJ 07656. Telephone (201) 261–5000.

REI. The nation's largest consumer cooperative. REI handles a wide variety of outdoor clothing and wilderness equipment and donates part of its yearly profit to wilderness and conservation organizations. It operates retail stores in a number of states. For a catalog write to REI, P.O. Box 88127, Seattle, WA 98138-2127, or call (800) 426–4840.

Sierra South Paddle Sports. One of California's most complete paddle sports stores. Located at 113000 Kernville Road, Box Y, Kernville, CA 93238. (800) 376–7303. Free catalog available.

Wyoming River Raiders. They call themselves the world's friendliest river supply company and have everything a paddler needs. Located at 601 Wyoming Boulevard, Casper, WY 82609. (800) 247–6068. Free catalog available.

None of the following stores have catalogs, but each is worth a visit, whether you are buying or merely gasping:

Adventurer Sport Shop, 427 Water Street, St. Charles, MO 63301

Algonquin Canoe Store, RR No. 1, Dwight P0A 1H0, Ontario, Canada

Appalachian Outfitters, 2938 Chain Bridge Road, Oakton, VA 22124

Baer's River Workshop, P.O. Box 443, Yawgoo Valley Road, Exeter, RI 02822

Berkshire Outfitters, Route 8, Cheshire Harbor, Adams, MA 01220

Brad Sheeler's Canoe Adventures, RD No. 6, Box 648, New Castle, PA 16101

The Boat House, 2855 Aqueduct Road, Schenectady, NY 12309

Canoe Country Outfitters, 6493 54 Avenue North, St. Petersburg, FL 33709

Canoe Pittsburgh, 74 South 20th Street, South Side, Pittsburgh, PA 15203

The Canoe Shop, 140 South River Road, Waterville, OH 43566

Canoesport, 940 North Main, Ann Arbor, MI 48104

Canoesport Texas, 6910-A Renwick, Houston, TX 77081

Cartwright and Danewell, M72W, Grayling, MI 49738

Chicagoland Canoe Base, 4019 North Narragansett, Chicago, IL 60634

Cold Brook Canoes, Route 28, Box 43, Boiceville, NY 12412

Country Paddlers, Route 16, Academy Street, Mexico, NY 13114

Curtis Enterprises, 4587 Clay Street, Hemlock, NY 14466

Eustis Outdoor Shop, 37826 State Road 19, Umatilla, FL 32784

Fresh Air Experience, 8537 109 Street, Edmonton T6G 1E4, Alberta, Canada

Great Outdoor Provision Co., Raleigh, NC (219) 833–1741; and Charlotte, NC (704) 523–1089

Indiana Camp Supply, 111 Center Street, Hobart, IN 46342

J.L. Waters & Co., 109 North College Street, Bloomington, IN 47401

Ketter Canoeing, 101 79th Avenue North, Minneapolis, MN 55444

Lumbertown Canoe & Kayak Specialties, 276 Ottawa Street, Muskegon, MI 49422

Midwest Mountaineering, 309 Cedar Avenue South, Minneapolis, MN 55454

Mountains and Rivers, 2320 Central S.E., Albuquerque, NM 87106

Ohio Canoe Adventures, 5128 Colorado Avenue, Sheffield Lake, OH 44054

O.L.F. Enterprise, 612 South Main Street, Elkhart, IN 46516

Ottawa Valley Canoe, 3980 Highway 17 West, RR2, Kinburn K0A 2H0, Ontario, Canada

Outdoor Action Ltd., 2205 West Wabash, Springfield, IL 62704

Pacific Water Sports, 16205 Pacific Highway South, Seattle, WA 98188

Pack N Paddle, 1217 E. Ogden, Ogden Mall, Naperville, IL 60563

Quietwater Canoes, Inc., 308 Hinton Street, Knightdale, NC 27545

Rivers Edge Canoe Outfitters, 3928 State Route 42 South, Waynesville, OH 45068

River Runner, 410 Meeting Street, West Columbia, SC 29169

Saco River Outfitters, 127 Marginal Way, Portland, ME 04101

The Small Boat Shop, 144 Water Street, South Norwalk, CT 06854

The Sports Connection, 1527 Horton Road, Jackson, MI 49203

Steam Boats, West U.S. 40, Box 2785, Steamboat Springs, CO 80477

Water Works Canoe Co., 385 Valley Street, Willimantic, CT 06226

Western Canoeing Inc., Box 115, 1717 Salton Road, Abbotsford V2S 4N8, BC, Canada

Wildwater Designs, 230 Penllyn Pike, Penllyn, PA 19422

Books and Videocassettes

Nearly all sporting goods and specialized canoe outfitters handle some books and possibly a few videocassettes on canoeing, but for the broadest range of both, write for the American Canoe Association book catalog, P.O. Box 1190, Newington, VA 22122.

Specialized Magazines

Widely available in sporting goods stores as well as by subscription, these magazines are of special interest to the paddler:

American Whitewater, specializing in whitewater canoeing and kayaking. Published by American Whitewater Affiliation, P.O. Box 85, Phoenicia, NY 12464, it is free to AWA members.

Canoe & Kayak, an excellent general-interest magazine for canoeists, kayakers, and rafters; published by Canoe America Associates, 10526 Northeast 68th, Suite 3, Kirkland, WA 98033.

Kanawa, the voice of canoeing in Canada. Trilingual. Published by the Canadian Recreational Canoeing Association, 1029 Hyde Park Road, Suite 5, Hyde Park, Ontario, Canada N0M1Z0; (519) 473–2109.

Paddler, a general-interest magazine for canoeists, kayakers, and rafters. Endorsed both by the American Canoe Association and Professional Paddlesports Association, it is free to ACA members. For inquiries write to P.O. Box 1341, Eagle, ID 83616.

APPENDIX 3

CANOE AND KAYAK SCHOOLS

Yes, you can learn basic canoeing skills by reading about the necessary strokes and practicing them on a real river in a real canoe with a real paddle. Assume, though, that you want to go beyond basics; you want to look at truly challenging whitewater and learn how to canoe the splash and thunder of the rapids. With more practice and more reading, you can probably achieve a fairly competent level, enough to handle Class II waters.

On the other hand, if you want to master Class II waters or achieve a good intermediate skill level, competent instruction properly given will get you there faster than you can learn on your own. What about going beyond this level and into the thrill and excitement of Class III? Again, you'll need some lessons. Luckily, some excellent sources of instruction are available throughout the nation. Most canoe clubs offer instruction classes, as do chapters of the Sierra Club and the Appalachian Mountain Club. In addition, a number of very fine canoe and kayak schools offer instruction for all skill levels.

Among the better paddling schools are these:

Ace Paddling Center, Box 1168, Pak Hill, WV 25901 (800–787–3982). Weekend and weekday lessons, all levels. Women's-only classes.

Adventure Canoes and Kayaks Paddling School, 11383 Pyrites Way, Rancho Cordova, CA 95670 (916–638–7900). Single and group instruction in canoes and kayaks; ACA certification classes; special clinics for kids, teens, women, and people over 40. Free brochure.

Adventure Quest, P.O. Box 184, Woodstock, VT 05091 (802–484–3939). Specializing in training for children ages seven through seventeen. Kayak, open and decked canoes, racing techniques. Free brochure.

Boulder Outdoor Center, 2510 North 47th Street, Boulder, CO 80301 (303–444–8420). Courses from beginner to advanced, river rescue seminars.

California Canoe and Kayak Schools, 8631 Folsom Boulevard, Sacramento, CA 95826 (800–366–9804). One- to four-day programs; personal or group instruction; ACA instructor development and certification programs. Kayak and canoe, solo and tandem. Free brochure.

Kayak & Canoe Institute, University of Minnesota, 121 Sport & Health Center, 10 University Drive, Duluth, MA 55812 (218–726–6533). Four-hour to five-day courses, open and decked canoes, all levels.

Nantahala Outdoor Center, U.S. 192 Box 41, Bryson City, NC 28713. Often cited as one of the nation's finest whitewater canoe schools. Basic to expert in kayak, solo canoe, tandem canoe, and decked canoe. Group and individual lessons. Special programs for kids, women, and handicapped, plus river rescue techniques and ACA Instructor Certification workshops. Free brochure.

New England Whitewater Center, Wyman Lake, Caratunk, ME 04925. Two- to five-day beginner courses. Women's and kid's classes.

Otter Bar Kayak School, Box 210C, Forks of Salmon, CA 96031 (916–462–4772). All levels of kayak instruction; basic, intermediate, and advanced. Free video and brochure.

The Outdoor Center of New England, 8 Pleasant Street, Millers Falls, MA 01349 (413–659–3926). River and sea kayaking; open and decked canoes; all levels. Special workshops for people over forty, women, teens, outdoor leaders, rescue techniques. Group and private lessons. Free brochure.

Riversport School of Paddling, 213 Yough Street, Confluence, PA 15424 (814–395–5744). Special kids' camp; clinics in slalom and squirting. Kayak, solo, and tandem canoe. All levels. Group and private instruction. Free information kit.

Rocky Mountain Outdoor Center's Paddling School, 10281 Highway 50, Howard, CO 81233 (800–255–5784). Two- and four-day classes; private instruction, all levels.

Saco Bound's Northern Waters School, Box 119-C, Center Conway, NH 03813 (603–447–2177). Basic and advanced instruction, tandem and solo; two- to five-day classes.

Sierra South Mountain Sports, P.O. Box Y, Kerriville, CA 93238 (619–376–3745). Class in all levels of kayaking and canoeing. Small classes and personalized instruction. Free brochure.

Snake River Kayak and Canoe, P.O. Box 3482, Jackson Hole, WY 83001 (800–824–5375). Clinic and personal instruction in basic skills. Free brochure.

Steamboat Springs Canope School, P.O. Box 775363, Steamboat Springs, CO 80477 (970–870–8127). Class for beginners to experts; wildlife interpretation classes.

Sundance Kayak School, 14894 Galice Road, Merlin, OR 97532 (503–479–8508). All levels of kayaking from beginner to expert; five-day beginners' program. Free brochure.

Whitewater Challengers Outdoor Adventure Center, P.O. Box 8, White Haven, PA 18661 (717–443–9532). Special two-day entry-level classes. Classroom and on-water instruction in whitewater kayaking. Free brochure.

Whitewater Specialty, N3894, Highway 55, White Lake, WI 54491 (715–883–5400). Group and private instruction available in kayak, solo canoe, and tandem canoe. Also instruction in rescue techniques, canoe poling, and quiet-water paddling. Send for free catalog.

W.I.L.D. W.A.T.E.R.S., Box 197A, HCR-01 Route 28 at the Glen, Warrensburg, NY 12885 (800–283–WILD). Beginning through advanced; kayak, solo, and tandem canoe; decked canoe; special programs for children seven through seventeen. Free brochure.

Zoar, P.O. Box 245 Mohawk Trail, Charlemont, MA 01339 (800–532–7483). All levels of training, two-day and three-day weekend sessions; midweek seminars. Training clinics for private groups.

Canadian Schools

The Adventure Begins/Outdoor Education Consultants, RR 3, Shelburne L0N 1S0, Ontario, Canada (519–925–3930). Kayak and canoe touring instruction, from weekend to week-long programs. Free catalog.

Madawaska Kanu Center, Box 635, Barry's Bay K0J 1B0, Ontario, Canada (613–756–3620). Adult classes for kayak and open canoe; up to expert level. Private instruction available. Free brochure.

River Run Paddling Centre, P.O. Box 179, Ontario, Canada K0J1C0 (613–646–2501). All levels of training, including wilderness travel in the Ottawa River area. Call for brochure.

Temagami Wilderness Center, RR #1(S) Temagami, P0H 2H0, Ontario, Canada (705–569–3733). Weekend and week-long workshops in canoeing and wilderness skills, from flat water to basic whitewater; survival techniques. Free brochure.

Wanapitei Wilderness Center, 393 Water Street, Suite 14, Peterborough K9H 3L7, Ontario, Canada (705–745–8314). Special youth and adult classes; two- and three-day clinics; novice to advanced canoe programs. Free brochure.

Wilderness Tours, Box 89, Beachburg K0J 1C0, Ontario, Canada (613–646–2291). Five-day beginner and intermediate classes for kayaks; group instruction.

APPENDIX 4

CANOE CLUBS

If there is one characteristic shared by the dozens of canoe and kayak clubs throughout the nation, it is this: They welcome your inquiries. In fact, if you call for information, be careful—they may try to seduce you into joining them.

Canoe clubs offer a wealth of information about canoes and paddles. Their experts can tell you why one specific item is better than another, and they can direct you to their region's rivers, liveries, and sporting goods shops that cater especially to paddlers.

The following canoe and kayak clubs are affiliated with the American Canoe Association. The list does not include outrigger canoe clubs devoted primarily to outrigger canoeing on coastal waters.

Alabama

Birmingham Canoe Club, P.O. Box 951, Birmingham 35201

Gunwale Grabbers, P.O. Box 19913, Birmingham 35219 (205–979–3064)

Alaska

Knik Kanoers & Kayakers, Inc., P.O. Box 101935, Anchorage 99510 (907–272–9351)

Arizona

Northern Arizona Paddler's Club, 611 North San Francisco Street, Flagstaff 86001 (602–774–0844)

Arkansas

Arkansas Canoe Club, P.O. Box 1843, Little Rock 72203

California

California National Olympic Canoe Club, P.O. Box 214845, Sacramento 95821-0845 (916–391–6912)

Monarch Bay Canoe Club, 24371 Barbados Drive, Danna Point

92629 (714–496–7792)

National Outdoor College, P.O. Box 962, Fair Oaks 95628 (916–633–7900)

Popular Outdoor Sports, 7675 Surrey Lane, Oakland 94605 (415–635–4051)

River City Paddlers, 428 J Street, Suite 400, Sacramento 95814 (916–965–3380)

Sequoia Canoe Club, P.O. Box 1164, Windsor 95492 (707–526–0940)

Sierra Club R.T.S., 695 Marshall Road, Vacaville 95687

Southern California Canoe Association, 8665 Nagle Avenue, Panorama City 91402

Ventura Olympic Canoe Club, 3427 Gloria Drive, Newbury Park 91320 (805–498–6954)

Western Waters Canoe Club, 840 Town and Country Village, San Jose 94128-2032 (408–298–6300)

Colorado

Colorado Rocky Mountain School, 1493 County Road, Carbondale 81623 (303–963–2562)

Colorado Whitewater Association, 7500 East Arapahoe Road, Englewood 80122 (303–770–0515)

Fibark Boat Races Inc., P.O. Box 762, Salida 81201 (303–539–3555)

Pikes Peak Whitewater Club, 20 Manitou Terrace, Manitou Springs 80829 (719–471–2640)

Rocky Mountain Canoe Club, 2185 South Acoma, Denver 80223 (303–698–9486)

Connecticut

Columbia Canoe Club, 38 Hunt Road, Columbia 06237

Connecticut Canoe Racing Association, 785 Bow Lane, Middletown 06457 (203–346–0068)

Farmington River Club, P.O. Box 475, Canton 06019

Housatonic Area C & K Squad, RR Box 307, West Cornwall 06796 (203–672–0293)

Delaware

Wilmington Trail Club, 106 Martindale Drive, Newark 19713

Florida

Atlantic Coast Kayak Club, 1 Northeast 39th Street, Ft.

Lauderdale 33334 (305–568–0280)

Florida Canoe & Kayak Association, P.O. Box 20892, West Palm Beach 33416 (407–686–8800)

Peninsula Paddling Club, 8571 Shady Glen Drive, Orlando 32819 (407–352–1711)

Seminole Canoe & Yacht Club, 4619 Ortega Farms Circle, Jacksonville 32205 (904–388–6734)

Georgia

Atlanta Whitewater Club, P.O. Box 33, Clarkston 30021 (404–299–3752)

Central Georgia River Runners, P.O. Box 5509, Macon 31208

Coastal Georgia Paddling Club, 505 Herb River Drive, Savannah 31406 (912–352–9121)

Georgia Canoeing Association, P.O. Box 7023, Atlanta 30357 (404–266–3734)

Illinois

Chicago Whitewater Association, 2750 Bernard Place, Evanston 60201 (708–328–0145)

Lincoln Park Boat Club, 2631 North Richmond, Chicago 60647 (312–278–5539)

Middle Fork Paddling Group, P.O. Box 8, Urbana 61801 (217–328–6666)

Northwest Passage Outing Club, 1130 Greenleaf Avenue, Wilmette 60091 (708–256–4409)

Prairie State Canoeists, 570 Webford, Des Plaines 60016-3317 (708–299–3977)

Indiana

Hoosier Canoe Club, 6212 Furnas Road, Indianapolis 46241 (317–856–6356)

South Bend Moving Water Club, 3220 East Jefferson Boulevard, South Bend 46615 (219–234–0191)

Wildcat Canoe Club, P.O. Box 6232, Kokomo 46904-6232

Iowa

Mississippi River Adventures, 922 North Third, Burlington 52601 (319–752–4142)

Kentucky

Bluegrass Wildwater Association, 453 Becky Place, Lexington 40502

Elkhorn Paddlers, 173 Lincoln Avenue, Lexington 40502
(606–277–0656)

Maine

Maine Canoe/Kayak Racing Organization, RFD 2 Box 268,
Orrington 04474 (207–825–4439)

Penobscot Paddle & Chowder Society, RFD 3, Box 840, Pittsfield
04967

UMM Outing Club, 9 O'Brien Avenue, Machias 04654
(207–255–3313)

Maryland

World Championships Inc., P.O. Box 689, McHenry 21541
(301–724–5541)

Massachusetts

Appalachian Mountain Club, Berkshire, 63 Silver Street, South
Hadley 01075 (413–536–1347)

Westfield River Wild Water Club, Ingell Road, Chester 01011
(413–354–9684)

Michigan

Lansing Oar & Paddle Club, P.O. Box 26254, Lansing 48909

St. Joseph Valley Paddlers, 23311 River Run Road, Mendon
49072 (616–467–7920)

Minnesota

Cascaders Canoe & Kayak Club, P.O. Box 61, Minneapolis 55458

Minnesota Canoe Association, Dinkytown Station, Minneapolis
55414 (612–725–3478)

Missouri

Kansas City Whitewater Club, 3727 Jefferson, Kansas City 64111
(816–753–5297)

Missouri Whitewater Association, 2305 White Ash Court,
Florrissant 63031 (314–837–8190)

Montana

Beartooth Paddlers Society, P.O. Box 20432, Billings 59104

Headwaters Paddling Association, Box 1392, Boseman 59715
(406–586–0072)

New Hampshire

Ledyard Canoe Club, P.O. Box 9, Hanover 03755 (603–646–2753)

New Jersey

Hunterdon County Canoe Club, County Park System, Highway 31, Lebanon 08833

Mohawk Canoe Club, RD 2, Lebanon 08833 (201–832–2570)

Monoco Canoe Club, 861 Colts Neck Road, Freehold 07728 (201–431–5678)

Wanda Canoe Club, Industrial Avenue, P.O. Box 723, Ridgefield Park 07660

New Mexico

Adobe Whitewater Club, P.O. Box 3835, Albuquerque 87190

New York

Heuvelton Canoe Club, 7 York Street, Heuvelton 13654 (315–344–7744)

Hilltop Hoppers Canoe / Kayak, 214 Helderberg Trail, Berne 12023 (518–872–2257)

Hudson River Whitewater Derby, Thirteenth Lake Road, North River 12856

International Canoe & Kayak Club of Oneonta, P.O. Box 163, Davenport 13750 (607–278–5990)

Ka-Na-Wa-Ke Canoe Club, 2849 Pleasant Valley Drive, Marcellus 13108

Kayak & Canoe Club of New York, P.O. Box 329, Phoenicia 12464 (914–688–5569)

Metropolitan Canoe & Kayak Club, P.O. Box 021868, Brooklyn 11202-0040 (718–482–2752)

Nissequogue River Canoe Club, 2930 Mill Road, Seaford 11783 (516–221–5614)

Rockaway Olympic Canoe & Kayak, 138 Beach 133rd Street, Belle Harbor 11694

Sebago Canoe Club, 1751 67th Street, Brooklyn 11204 (718–241–3683)

Sons of the Legion, Arden Kelsey Post 907, Candor 13743

The Tenandeho Canoe Association, Inc., 718 B Bruno Road, Clifort Park 12065 (518–877–6277)

North Carolina

Carolina Canoe Club, Box 12932, Raleigh 27605

Catawba Valley Outing Club, 774 Fourth Street Drive SW, Hickory 28602 (704–322–2297)

Nantahala Racing Club, US19W, Box 41, Bryson City 28713 (704–488–9017)

Triad River Runners, P.O. Box 11283, Bethabara Station, Winston-Salem 27116-1283

Triangle Paddlers, Inc., P.O. Box 20902, Raleigh 27619

Ohio

Dayton Canoe Club, 1020 Riverside Drive, Dayton 45405 (513–222–9392)

Keel Haulers Canoe Club, 1649 Allen Drive, Westlake 44145 (216–871–1758)

Scenic Scioto Canoe Club Inc., 1720 Coles Boulevard, Portsmouth 45662 (614–353–5105)

Toledo River Gang, 626 Louisiana Avenue, Perrysburg 43551 (419–874–9782)

Oregon

Lower Columbia Canoe Club, 14490 Northwest Hunters Drive, Beaverton 97006 (503–629–8124)

Oregon Canoe & Kayak Club, P.O. Box 692, Portland 97207 (503–629–1863)

South Oregon Association of Kayakers, 5168 Glen Echo Way, Central Point 97502 (503–664–5669)

Pennsylvania

Benscreek Canoe Club, P.O. Box 2, Johnstown 15907

Buck Ridge Ski Club, P.O. Box 179, Bala Cynwd 19004

Canoe Club of Greater Harrisburg, 180 Andersontown Road, Dover 17315

Conewago Canoe Club, 670 B Trolley Drive, Dallastown 17313 (712–244–8440)

Keystone Canoe Club, P.O. Box 377, Blandon 19510 (215–670–0829)

Keystone River Runners, RD 6, Box 359, Indiana 15701 (412–349–2805)

Lancaster Canoe Club, 339 North George Street, Millersville 17551 (717–872–4413)

Lehigh Gorge Outdoor Club, 243 Main Street, White Haven 18661 (717–443–8075)

Lehigh Valley Canoe Club, P.O. Box 2726, Lehigh Valley 18001 (215–559–9595)

PACK, 917 Pine Hill Road, Lititz 17543

Philadelphia Canoe Club, 4900 Ridge Avenue, Philadelphia 19128 (215–844–6727)

Three Rivers Paddling Club, 500 Sixth Street, Patterson Heights, Beaver Falls 15010 (412–843–5152)

Western Pennsylvania Paddle Sport Association, P.O. Box 8857, Pittsburgh 16003

Rhode Island

Rhode Island Canoe Association, 193 Pettaconsett Avenue, Warwick 02888 (401–781–5187)

Westerly YMCA Canoe & Kayak Club, 95 High Street, Westerly 02871 (401–596–2894)

South Carolina

Foothills Canoe Club, P.O. Box 6331, Greenville 29606 (803–268–7275)

Palmetto Paddlers, Inc., 5938 Woodvine Road, Columbia 29206 (803–787–7999)

Tennessee

Bluff City Canoe Club, Box 40523, Memphis 38104 (901–795–3988)

Chota Canoe Club, 1407 Woodcrest Drive, Knoxville 37918 (615–689–2664)

Tennessee Scenic Rivers Association, 4414 Leland Lane, Nashville 37204 (615–329–3563)

Texas

Bayou City Whitewater Club, P.O. Box 980782, Houston 77098 (713–224–7554)

Houston Canoe Club, P.O. Box 925516, Houston 77250 (713–467–8857)

North Texas River Runners, 215 Lakeshore Drive, Waxahachie 75165 (214–937–8835)

Texas Canoe Racing Association, 9706 Brookshire, Houston 77041 (713–939–7159)

Vermont

Club Adventure, P.O. Box 184, Woodstock 05091 (802–484–3939)

Northern Vermont Canoe Cruise, 11 Discovery Road, Essex Junction 05452 (802–878–6828)

Virginia

Canoe Cruisers Association, 2420 North George Mason Drive, Arlington 22207 (703–533–8334)

Coastal Canoeists, Box 566, Richmond 23204 (804–282–2634)

Mid-Atlantic Paddlers Association, 154 Pacific Drive, Hampton 23666 (804–838–8998)

Richmond River Runners, P.O. Box 11775, Richmond 23204 (804–323–3035)

Washington Canoe Club, 4600 South Four Mile Run Drive, No. 620, Arlington 22204 (703–521–7069)

Washington

Seattle Canoe Club, 5900 West Green Lake Way North, Seattle 98115 (206–522–1774)

Spokane Canoe & Kayak Club, West 4625 Bonnie Drive, Spokane 99204 (509–624–8384)

Washington Kayak Club, 4257 123rd Avenue SE, Bellevue 98006 (206–746–6726)

Wisconsin

Green Bay Paddlers United, 13601 Marshek Road, Mariel 54227 (414–863–8458)

Hoofers Outing Club, Wisconsin Memorial Union, Madison 53706 (608–262–1630)

Spirit of America Canoe & Kayak, 240 Broadway, Platteville 53818 (608–348–8523)

Wausau Area Canoe/Kayak Organization, P.O. Box 14, Wausau 54402

INDEX

About the Author

Herb Gordon has been paddling North American waterways for more than 30 years. He is currently a national wilderness trip leader for the Sierra Club's Atlantic chapter. An acid downhill skier, he is also the author of *Essential Skiing,* (Lyons & Burford, 1996), as well as *The Canoe Book* (McGraw Hill, 1978). During his twenty years as a writer and senior producer at NBC News he won the coveted Peabody award three times for his documentaries. His freelance articles and photographs have appeared in such publications as the *New York Times,* the *Los Angeles Times, Skiing* magazine, the *Reader's Digest,* and *Field & Stream.*

Despite his "lifelong and unquenchable love of the wilderness," Herb and his wife, Gail, and their twin red-headed daughters, Hilary and Rebecca, make their home in a charming old brownstone on Manhattan's Upper West Side.